Performance and Behavior of Family Firms

Special Issue Editor
Esra Memili

MDPI • Basel • Beijing • Wuhan • Barcelona • Belgrade

MDPI

Special Issue Editor
Esra Memili
University of North Carolina at Greensboro
USA

Editorial Office
MDPI AG
St. Alban-Anlage 66
Basel, Switzerland

This edition is a reprint of the Special Issue published online in the open access journal *International Journal of Financial Studies* (ISSN 2227-7072) from 2014–2015 (available at: http://www.mdpi.com/journal/ijfs/special_issues/family_firms).

For citation purposes, cite each article independently as indicated on the article page online and as indicated below:

Lastname, F.M.; Lastname, F.M. Article title. *Journal Name*. **Year**. *Article number, page range.*

First Edition 2018

ISBN 978-3-03842-781-0 (Pbk)
ISBN 978-3-03842-782-7 (PDF)

Table of Contents

About the Special Issue Editor

Esra Memili, PhD, is an Associate Professor of Entrepreneurship and Margaret Van Hoy Hill Dean's Notable Scholar at the Bryan School of Business and Economics at University of North Carolina, Greensboro. Dr. Memili's accepted and/or published manuscripts have appeared in Entrepreneurship Theory and Practice, Family Business Review, Small Business Economics, Journal of Small Business Management, Global Strategy Journal, Journal of Family Business Strategy, Long Range Planning, Academy of Management Best Paper Proceedings, and others. She is an Associate Editor of Journal of Family Business Strategy, an ERB member of Family Business Review, Journal of Management Studies, Journal of Leadership and Organizational Studies, and International Journal of Management and Enterprise Development, a Guest Editor for Special Issues on family firms of International Journal of Financial Studies and Journal of Family Business Management, and a recent Guest Editor of Entrepreneurship and Regional Development journal's Special Issue on Family Firms.

International Journal of
Financial Studies

MDPI

Editorial

Performance and Behavior of Family Firms

Esra Memili

Bryan School of Business and Economics, University of North Carolina at Greensboro, 370 Bryan, Greensboro, NC 27402, USA; e_memili@uncg.edu; Tel.: +1-662-617-1459

Academic Editor: Nicholas Apergis
Received: 21 July 2015; Accepted: 1 September 2015; Published: 9 September 2015

Abstract: This Guest Editor's note reflects on the contributions of each article in the Special Issue on family firms' behavior and performance. Building on this, several under-researched areas concerning family involvement in businesses are identified and the resulting impact on firm behavior and performance is explained. Finally, future research directions and insights for practitioners are outlined.

Keywords: family firm; family involvement; firm performance; firm behavior

1. Introduction

I am pleased to announce the first Special Issue on Family Firms in the *International Journal of Financial Studies*. The focus of articles in this Special Issue is mostly on family enterprises' behavior and performance. In addition, one article provides a review of the definition of family firms in the literature. This Guest Editor's note synthesizes the contributing authors' propositions and findings regarding family firms in different parts of the world and suggests future research directions.

Indeed, a large number of firms around the world exhibit family involvement in various ways (e.g., family ownership), which can significantly impact their strategies, behavior, and performance. When family business members have intentions to pursue particularistic goals and strategies, they are more likely to be influential on firm strategies, behavior, and performance. Such intentions can lead to strategic behaviors that are often oriented toward preserving the economic and socioemotional wealth of the firm for the family in the long run. Consequently, family firm behavior is expected to be distinct from those in non-family firms and among family firms. Since family firms are key value creators around the globe (Bertrand and Schoar [1]), we invited researchers to shed light on how families use their influence to affect the behavior and performance of firms. Taking a closer look at the effects of family involvement on these companies across the world helps us also appreciate the research progress made to date and identify the areas deserving future research. This Guest Editor's note provides such a discussion, distilling key findings and how they could enrich future theory building and testing.

This Special Issue on Family Firms and the Guest Editor's Note can guide future research in several ways. First, the importance of family governance to explain how families control corporations differently is highlighted. By doing so, this Special Issue draws attention to the differences between publicly traded family and non-family firms that are likely to have an impact on firm behavior performance. Second, this Special Issue helps us better understand how family involvement in the business can influence firm behavior and performance. This improves our understanding of the heterogeneity among family firms. Third, new insights and future research directions regarding behavior and performance differences between family and non-family firms as well as among family firms themselves are provided.

The remainder of the Guest Editor's Note will progress as follows: First, this Editor's Note will summarize each article in the Special Issue. Then, key propositions and findings and their theoretical and practical implications are evaluated. This allows identification of several under-researched areas

Int. J. Financial Stud. **2015**, *3*, 423–430

that require close scholarly attention. In the final section of the Guest Editor's note, promising future research directions and insights for practitioners are discussed.

2. Articles

2.1. Definition of Family Business

Since the findings on behavior and performance in previous studies might be affected by the family firm definition, the review of Harms [2] is particularly important in this Special Issue. Harms [2] identifies six different clusters by focusing on the most frequently used definitions in previous research.

Components of Involvement and Essence Approaches have been grouped together since this categorization by Chua, Chrisman and Sharma [3] suggests that components factors, such as ownership or control, have to be combined with elements depicting the essence of family businesses, such as visions and intentions. Studies based on Chua *et al.* [3] and more recent updates (e.g., Chrisman *et al.* [4]) systematically differentiate between family and non-family firms as well as among family businesses themselves, suggesting that components and essence factors are jointly crucial to account for family firms' uniqueness.

Definitions with *Empirical Focus* are explicitly geared toward conducting empirical analyses. First introduced by Anderson and Reeb [5] and extended by Villalonga and Amit [6], this definitional approach specifies operational criteria to empirically measure family business characteristics, especially those with effects on the relationship between family ownership and firm performance. Definitions applied before the publication of the aforementioned definitional concepts as well as those intended to account to specific research designs are summarized under *Other Definitions*. *Self-Developed Definitions* categorize studies in which the authors neglected previous definitions and based their studies on new sub-classification and self-developed approaches. In contrast to those assigned to the other clusters, studies *Without Explicit Definition* did not refer to any family firm definition or solely pointed to the used data source without defining the object of investigation. Furthermore, Harms [2] assigned some studies to the cluster F-PEC or "Familiness" (*i.e.*, family influence by power, experience, and culture) (Astrachan *et al.* [7]), which contains all studies targeted at discussing "soft factors", such as family's values or commitment to the business. These definitions partly build on the components of involvement or essence approach, but highlight the importance of experience and culture to explain family firms' distinctiveness.

2.2. Financial Performance in Family versus Non-Family Publicly Traded Firms

A prominent stream of research shows that family firms may outperform non-family firms around the world (e.g., Anderson and Reeb [5]; Andres [8]). While investigating the performance differences between not only family and non-family firms, but also among family firms, studies also draw attention to different family involvement configurations (e.g., founding family control *vs.* descendant family control, family *vs.* non-family CEO, the degree of board independence, and family firm types), which may lead to performance differences not only between family and non-family firms, but also among family firms as well (Anderson and Reeb [5,9]; Villalonga and Amit [6]). Research to date shows that these different configurations of family ownership and management can be associated with firm value positively or negatively or exhibit no relationship (O'Boyle *et al.* [10]; Peng and Jiang [11]). Hence, findings are mixed concerning the performance differences between founder-controlled and descendant-controlled family firms.

On the one hand, research shows that founder-controlled firms can outperform not only non-family firms, but also descendant-controlled family firms (Andres [8]; Miller and Le Breton-Miller [12]; Villalonga and Amit [6]). According to Miller and Le Breton-Miller [12], the success factors in founder-controlled firms are family owners' voting rights deriving from significant equity rights, a strong CEO without complete voting control and accountable to independent directors, multiple family members serving as managers, and transgenerational succession intentions.

Int. J. Financial Stud. **2015**, *3*, 423–430

Morck *et al.* [13] show that heir-controlled Canadian firms exhibit low financial performance, which can be a factor that impedes economic growth. This may stem from the entrenchment of unqualified family managers (Morck *et al.* [13]). The descendants may also pursue the private benefits of control when they are wealthy enough to do so through inherited wealth. Another reason may be that the positive effects of family influence tend to be weaker in later generations when family influence is more dispersed or fractionalized (Gomez-Mejia *et al.* [14]).

Some scholars, however, argue the opposite by showing that descendant-controlled firms are more efficient and profitable than founder-controlled firms even though founder-controlled firms tend to grow faster and invest more in capital assets and research and development (McConaughy *et al.* [15]; McConaughy *et al.* [16]). Similarly, Morck *et al.* [13] show that firm performance becomes lower when the firm is run by a member of the founding family than when it is run by an officer unrelated to the founder in older firms. According to Sraer and Thesmar [17], family firms largely outperform non-family firms regardless of being controlled by the founding or descendant families in control in France. However, Miller *et al.* [18] show that only businesses with a lone founder, rather than a founding family, outperform others among *Fortune 1000* firms. Miller and Le Breton-Miller [12] observe that family-controlled businesses perform well when they mitigate agency costs and foster stewardship behaviors among leaders.

In this Special Issue, five articles take a closer look at the impact of family involvement on firm performance within different contexts in different countries (*i.e.*, US, Poland, Mexico, and China), giving us the comparison opportunity across different parts of the world.

First, Noguera and Chang [19] examine Real Estate Investment Trust (REIT) founders *versus* successors through the lens of the socioemotional wealth (SEW) perspective. The authors show that founders preserve SEW by appointing a descendant as the REIT CEO and using the family name to identify the REIT. On the one side, REITs led by successors underperform other REITS (led by professional managers after succeeding the REIT founder or REITs led by their founders) and independent board members are not positively influential in REITs' governance. On the other side, the family identification through the use of family name in REIT influences performance positively.

The paper by Lipiec [20] examines how publicly-traded family firms perform during economic downturns compared to non-family firms in the construction sector in Poland. The author shows that publicly-traded family firms significantly outperform non-family peers during economic crisis and presents future research directions in regards to the determinants of performance in these outperforming family firms.

The article by San Martin-Reyna and Duran-Encalada [21] shows a positive link between family ownership concentration and performance among publicly-traded firms in Mexico. In addition, lower levels of debt and less participation by independent directors in family businesses strengthens this positive link. Nevertheless, in non-family firms, higher levels of participation by independent directors and debt contribute to better performance.

Relevant to San Martin-Reyna and Duran-Encalada's [21] work, the article by Luo and Liu [22] in this Special Issue, examines publicly-traded family firms in China. The authors show that there is an inverted U-shaped relationship between family ownership concentration and corporate value, and board independence positively moderates this relationship, suggesting interest-alignment effects of family ownership concentration up to an optimum level. After an optimum level, entrenchment effects prevail.

Consistent with Luo and Liu's [22] work, Memili and Misra [23] examine the S&P 500 firms and show the moderation effects of corporate governance provisions on the inverted U-shaped links between family involvement (*i.e.*, family ownership and family management) in publicly-traded firms and firm performance by drawing upon agency theory, with a focus on principal-principal agency issues, and the extant family governance literature. Hence, both family involvement and the use of governance provisions are influential on firm performance in publicly-traded firms in the US.

2.3. Family Firm Behavior

Aside from the performance outcomes of family involvement, the Special Issue presents two articles on Family Firm Behavior in the forms of Corporate Social Responsibility (CSR) and Succession.

2.3.1. CSR in Family Firms

CSR studies focusing on family firms suggest that family business owners' greater commitment to the family firm, direct contact with customers, proactiveness in nurturing relationships with all stakeholders, long-term orientation, involvement in the community, and reputation concerns can facilitate CSR activities (Bingham *et al.* [24]; Deniz and Suárez [25]; Dyer and Whetten [26]; Uhlaner *et al.* [27]).

In this Special Issue, Hirigoyen and Poulain-Rehm [28] demonstrate that publicly-traded family businesses in Europe, Asia, and North America do not differ from non-family firms in CSR activities in the forms of human resources (*i.e.*, industrial relations, employment relations, and working conditions), human rights (*i.e.*, freedom of association, promotion of collective bargaining, non-discrimination, equality, elimination of child or any forced labor as well as harassment, and protection of personal data), community involvement, protection of environment, and business relations (*i.e.*, rights and interests of customers, integration of social and environmental standards in the selection of suppliers, and respect for competition rules). The authors also show a negative relationship between family governance and corporate governance practices in terms of the balance of power and effectiveness of board, audit and control mechanisms, engagement with shareholders, and executive compensations.

2.3.2. Succession in Family Firms

Intra-family succession is critical for family firms' longevity. Boyd and colleagues [29] develop a conceptual model of incumbent decisions on succession in family firms by drawing upon the theory of planned behavior and socioemotional wealth (SEW). The authors suggest that family, firm, industry, and cultural contexts can shape concerns about family and business, in turn affecting attitudes toward the type of succession, norms, and perceived behavioral control. These can consequently determine the intention toward a particular type of succession.

3. Discussion and Conclusions

There has been a prominent stream of research investigating whether family firms outperform non-family firms. The general conclusion has been that they do. However, performance differences also depend upon the type of family involvement (e.g., founder control) (e.g., Anderson and Reeb [5]; Miller *et al.* [18]; Villalonga and Amit [6]). There has been also an increase in research examining family firm performance and its antecedents, owing to the critical role of firm value in buy-out decisions, tax payments, executive compensation, capital raising strategies, and selling the company (Villalonga [30]). The articles in this Special Issue (e.g., Lipiec [20]; San Martin-Reyna and Duran-Encalada [21]) are in line with studies showing that family ownership and management can enhance firm value since the controlling family can provide superior oversight through lengthy tenure, investment in long-term projects, or exhibit reputation concerns that diminish the possibility of questionable or irresponsible business practices (Anderson and Reeb [5]; Dyer and Whetten [26]). Nevertheless, family involvement can also result in negative firm behavior and performance, if principal-principal agency problems prevail, particularly after an optimum level of family ownership and/or management (e.g., Luo and Liu [22]; Memili and Misra [23]).

Existing research generally explores the use of various governance mechanisms and performance differences between family firms and non-family firms and among family firms by drawing upon agency theory with a focus on principal-principal agency issues (e.g., Memili [31]; Memili and Misra [23]). However, institutional factors tend to play a role in governance systems as well. Accordingly, a recent review by Gedajlovic *et al.* [32] suggests that the effects of family firm governance may depend on the existence of institutional factors. Indeed, family owners and managers may have more or less power than their peers in different countries (Memili [31]). For example, in the US, family owners and managers may not have as high levels of discretion power as peers in some other countries owing to effective investor protection. Accordingly, Peng and Jiang [11] suggest that the impact of family ownership and control on firm value is associated with the level of shareholder protection ensured by legal and regulatory institutions of a country. On the one hand, when there is effective investor protection, family owners tend to dilute their equity to attract minority shareholders and delegate management to professional managers (Peng and Jiang [11]). In this case, family owners and managers do not have the need or motivation to use control enhancing governance mechanisms to enhance their power. On the other hand, when the legal system is weak, ownership becomes more concentrated by family owners who would seek to ensure their control by participating in management (Peng and Jiang [11]). However, the negative aspect of the enhanced power of the controlling family in an environment characterized by weak legal investor protection is the likelihood of principal-principal agency problems such as expropriation of non-controlling shareholder wealth and entrenchment of the controlling family. Therefore, future research would benefit from exploring the relative effects of institutionalization *versus* family influence on firm performance through the lens of institutional theory within the context of different countries' legal regimes.

The meta-analytic approaches for examining the link between family involvement in corporations and firm performance will be particularly helpful to reconcile the inconsistencies in prior findings through a quantitative integration of the results of previous studies. This can allow for calculating an overall effect through consolidating available empirical evidence into a single quantitative effect size, and testing the role of various contingency factors, such as sample differences, study design differences, measures, regions, and more. The meta-analytic review (e.g., O'Boyle *et al.* [10]; Wagner *et al.* [33]) can thereby help integrate available empirical evidence, while at the same time identifying under-researched areas. More specifically, this type of review can highlight the importance of different forms of family involvement in publicly-traded firms to explain how families control corporations differently. By doing so, it can contribute to a better understanding of the differences between publicly-traded family and non-family firms that are likely to have an impact on firm performance. Second, it can add to the literature by reviewing different publicly-traded family firm governance contexts and contingencies that can influence firm performance. By this, our understanding of the heterogeneity among family firms (Melin and Norqvist [34]) will be improved. Third, new insights and future research directions regarding corporate governance differences between family and non-family firms as well as among family firms can be provided.

This Guest Editor's Note summarizes the articles in the Special Issue, explains the relevance as well as differences among the articles, and draws attention to different contexts (e.g., the extent of institutionalization and the legal environment) that may play a role in family firm behavior and performance. If publicly traded family firms can capitalize on the positive effects of family involvement and mitigate agency problems, they can achieve superior performance. Publicly traded family firms concerned with maximizing shareholder value and attaining competitive advantages through family control will be sought after by investors and reap the benefits of positive corporate image.

Conflicts of Interest: The author declares no conflict of interest.

References

1. Bertrand, M.; Schoar, A. The role of family in family firms. *J. Econ. Perspect.* **2006**, *20*, 73–96. [CrossRef]
2. Harms, H. Review of Family Business Definitions: Cluster Approach and Implications of Heterogeneous Application for Family Business Research. *Int. J. Financ. Stud.* **2014**, *2*, 280–314. [CrossRef]
3. Chua, J.H.; Chrisman, J.J.; Sharma, P. Defining the family business by behavior. *Entrep. Theory Pract.* **1999**, *23*, 19–39.
4. Chrisman, J.J.; Chua, J.H.; Sharma, P. Trends and directions in the development of a strategic management theory of the family firm. *Entrep. Theory Pract.* **2005**, *29*, 555–576. [CrossRef]

5. Anderson, R.C.; Reeb, D.M. Founding-family ownership and firm performance: Evidence from the S&P 500. *J. Financ.* **2003**, *58*, 1301–1328.

6. Villalonga, B.; Amit, R. How do family ownership, management, and control affect firm value? *J. Financ. Econ.* **2006**, *80*, 385–417. [CrossRef]

7. Astrachan, J.H.; Klein, S.B.; Smyrnios, K.X. The F-PEC scale of family influence: A proposal for solving the family business definition problem. *Fam. Bus. Rev.* **2002**, *15*, 45–58. [CrossRef]

8. Andres, C. Large shareholders ad firm performance: An empirical examination of founding-family ownership. *J. Corp. Financ.* **2008**, *14*, 431–445. [CrossRef]

9. Anderson, R.C.; Reeb, D.M. Who Monitors the Family? Available online: http://papers.ssrn.com/sol3/papers.cfm?abstract_id=369620 (accessed on 21 July 2015).

10. O'Boyle, E.H.; Pollack, J.M.; Rutherford, M.W. Exploring the relation between family involvement and firms' financial performance: A meta-analysis of main and moderator effects. *J. Bus. Ventur.* **2012**, *27*, 1–18. [CrossRef]

11. Peng, M.W.; Jiang, Y. Institutions behind family ownership and control in large firms. *J. Manag. Stud.* **2010**, *47*, 253–273. [CrossRef]

12. Miller, D.; le Breton-Miller, I. Family governance and firm performance: Agency, stewardship, and capabilities. *Fam. Bus. Rev.* **2006**, *19*, 73–88. [CrossRef]

13. Morck, R.; Strangeland, D.A.; Yeung, B. *Inherited Wealth, Corporate Control and Economic Growth: The Canadian Disease?* Working Paper 6814; National Bureau of Economic Research: Cambridge, MA, USA, 1998.

14. Gómez-Mejía, L.R.; Hynes, K.T.; Núñez-Nickel, M.; Moyano-Fuentes, H. Socioemotional wealth and business risk in family-controlled firms: Evidence from Spanish olive oil mills. *Adm. Sci. Q.* **2007**, *52*, 106–137.

15. McConaughy, D.L.; Phillips, G.M. Founders *versus* descendants: The profitability, efficiency, growth characteristics, and financing in large, public, founding-family-controlled firms. *Fam. Bus. Rev.* **1999**, *12*, 123–132. [CrossRef]

16. McConaughy, D.L.; Walker, M.C.; Henderson, G.V.; Mishra, C.S. Founding family controlled firms: Efficiency and value. *Rev. Financ. Econ.* **1998**, *7*, 1–19. [CrossRef]

17. Sraer, D.; Thesmar, D. Performance and behavior of family firms: Evidence from the French stock market. *J. Eur. Econ. Assoc.* **2007**, *5*, 709–751. [CrossRef]

18. Miller, D.; le Breton-Miller, I.; Lester, R.H.; Cannella, A.A. Are family firms really superior performers? *J. Corp. Financ.* **2007**, *13*, 829–858. [CrossRef]

19. Noguera, M.; Chang, E.P.C. Socio Emotional Wealth Preservation in the REIT Industry: An Exploratory Study. *Int. J. Financ. Stud.* **2014**, *2*, 220–239. [CrossRef]

20. Lipiec, J. Capital Asset Pricing Model Testing at Warsaw Stock Exchange: Are Family Businesses the Remedy for Economic Recessions? *Int. J. Financ. Stud.* **2014**, *2*, 266–279. [CrossRef]

21. San Martin-Reyna, J.M.; Duran-Encalada, J.A. Effects of Family Ownership, Debt and Board Composition on Mexican Firms Performance. *Int. J. Financ. Stud.* **2015**, *3*, 56–74. [CrossRef]

22. Luo, J.H.; Liu, H. Family-Concentrated Ownership in Chinese PLCs: Does Ownership Concentration Always Enhance Corporate Value? *Int. J. Financ. Stud.* **2014**, *2*, 103–121. [CrossRef]

23. Memili, E.; Misra, K. Corporate Governance Provisions, Family Involvement, and Firm Performance in Publicly Traded Family Firms. *Int. J. Financ. Stud.* **2015**, *3*, 194–229. [CrossRef]

24. Bingham, J.B.; Dyer, W., Jr.; Smith, I.; Adams, G.L. A Stakeholder Identity Orientation Approach to Corporate Social Performance in Family Firms. *J. Bus. Ethics* **2011**, *99*, 565–585. [CrossRef]

25. De Ia Cruz Déniz Déniz, M.; Suárez, M. Corporate Social Responsibility and Family Business in Spain. *J. Bus. Ethics* **2005**, *56*, 27–41. [CrossRef]

26. Dyer, W.G.; Whetten, D.A. Family firms and social responsibility: Preliminary evidence from the S&P 500. *Entrep. Theory Pract.* **2006**, *30*, 785–802.

27. Uhlaner, L.M.; van Goor-Balk, H.J.M; Masurel, E. Family business and corporate social responsibility in a sample of Dutch firms. *J. Small Bus. Enterp. Dev.* **2004**, *11*, 186–194. [CrossRef]

28. Hirigoyen, G.; Poulain-Rehm, T. The Corporate Social Responsibility of Family Businesses: An International Approach. *Int. J. Financ. Stud.* **2014**, *2*, 240–265. [CrossRef]

29. Boyd, B.; Botero, I.C.; Fediuk, T.A. Incumbent Decisions about Succession Transitions in Family Firms: A Conceptual Model. *Int. J. Financ. Stud.* **2014**, *2*, 335–358. [CrossRef]

30. Villalonga, B. *Note on Valuing Control and Liquidity in Family and Closely Held Firms*; Harvard Business School Publishing: Boston, MA, USA, 2009.

Int. J. Financial Stud. **2015**, *3*, 423–430

31. Memili, E. Control-Enhancing Corporate Governance Mechanisms: Family *versus* Non-family Publicly Traded Firms. Doctoral Dissertation, Mississippi State University, Mississippi State, MS, USA, 2011.

32. Gedajlovic, E.; Carney, M.; Chrisman, J.J.; Kellermanns, F.W. The adolescence of family firm research taking stock and planning for the future. *J. Manag.* **2012**, *38*, 1010–1037. [CrossRef]

33. Wagner, D.; Block, J.H.; Miller, D.; Schwens, C.; Xi, G. A meta-analysis of the financial performance of family firms: Another attempt. *J. Fam. Bus. Strategy* **2015**, *6*, 3–13. [CrossRef]

34. Melin, L.; Nordqvist, M. The reflexive dynamics of institutionalization: The case of the family business. *Strateg. Organ.* **2007**, *5*, 321–333. [CrossRef]

International Journal of
Financial Studies

MDPI

Article

Corporate Governance Provisions, Family Involvement, and Firm Performance in Publicly Traded Family Firms

Esra Memili [1,*] and Kaustav Misra [2]

[1] Bryan School of Business and Economics, University of North Carolina-Greensboro, 370 Bryan, Greensboro, NC 27402, USA
[2] College of Business and Management, Saginaw Valley State University, C326, 7400 Bay Road, University Center, MI 48710, USA; kmisra@svsu.edu
* Author to whom correspondence should be addressed; e_memili@uncg.edu; Tel.: +1-662-617-1459.

Academic Editor: Nicholas Apergis
Received: 2 April 2015; Accepted: 1 July 2015; Published: 17 July 2015

Abstract: This study examines the moderation effects of corporate governance provisions on the link between family involvement (*i.e.*, family ownership and family management) in publicly-traded firms and firm performance by drawing upon agency theory, with a focus on principal-principal agency issues, and the extant family governance literature. We develop and test the hypotheses on 386 of the S&P 500 firms longitudinally. Findings support the hypotheses suggesting the moderation effects of the use of provisions (a) protecting controlling owners in terms of their sustainability of controlling status, and (b) protecting management legally on the inverted U-shaped relationship between family ownership and firm performance. We also found support for the moderation effects of provisions (c) protecting controlling owners in terms of their voting rights, (d) protecting noncontrolling owners, and (e) protecting management monetarily on the inverted U-shaped relationship between family management and firm performance. By this, our study provides empirical support for the principal-principal agency perspective on the corporate governance in publicly-traded family firms. As such, it suggests new avenues of research for both the corporate governance literature, as well as for the theory of the family firm. Our study also offers insights to policy directed toward monitoring the actions of large shareholders such as family and enhancing the overall shareholder value in publicly-traded family firms.

Keywords: corporate governance; principal-principal agency theory; governance provisions; family firms; firm performance

JEL Classification: G32

---

1. Introduction

Many corporations in the U.S. and around the world exhibit family involvement (Aguilera *et al.* [1], Villalonga and Amit [2,3]). The involvement of family in the firm is usually through ownership and management (Chrisman *et al.* [4], Neubauer *et al.* [5], Siebels *et al.* [6]). Since these can lead to the pursuit of family-centered goals and associated strategies (Carney [7]), family firm behavior and performance tend to differ from not only those in nonfamily firms, but also other family firms (Miller *et al.* [8]). Examining the use of corporate governance provisions can improve our understanding of the relationship between family involvement and firm performance in publicly-traded family firms. Research generally draws attention to principal-principal agency problems between controlling and noncontrolling shareholders in corporate family enterprises. This is because of families' stock ownership being relatively more than that of minority shareholders and control over the business through involvement in management and board of directors. By this, families are able to pursue family-centered goals (e.g., behaving altruistically toward family members) which may not be beneficial for noncontrolling owners (Ali *et al.* [9], Maury [10]). The use of control enhancing corporate governance provisions, such as unequal voting rights in favor of the controlling family, can further enhance the family's ability to pursue noneconomic and economic goals primarily benefiting the family, if they intend to do so. Gompers and colleagues [11] show that governance provisions (*i.e.*, provisions allowing management to resist shareholder activism, and prevent or delay takeovers) can lead to higher agency costs (Daily *et al.* [12], Daily *et al.* [13]). They also suggest the use of such provisions can be related to performance differences among firms. However, the authors do not distinguish between family and nonfamily firms. A recent work by Memili, Misra, and Chrisman [14] classifies these governance provisions by considering family firm idiosyncrasies. There has been a stream of research investigating whether family firms outperform nonfamily firms. There seems to be mixed findings and performance differences tend be a function of the type of family involvement (e.g., founder control) (e.g., Anderson and Reeb [15–17], Miller *et al.* [18], Villalonga and Amit [2,3]). For instance, Villalonga and Amit [19] found that the impact of control enhancing mechanisms on firm performance depends on the mechanism used. Nevertheless, only a few of the governance provisions such as voting agreements, dual-class stock, cross-holdings, pyramids [1], and their impact on firm performance have been investigated in publicly traded family firms (e.g., Villalonga and Amit [2,3]). These provisions generally elevate voting rights of the families even at low levels of equity ownership (Villalonga and Amit [3]). Hence, more research is needed concerning governance provisions in order to better understand corporate governance in publicly-traded family firms.

There has been a call for studies examining family firm performance and its antecedents, owing to the critical role of firm value in buy out decisions, tax payments, executive compensation, capital raising strategies, and selling the company (Villalonga [21]). Family ownership and management can enhance firm value since the controlling family can provide superior oversight through lengthy tenure, invest in long-term projects, or exhibit reputation concerns that diminish the possibility of questionable or irresponsible business practices (Anderson and Reeb [17], Dyer and Whetten [22]). However, the use of control enhancing mechanisms, which may be driven by intentions to maintain family control to preserve socioemotional wealth (Chrisman *et al.* [23], Gomez-Mejia *et al.* [24]), may also negatively influence the effects of family ownership and management on firm performance. To date, the interaction effects of family involvement and control enhancing governance provisions on firm performance have not been fully investigated. Instead, the focus has been mostly on the direct effects of some of the governance mechanisms on firm performance (Daily *et al.* [12]). Control enhancing mechanisms within the context of publicly traded family firms require more research attention, since some of them may be associated with principal-principal agency costs (Chrisman *et al.* [25], Crutchley *et al.* [26], Morck *et al.* [27]) through enhancing the power, authority, and legitimacy of the family. However, we do not know enough about the factors that enhance or mitigate controlling owners' ability and willingness to pursue policies that lead to the expropriation of minority shareholder wealth and entrenchment in family firms (Chrisman *et al.* [25]).

In an attempt to fill these gaps, this paper [2] applies agency theory (Fama and Jensen [29], Jensen and Meckling [30]) and the extant family governance literature to develop and test the model in this paper. The model in this paper addresses the research question: "How do governance provisions affect the link between family involvement (*i.e.*, family ownership and family management) and firm

---

[1] According to Morck and Steier [20], a pyramid is a structure prevalent around the world except in the U.S. and U.K. in which a shareholder, usually a family, controls a single company and this company then holds control blocks in other companies and each of these companies holds control blocks in even more companies, which is rare in the U.S.

[2] Has been originally developed as part (*i.e.*, Essay 2) of a dissertation (Memili [28]) by one of the co-authors of this manuscript.

performance?" and hence demonstrates how the use of these provisions moderates the relationships between family involvement (*i.e.*, family ownership and management) and firm performance.

This paper contributes to the literature in several ways. First, the model in this paper illustrates the interplay between family involvement and corporate governance provisions in influencing firm performance when studies mostly focus on the direct effects of family involvement components or governance provisions on firm performance. Indeed, both family involvement and the use of governance provisions are likely to be influential on firm performance in publicly-traded firms. Hence, the model reflects the reality better. Second, this paper contributes to a better understanding of the differences among family firms, shedding light on to the heterogeneity among family firms. Third, findings of this paper inform us about the principal-principal agency costs since some of the provisions may be associated with agency problems in publicly-traded family firms by elevating the power of the controlling family which can enable the family to act opportunistically, if they intend to. Fourth, we test our hypotheses longitudinally, allowing stronger causal inference and increased statistical power over cross sectional design.

In the remainder of this paper, a theoretical overview is provided and hypotheses are developed. Then, the hypotheses are tested. Finally, results, future research opportunities, and implications for practice are discussed.

2. Theoretical Overview

2.1. Principal-Principal Problems in Publicly Traded Family Firms

Principal-principal agency problems in publicly traded family firms are different from principal-agent problems in privately held family firms, owing to the co-existence of controlling and minority shareholders (Gomez-Mejia *et al.* [31]). Unlike minority shareholders, family not only has relatively higher levels of equity ownership, but also often has management and board representation as well. Thereby, interests of owners and managers are more aligned than those in nonfamily publicly-traded firms. Nevertheless, controlling family owners and managers tend to hold family-centered interests which may not benefit minority shareholders (Morck and Yeung [32]). Principal-principal agency problems are in the forms of expropriation of noncontrolling shareholder wealth and entrenchment of controlling family.

Concentrated control can be beneficial in monitoring agents (who may also be owners), but can enable expropriation of minority shareholder wealth (Anderson and Reeb [15,33], Andres [34], Johnson *et al.* [35], La Porta *et al.* [36]). Expropriation within the weak governance context appears when majority owners control the firm and restrict noncontrolling owners' rights to appropriate returns on their investments (Dharwadkar *et al.* [37], Young *et al.* [38]). This can be through tunneling with non-arm's-length and related-party transactions (Johnson *et al.* [35], Shleifer and Vishny [39], Young *et al.* [38]), transfer pricing (*i.e.*, a related-party transaction) which can occur by managers forming independent companies that they own personally and selling the products of the main company they manage to the independent firms at below market prices or *vice versa*, misallocation of company funds which can be through self-dealing transactions such as exclusive dividends, high compensation, loan guarantees using the firm's assets as collateral, or sub-optimal investment decisions that create empire building opportunities for family members (*i.e.*, excessive expansion). These consequently can lower shareholder value. The management can also prefer excessive cash holdings rather than investing or distributing dividends (Shleifer and Vishny [39]).

In addition, managerial resistance to takeovers in order to protect the private benefits of family control can lower shareholder wealth (Mahoney and Mahoney [40], Mahoney *et al.* [41,42], Cremers and Nair [43]). Shareholders usually can gain from above average returns from corporate takeovers owing to the economies of scale and synergies attained from combining corporate resources (Jensen and Ruback [44], Berkovitch and Narayanan [45], Bechuk [46]). Takeovers can also enhance cash flows, market power in product markets, tax advantages, and avoidance of bankruptcy (Jensen and

Ruback [44], Jensen [47]). However, transfer of control may not be favorable for the controlling family owing to self- and family-interest at the expense of shareholders (Jensen and Ruback [44]). Consistent with this, Gompers *et al.* [11] show that the provisions in the U.S. are associated with lower firm value.

The expropriation can be even more problematic, if the controlling owners are wealthy enough and they simply prefer to maximize private benefits of control rather than shareholder wealth. Even when a legal system, such as that in the U.S., provides investor protection, the controlling owners may still treat family members exclusively, limit innovation, avoid diversification, restrict dividends, and refrain from expansion through raising capital (Anderson and Reeb [15,16], Gomez-Mejia *et al.* [48], La Porta *et al.* [49], Young *et al.* [38]).

Aside from the expropriation problem, managerial entrenchment (*i.e.*, a manager remains active in management and resists transfer of control even though he/she is no longer competent or qualified to run the firm of family members) is likely to occur in family firms (Anderson *et al.* [50], Anderson and Reeb [15], Claessens *et al.* [51], Crutchley [26], Gomez-Mejia *et al.* [31], Morck and Yeung [32], Shleifer and Vishny [39], Walsh and Seward [52], Westhead *et al.* [53]).

Gomez-Mejia *et al.* [31] argue that family firms may be more prone to managerial entrenchment because family ties and emotions may be influential in appointment and tenure of executives, lowering the effectiveness of monitoring and resulting in biased judgments of executive performance. For example, Miller and Le Breton-Miller [54] also draw attention to long-term CEO tenures in family firms.

The variant equity levels of the controlling family and minority shareholders can result in conflicts (Gilson and Gordon [55], Villalonga and Amit [2]). In large US corporations, founding families tend to be the only blockholders whose control rights exceed their cash-flow rights (Villalonga and Amit [56]). The discrepancy between family's control rights and ownership tends to exacerbate the agency problem of the expropriation of noncontrolling owners since families bear only a fraction of the costs associated with the private benefits they reap (Ang *et al.* [57], Claessens *et al.* [51], Jensen and Meckling [30], Miller and Le Breton-Miller [54], Villalonga and Amit [3]). Moreover, family owners may be driven by the noneconomic benefits of control rather than wealth. Family-oriented noneconomic goals can be the preservation of family harmony, identity, dynasty, social capital, reputation, and ability to be altruistic toward family members (Berrone *et al.* [58], Chrisman *et al.* [25], Gomez-Mejia *et al.* [24,48]). The achievement of these goals creates socioemotional wealth for the family and elevates their intention to sustain family control (Chua *et al.* [59], Gomez-Mejia *et al.* [24]). The loss of socioemotional wealth, however, can result in diminished intimacy, lowered status, and inability to meet family's expectations (Gomez-Mejia *et al.* [24]). Hence, family firms could be willing to accept greater performance hazard in order to preserve socioemotional wealth rooted in noneconomic goals (Chrisman *et al.* [60], Gomez-Mejia *et al.* [24]). Gomez-Mejia *et al.* [24] show that family firms may be willing to accept risk to their performance to avoid the loss of socioemotional wealth, but at the same time be risk averse in making other business decisions. Hence, family-centered noneconomic goals may not be beneficial for nonfamily stakeholders (Chrisman *et al.* [23]).

Additionally, family firm leaders often desire to pass on a sustainable legacy to future generations of the family (Dyer and Whetten [22]), which leads to parsimony in resource conservation and allocation (Carney [7]), particularly when a family's equity ownership constitutes a significant portion of the family's wealth (Wright *et al.* [61]). In these cases, family owners and/or managers may be reluctant to support innovation or other risky investments necessary to maximize firm performance and growth (Morck and Yeung [32], Wright *et al.* [61]). Accordingly, researchers (e.g., Daily *et al.* [12], Mishra and McConaughy [62]) suggest that the risk aversion of family owners may cause them to forego profitable growth opportunities, limiting the growth of the firm. Family's reducing risk exposure at the expense of other shareholders' potential higher returns may consequently create conflict of interests.

Furthermore, controlling shareholders either actively participate in management or are positioned to assure that management and even the board serves their interests (Brecht *et al.* [63], Combs [64], Demsetz and Lehn [65], Herman [66], Jones *et al.* [67]). This is in line with family owner and managers' particularistic tendencies with regard to whom they personally choose to work within their organizations (Carney [7]). In addition, there may be generational differences in the agency costs between family and nonfamily firms (Villalonga and Amit [2,19]). While founding families may be concerned with value for all shareholders, the descendants may be shifting their focus toward engaging in power struggles, which can foster relational conflict and harm performance (Kellermanns and Eddleston [68], Kellermanns and Eddleston [69]).

Hence, principal-principal agency problems arising between controlling and noncontrolling shareholders can result in more detrimental effects than the principal-agent agency problems in publicly traded family firms (Ali *et al.* [9]).

2.2. Corporate Governance Provisions

Governance provisions are an important part of corporate governance in today's corporate environment in the U.S. and many other countries around the world. In the 1980s, hostile takeovers started in the U.S. (Holstrom and Kaplan [70]). Hostile takeovers are orchestrated by an outside entity by making a tender offer (*i.e.*, a price for their stock, which is higher than the current market price) to shareholders of a target firm without involving the target's management and board (Davis [71]). When the raider firm acquires a substantial ownership position to exercise control, it may merge with the target firm, liquidate its assets to finance the takeover, replace top management and board, or sell off some of the divisions (Davis [71]). Takeover threats constitute an external governance provided by the market for corporate control and discipline corporate management (Davis [71], Sundaramurthy [72], Cremers and Nair [43]). Consequently, takeovers generally benefit shareholders of target and acquiring companies through facilitating constructive organizational restructuring and generating substantial gains (Jensen [47], Berkovitch and Narayanan [45], Cremers and Nair [43]). Then, hostile takeovers declined substantially, while at the same time executive stock options and the greater involvement of boards of directors and shareholders took place in the corporate world. Through these changes, corporate governance mechanisms became more important than ever (Holstrom and Kaplan [70]). Gompers *et al.* [11] suggest that governance provisions generally allow management to resist shareholder activism, and prevent or delay takeovers. The activist shareholders pressure the management of the poorly performing firms in their portfolio for improvement of performance and shareholder value (Gillan and Starks [73]). However, families, who control publicly traded firms and are expected to be unwilling to let go of control and utilize control enhancing governance provisions in order to enhance and sustain their power.

Gompers *et al.* [11] identify 24 governance provisions used in corporations in the U.S. The authors divide governance provisions into five groups based upon the purpose of their usage: tactics for delaying takeovers (delay), director/officer protection (protection), voting rights (voting), state laws (state), and other takeover defenses (other). However, the authors do not differentiate between family and nonfamily firms nor consider the differences between controlling family and noncontrolling owner groups and their distinct characteristics, interests, and rights within the context of family firms. In this paper, we use Memili and colleagues' [14] classification of governance provisions based on the purpose of usage and the existence of different interest groups (*i.e.*, controlling owners, noncontrolling owners, and management and board) within the context of family firms, as can be seen in Table 1.

Table 1. Corporate Governance Provision Definitions. (Gillan *et al.* [74], Gompers *et al.* [11], Mahoney *et al.* [42], Memili *et al.* [14]).

Provisions protecting controlling owners through enhancing voting rights	
Provisions	**Definitions**
Unequal Voting Rights	To limit voting rights of some shareholders and expand those of others.
Cumulative Voting	Allows shareholders to concentrate their votes and helps minority shareholders to elect directors.
Supermajority	Voting requirements for approval of mergers.
Provisions protecting controlling owners through sustaining controlling status	
Provisions	**Definitions**
Blank Check	A preferred stock over which the BOD has broad authority to determine voting, dividend, conversion, and other rights. It is used to prevent takeover by placing this stock with certain friendly investors.
Business Combination Law	Requires a waiting period for transactions such as mergers, unless the transaction is approved by the BOD.
Poison Pills	Give the holders of the target firm's stocks the right to purchase stocks in the target at a discount and to sell shares at a premium if ownership changes. This makes the target unattractive.
Bylaw	Amendment limitations limit shareholders' ability to amend the governing documents of the company.
Charter	Limitations to change the governing documents of the company.
Fair Price	Requires a bidder to pay to all shareholders the highest price paid to any during a period of time before the commencement of an offer. This makes an acquisition more expensive.
Anti-greenmail	Prohibits a firm's controlling owners/managers from paying a raider "greenmail", which involves the repurchase of blocks of company stock, at a premium above market price, in exchange for an agreement by the raider not to acquire the firm. Eliminating greenmail may discourage potential bidders from considering the target firm for a takeover. Hence, it can be used as an antitakeover device.
Provisions protecting noncontrolling owners	
Provisions	**Definitions**
Cash-out Laws	Shareholders can sell their stakes to a controlling shareholder at a price based on the highest price of recently acquired shares. It works as fair-price provisions extended to nontakeover situations.
Secret Ballot	Confidential voting. Either an independent third party or employees sworn to secrecy count proxy votes and management does not look at proxy cards.

Table 1. *Cont.*

Provisions protecting management and directors' positions	
Provisions	Definitions
Classified Board	The board is split into different classes, with only one class up for election in a given year. Hence, an outsider who gains control of a corporation may need to wait a few years in order to be able to gain control of the board.
Special Meeting Limitations	Bidders must wait until the regularly scheduled annual meeting to replace BOD or dismantle takeover defenses.
Written Consent Limitations	Bidders must wait until the regularly scheduled annual meeting to replace BOD or to dismantle takeover defense.
Directors' Duties	Provides BOD with a legal basis for rejecting a takeover that would have been beneficial to shareholders.
Provisions protecting management and directors monetarily	
Provisions	Definitions
Compensation Plans	In case of a change in control, this provision allows participants of incentive bonus plans to cash out options or accelerate the payout of bonuses.
Golden Parachutes	Severance agreements that provide cash or noncash compensation to senior executives upon an event such as termination, demotion, or resignation following a change in control.
Severance	Agreements assuring executives of their positions or some compensation and are not contingent upon a change in control.
Provisions protecting management and directors legally	
Provisions	Definitions
Contracts	Indemnifies officers and directors from certain legal expenses and judgments resulting from lawsuits.
Indemnification	Indemnify officers and directors from certain legal expenses and judgments resulting from lawsuits pertaining to their conduct.
Limitations on Director Liability	Limit directors' personal liability.

3. Hypotheses

3.1. Family Involvement and Firm Performance

Family business studies generally suggest a nonlinear (*i.e.*, an inverted U-shaped) relationship between family involvement and firm performance (e.g., Sciascia and Mazzola [75], Anderson and Reeb [15,16], Claessens *et al.* [51], Morck *et al.* [27], Short and Keasey [76]). One reason for the nonlinear inverted U-shaped relationship between family involvement and firm performance may be the family's tendency to pursue noneconomic goals as family ownership and management increase (Sciascia and Mazzola [75], Chrisman *et al.* [25]). They are able to do so owing to the legitimacy and power obtained through ownership and management positions they hold in the company (Chrisman *et al.* [25]). When the level of family management increases along with the level of family ownership, the noneconomic goals are likely to be aligned with the interests of both owners and managers, resulting in a relatively lower cost of adopting the goals and lower resistance by management and/or noncontrolling owners (Chrisman *et al.* [25]). The largest shareholder may become entrenched and better able to extract value (Claessens *et al.* [51]), which may consequently harm not only firm performance, but also the economy in a broader sense (Chrisman *et al.* [25], Morck *et al.* [77], Morck and Yeung [32]). For example, Morck *et al.* [27] show that heir-controlled Canadian firms exhibit low financial performance owing to the expropriation of noncontrolling owners' wealth and the entrenchment of poorly performing managers whose firms continue to survive through access to capital and insulation from competition via political influence. Accordingly, when controlling owners' voting rights and controlling status are enhanced while also having managers' and directors' positions secured through the use of governance provisions, controlling owners' and managers' ability to pursue the family agenda and engage in opportunistic actions can increase.

Therefore, after a certain point, family ownership and management may lead to the adoption of family-centered goals and strategies which may diminish shareholder value since the benefits of the pursuit of family-centered noneconomic goals are usually not transferrable to nonfamily members. Furthermore, principal-principal agency costs deriving from the controlling owners' and managers' expropriation of noncontrolling shareholder wealth and their entrenchment are likely to increase, which can consequently harm firm performance (Chrisman *et al.* [25]).

Additionally, according to Dyer [78], certain governance mechanisms may be associated with more or fewer agency problems. Indeed, certain provisions protecting management and family shareholder rights can make firms susceptible to principal-principal agency problems in publicly traded family firms since they strengthen the controlling family business members' ability, power, and legitimacy to entrench themselves and extract value (Burkart *et al.* [79], Claessens *et al.* [51]). This is relevant to Alchian and Demsetz' [80] agency concern regarding "Who will monitor the monitor?"

Since governance provisions differentially affect the balance of power in the firm (Gompers *et al.* [11]), the frequency of the use of provisions protecting controlling owners, noncontrolling owners, and management are also likely to interact with family involvement components (*i.e.*, family ownership and family management) to determine firm performance. Specifically, higher frequency of the use of provisions protecting controlling owners, management and directors, and others indicating higher management, director, and family shareholder power and ability to pursue family-centered noneconomic goals exclusively benefiting family members, are likely to weaken the positive effects and strengthen the negative effects of family involvement components on firm performance. Additionally, higher frequency of the use of provisions protecting noncontrolling owners and others, indicating a higher level of noncontrolling owners' rights, are likely to strengthen the positive effects and weaken the negative effects of family involvement components on firm performance. Owing to a prominent stream of research showing an inverted U-shaped relationship between family involvement and firm performance, this paper attempts to explore a relatively less investigated area (*i.e.*, the moderators which may influence this relationship) in order to extend this line of research.

3.2. Moderation Effects of the Provisions Protecting Controlling Owners

The higher frequency of the use of provisions, which create a wedge between controlling owners' voting rights and their cash-flow rights (*i.e.*, unequal voting rights, cumulative voting, and supermajority) as well as secure sustainability of their controlling status through delaying or preventing takeovers (*i.e.*, blank check, business combination law, poison pill, bylaw and charter, fair price, and antigreenmail), can elevate family owners' and managers' power. This can exacerbate expropriation of noncontrolling owners' wealth through strengthening the controlling family's ability to reap the private benefits of control and entrench themselves in ownership and management positions (Anderson and Reeb [15,33], Andres [34], Gomez-Mejia *et al.* [31], Shleifer and Vishny [39]), weakening the positive effects and strengthening the negative effects of family ownership and family management on firm performance. The moderating effects of the use of provisions protecting controlling owners in terms of their voting rights are expected to lead to a shift of the inverted U-shaped curve representing the relationship between family involvement (*i.e.*, family ownership and family management) and firm performance.

Moreover, additional discretionary power, attained through the provisions protecting controlling owners, can allow both family owners and managers to pursue family agendas primarily benefiting the family and to consume perks, thereby reducing firm performance and noncontrolling shareholder value. At relatively smaller percentages of ownership of shares and higher voting rights, family owners' incentive to consume perks, rather than to maximize firm value increases since they gain 100 percent of the amount spent on perks, but their percentage of share in firm profits are only reduced according to their percentage share of the firm. Hence:

Hypothesis 1. The use of provisions protecting controlling owners in terms of their (1a) voting rights and (1b) sustainability of controlling status will negatively moderate the inverted U-shaped relationship between family ownership and firm performance.

Hypothesis 2. The use of provisions protecting controlling owners in terms of their (2a) voting rights and (2b) sustainability of controlling status will negatively moderate the inverted U-shaped relationship between family management and firm performance.

3.3. Moderation Effects of the Provisions Protecting Noncontrolling Owners

These provisions (*i.e.*, cash-out laws and secret ballot) protect noncontrolling owners by elevating the value of noncontrolling owners' shares while selling to a controlling owner and assuring confidentiality in voting. Particularly, the secrecy of voting, which gives noncontrolling owners' a voice in firm governance, can constitute an internal control mechanism by monitoring controlling owners' actions and allowing potentially beneficial takeovers to take place by weakening the controlling family owners and managers' resistance and prevention tactics. As a result, the use of these provisions can democratize the dominant family governance context by lowering the risk of expropriation of noncontrolling owners' wealth and entrenchment of the family and facilitate raising capital through attracting outside investors. Hence, the higher use of these provisions is expected to strengthen the positive effects and weaken the negative effects of family involvement on performance. This is expected to lead to a shift of the inverted U-shaped curve representing the relationship between family involvement (*i.e.*, family ownership and family management) and firm performance.

Hypothesis 3. The use of provisions protecting noncontrolling owners will positively moderate the inverted U-shaped relationship between (3a) family ownership and firm performance, and (3b) family management and firm performance.

3.4. Moderation Effects of the Provisions Protecting Management and Directors

These provisions (*i.e.*, classified board, special meeting, written consent, directors' duties, compensation plans, golden parachute, severance, contracts, indemnification, and limitations on director liability) protect managers and directors in terms of their position in the firm, monetarily, and legally. Family owners are often involved in management to exert family influence on the business (Brecht *et al.* [63]). When they are not actively involved in the management of the firm, they appoint well trusted associates to represent them (Combs [64], Jones *et al.* [67]). When managers' and directors' positions in the firm are insulated from proxy fights and takeovers, they have more freedom to act according to the controlling family's family-centered expectations and/or their own personal gains, which may not always be beneficial for firm performance. Hence, the use of provisions protecting managers and directors in terms of their positions in the firm combined with family's dominance in ownership and/or management can enhance the family's pursuing family agendas and exacerbate expropriation of noncontrolling owners' wealth and entrenchment of the controlling family, which can consequently harm firm performance.

Moreover, as discussed and hypothesized in the previous section, family controlled publicly traded firms are expected to use provisions protecting managers and directors monetarily and legally less frequently than nonfamily firms. However, when/if they are used, they are expected to weaken the positive effects of family involvement on firm performance and strengthen the negative effects, which can shift the inverted U-shaped curve representing the relationship between family involvement (*i.e.*, family ownership and family management) and firm performance. In the absence of the concern for the monetary and legal consequences of wrongdoings, managers and directors are more likely to be in compliance with the controlling family's family-oriented expectations in their actions even if they may not be beneficial for the shareholders and firm value in general.

Hypothesis 4. The use of provisions protecting management (4a) in terms of their position in the firm, (4b) monetarily, and (4c) legally will negatively moderate the inverted U-shaped relationship between family ownership and firm performance.

Hypothesis 5. The use of provisions protecting management (5a) in terms of their position in the firm, (5b) monetarily, and (5c) legally will negatively moderate the inverted U-shaped relationship between family management and firm performance.

4. Methodology

4.1. Data

Panel data regarding governance provision usage in firms is obtained from a larger project designed to investigate all the companies incorporated in the U.S. in the Investor Responsibility Research Center books in terms of their usage of 20 out of 24 control enhancing governance mechanisms (Gompers *et al.* [11]). Accounting, market, ownership, and management data is obtained from Thompson Reuters Thompson One Corporate Development database. Family business members are identified by using the Hoover's database and annual reports in Mergent Online. Data is analyzed on a restricted sample of firms based on publicly available data for 2001 to 2007. We conducted several tests to select the appropriate model for this paper. Consistent with previous studies investigating publicly traded family firms, the sample comes from the firms listed in S&P 500 (e.g., Anderson and Reeb [15,16,33], Short *et al.* [81]). Missing data lowered the sample size to 386.

4.2. Variables

4.2.1. Dependent Variable

Firm performance is measured by the Tobin's q (Chung and Pruitt [82]) with accounting data provided by Thomson Reuters. The use of this firm performance measurement in this paper follows Anderson and Reeb [33], Villalonga and Amit [2,3,56] and Miller *et al.* [18]. Tobin's q is the ratio of the firm's market value to replacement value of its assets (Villalonga and Amit [2], Miller *et al.* [18]). The formula for Tobin's q (Miller *et al.* [18]) is as follows: ((commonshares outstanding × calendar year closing price) + (current liabilities-current assets) + (long-term debt) + (liquidating value of preferred stock))/total assets. For robustness checks, we also collected data regarding other firm performance measures concerning profitability such as Return on Assets (ROA = Net Income/Average Total Assets), Return on Equity (ROE = Net Income/Shareholders' Equity), and Return on Investment (ROI = Net Income/Total Assets) (Carton and Hofer [83]).

4.2.2. Independent Variables

Family ownership (FO) is the percentage of total firm ownership held by members of a family. *Family management (FM)* is the number of individual family members who are in top management and/or the board of directors. The *squared family ownership (FO^2)* and the *squared family management (FM^2)* variables are used to indicate nonlinear relationships between independent variables and dependent variable. For robustness tests, the proportion of number of family managers and/or the board of directors *(PFM)* to total number of managers and/or the board of directors is also calculated.

17

4.2.3. Moderators

Moderators consist of six categories of governance provisions that group the 20 of the 24 provisions (Business Combination Law and Cash-out Laws which were missing in the dataset) identified by Gompers *et al.* [11] according to the purposes of their usage by firms. Judgment-based categorization (Perreault and Leigh [84]) of the governance provisions is used. The validity of this categorization was confirmed by three expert judges who assessed the degree to which the provisions represent the categories (Netemeyer *et al.* [85]).

The first moderator is the *frequency of the use of governance provisions protecting controlling owners through voting rights (VOTING)*. This variable involves the following provisions: (1) Unequal voting rights; (2) Cumulative voting; and (3) Supermajority. The second moderator is the *frequency of the use of governance provisions protecting controlling owners through sustaining control status (STATUS)* and includes the following provisions: (1) Blank check; (2) Poison pill; (3) Bylaw; (4) Charter; (5) Fair price; and (6) Antigreenmail. The third moderator, the *frequency of the use of governance provisions protecting noncontrolling owners (NONCONTROLLING)* includes provisions concerning: (1) Secret ballot. The fourth moderator is the *frequency of the use of governance provisions protecting management and directors in terms of their position (POSITION)*. This variable involves the following provisions: (1) Classified board; (2) Special meeting; (3) Written consent; and (4) Director's duties. The fifth moderator, the *frequency of the use of governance provisions protecting management and directors monetarily (MONETARY)* includes provisions concerning: (1) Compensation plans; (2) Golden parachute; and (3) Severance. The sixth moderator is the *frequency of the use of governance provisions protecting management and directors legally (LEGAL)*. This variable involves the following provisions: (1) Contracts; (2) Indemnification; and (3) Limitations on director liability.

In a given year, provisions that are used by a firm are coded as "1" and provisions not used are coded as "0". The frequency of the use of each category is calculated by adding usage/no usage figures (*i.e.*, 1/0) in each category. For robustness tests, particularly when one provision group (*i.e.*, NONCONTROLLING) included only one provision due to missing provision data, categorical provision group variables are also included (1 = at least one mechanism present; 0 = none).

4.2.4. Control Variables

We controlled for the variables that are expected to influence firm performance. Larger companies may have performance advantages over small and medium size firms owing to economies of scale, consequently affecting their firm performance (Hansen and Wernerfelt [86]). Hence, *firm size (FS)* is controlled and measured via the log of the number of employees following Dewar and Dutton [87]. In addition, older firms may have the advantage of being established with a history of past successes, which can influence their performance (Hansen and Wernerfelt [86]). *Firm age (FA)* is measured as the number of years the firm has been in existence since founding. Additionally, family firms may have competitive advantages in some industries compared to others (Chrisman *et al.* [25]), which can influence their performance. We measure *primary firm industry (FI)* by classifying all firms into one of four industrial categories: (1) retail; (2) service; (3) manufacturing; and (4) other, following Chrisman *et al.* [25]. Three categorical variables, coded 1/0, are created to indicate retail, service, and manufacturing firms. Firms in other industries are coded as zero for each variable. For further specification of industry, four-digit SIC codes and sector names are also identified and entered for each firm. Additionally, *generational majority in management and board* is controlled since family influence tends to be weaker when family influence is more dispersed or fractionalized owing to the involvement of later generations (Schulze *et al.* [88], Gomez-Mejia *et al.* [24]). Two categorical variables, coded 1/0, are created to indicate first generation *(GEN1)* and second generation or later *(GEN2)*. Nonfamily firms are those coded as zero for each of these two variables. Institutional owners such as mutual or pension funds may also play a significant role in corporate decision making (Anderson and Reeb [33]), which can consequently affect firm performance. *Institutional ownership (IO)* is the percentage of overall institutional ownership of voting shares outstanding. Similarly, ownership by other insiders can also influence decision making and firm performance (Anderson and Reeb [33]). Hence, *other insiders' ownership (OIO)*, which is the equity holdings of top managers and directors minus family ownership, is controlled to capture the incentive effects of other insiders' ownership (Anderson and Reeb [33]). Firm risk (*i.e.*, return volatility) may be another factor that can influence firm performance (Anderson and Reeb [15,33]) since high level of risk may result in either above average returns or a large amount of losses. *Firm risk (FR)* is measured as the standard deviation of stock returns for the previous 60 months, following Anderson and Reeb [15,33]. Also, investment into R&D and internationalization may lead firms to high or low performance (Decarolis and Deeds [89], Graves and Langowitz [90]). Hence, these variables are controlled. *R&D (RD)* level will be calculated via R&D/sales ratio (Miller *et al.* [18]). *Internationalization (INT)* is measured as the percentage of foreign revenue (100%-percentage of domestic revenue).

4.3. Analyses

Table 2 provides the means, standard deviations, and correlations of the variables used in the study. This is a balanced time series panel model. As a result, many observations have censored or truncated data which is important to recognize in the model. Hence the Tobit model would seem to be a sensible approach, because it was designed to accommodate such issues (Greene [91]). The basic choice is between a pooled model and fixed or random effects model. The difference between the random effect and fixed effect model is straightforward. The random effect estimator is the most efficient and it is consistent under the assumption that the effect from companies must be uncorrelated with other explanatory variables. The fixed effect estimators do not require this assumption (Caselli and Coleman [92]). Before selecting the correct model for the analysis, a series of tests were employed to confirm the correct econometric model for this paper. The Breusch-Pagan and Hausman tests confirm the model specification. Both of these tests confirm that both the pooled model and fixed effect model is adequate for this sample. Therefore we employed Fixed Effects Tobit Model to evaluate the hypotheses in this paper.

Since this is a time series dataset, it is reasonable to expect the lag effects in the model. To select the right model, we performed a series of time series tests and used AIC (Akaike Information Criteria) values in order to select the appropriate model (Enders [93]). We tested three models with various specifications, such as independent variables with no lags, with one lag and then with two lags and then compare their AIC values. The independent variable with first lag had the lowest AIC values. Hence, we used independent variables with first lag in this paper. Table 3 presents the results of the Fixed Effects Tobit Models, with firm performance as the dependent variable.

Hypotheses 1a through 5c are tested via Tobit Fixed Effects panel data analysis for first lagged the controls, independent variables, moderators, and interactions. NLOGIT version 4.0 Econometric software is used. NLOGIT4 selected the estimation model as the Fixed Effects estimation model. Tobit Fixed Effects estimation is used to adjust for a large number of zero observations (Maddala [94]). Prior to running the analyses, the variables' normality of their distributions is examined by graphing the distributions and examining the skewness and kurtosis in Excel. The variables which are not normally distributed are transformed (e.g., log of firm size). Additionally, Variance Inflation Factors for the variables are calculated. Additionally, Variance Inflation Factors for the variables are calculated. VIFs range between 1.10 and 3.24. Collinearity was not a problem since all VIFs were less than 10.

Table 2. Descriptive and Correlations.

	M	SD	1	2	3	4	5	6	7	8	9	10	11	12	13	14	15	16	17	18	19	20	21	22	23	24
1. VOT	0.29	0.50	1																							
2. STA	2.06	1.04	0.05	1																						
3. NON	0.21	0.41	−0.06	0.01	1																					
4. POS	1.64	1.15	0.07	0.37	0.05	1																				
5. MON	1.57	0.66	0.03	0.22	0.07	0.14	1																			
6. LEG	0.96	0.97	0.09	0.05	0.02	−0.17	0.03	1																		
7. OTH	0.04	0.22	0.03	0.19	0.11	0.06	0.08	0.03	1																	
8. GEN1	0.05	0.23	0.08	−0.03	−0.05	−0.02	−0.11	−0.04	0.01	1																
9. GEN2	0.14	0.35	−0.00	−0.11	−0.05	−0.08	−0.19	0.09	−0.04	−0.09	1															
10. RET	0.09	0.29	−0.04	−0.09	−0.12	0.03	−0.04	−0.08	−0.03	0.06	0.05	1														
11. SER	0.27	0.45	−0.01	−0.02	−0.03	0.10	−0.05	−0.06	−0.03	0.01	−0.03	−0.21	1													
12. MAN	0.38	0.48	−0.00	0.04	0.05	−0.07	−0.06	0.06	0.06	−0.08	0.01	−0.27	−0.49	1												
13. IO	32.29	11.21	−0.02	0.08	−0.07	0.05	0.17	−0.03	0.03	−0.05	−0.07	0.11	−0.07	0.03	1											
14. FA	59.19	44.63	0.09	0.09	0.08	0.04	0.06	0.13	0.02	−0.15	0.09	−0.09	0.03	0.05	−0.27	1										
15. FSL	4.23	0.56	−0.07	0.00	0.29	0.03	−0.07	0.09	0.05	−0.05	−0.01	0.16	0.03	0.05	−0.19	−0.27	1									
16. OIO	3.99	6.79	−0.01	−0.16	−0.19	−0.10	−0.01	−0.07	−0.13	0.02	−0.02	−0.09	−0.02	−0.02	−0.02	−0.15	−0.17	1								
17. FR	43.84	46.59	−0.03	−0.04	−0.11	−0.02	−0.03	−0.17	−0.02	0.03	−0.10	0.02	−0.02	0.06	−0.05	0.15	−0.26	0.19	1							
18. FO	1.69	6.21	0.00	−0.10	−0.07	−0.08	−0.33	0.06	−0.03	0.33	0.45	0.06	0.07	−0.05	−0.01	−0.01	−0.21	−0.01	0.01	1						
19. FOS	41.42	213.33	−0.00	−0.10	−0.05	−0.85	−0.29	0.05	−0.03	0.29	0.29	0.03	0.09	−0.05	−0.05	−0.20	−0.02	0.00	−0.08	0.93	1					
20. FM	0.39	0.96	−0.00	−0.16	−0.04	−0.12	−0.23	0.07	−0.06	0.36	0.69	0.12	−0.04	−0.04	0.00	−0.12	0.01	0.00	−0.14	−0.06	0.44	1				
21. FMS	1.06	3.55	−0.01	−0.18	−0.18	−0.12	−0.20	0.07	−0.05	0.19	0.56	0.14	−0.04	−0.03	−0.00	−0.10	0.02	0.00	−0.10	−0.05	0.49	0.92	1			
22. FP1	1.80	3.82	−0.06	−0.07	0.02	−0.09	−0.13	0.03	−0.04	−0.01	0.09	0.01	−0.03	0.11	−0.10	−0.05	−0.03	−0.06	0.06	0.05	−0.03	−0.03	0.06	1		
23. RD	0.03	0.00	−0.05	−0.06	−0.02	−0.08	0.02	−0.03	−0.01	−0.02	−0.11	−0.13	−0.16	0.40	−0.19	0.18	−0.20	−0.26	0.12	0.33	−0.10	−0.07	−0.10	0.09	1	
24. INT1	33.97	22.28	0.04	−0.07	−0.04	0.01	0.10	0.10	−0.05	0.04	−0.02	−0.16	−0.06	0.24	−0.14	0.01	−0.2	0.00	−0.05	−0.05	0.14	−0.02	−0.4	−0.10	−0.04 0.28	1

Variables: VOTING: The frequency of the provisions protecting controlling owners' voting rights; RETAIL: Retail industry; FOS: Family ownership squared; STATUS: The frequency of the provisions protecting controlling owners' controlling status; SERVIC: Service industry; FM: Family management; NONCON: The frequency of the provisions protecting noncontrolling owners; MANUF: Manufacturing industry; FMS: Family management squared; POSITIO: The frequency of the provisions protecting managers and directors' positions; FA: Firm age; FP1: Firm performance; MONETA: The frequency of the provisions protecting managers and directors monetarily; FSL: Log of firm size; RD: Research and development; LEGAL: The frequency of the provisions protecting managers and directors legally; OTH: Other provisions; OIO: Other insiders' ownership; INT1: Internationalization; GEN1: First generation's majority in management and board; FR: Firm risk; IO: Institutional ownership; GEN2: Second or later generation's majority in management and board; FO: Family ownership.

Table 3. Results of Analyses.

H1a-H5c with DV: FP1 (Firm Performance)	Model 1	Model 2	Model 3	Model 4
Control Variables (First lagged)				
GEN1 (Generational majority in management and board)	0.21	−0.81 *	1.26 *	−2.76 ***
GEN2 (Generational majority in management and board)	−0.22	−0.11	0.99	−2.46 ***
RETAIL	0.87	1.05 *	0.95*	0.96 *
SERVICE	0.52 +	−0.23	0.42	−0.31
MANUFACTURING	0.73 **	0.73 *	0.70 **	0.52 +
IO (Institutional Ownership)	0.01	0.01 ***	0.01	0.01 ***
FA (Firms Age)	−0.01	−0.01 *	−0.01	−0.01 +
FSL (Log of Firm Size)	−0.58 ***	0.04 +	−0.60 ***	0.01 +
OIO (Other Insiders' Ownership)	0.04 ***	−0.04	0.04 ***	−0.04
RD (Research and Development)	0.82	0.04	0.30	0.04
FR (Firm Risk)	0.01 ***	0.01 +	0.01 **	0.04 +
INT1 (Internationalization)	0.01	0.01 ***	0.01	0.04 ***
Independent Variables (First lagged)				
FO (Family Ownership)		0.91	−0.03	0.02
FOS (Family Ownership Squared)		−0.01 *	0.01	−0.02 **
FM (Family Management)		1.1 *	−0.81	5.22 ***
FMS (Family Management Squared)		−0.18 +	0.13	−0.65 ***
Moderators (First lagged)				
VOTING (Frequency of the use of provisions protecting owners through voting rights)			−0.11	0.29
STATUS (Frequency of the use of provisions protecting owners through sustaining control status)			0.01	−0.02
NONCONTR (Frequency of the use of provisions protecting noncontrolling owners)			0.11	−0.51 +
POSITION (Frequency of the use of provisions protecting managers' positions)			−0.01	−0.11
MONETARY (Frequency of the use of provisions protecting managers monetarily)			−0.20 *	−0.22
LEGAL (Frequency of the use of provisions protecting managers legally)			0.10	−0.08
Interactions (First lagged)				
FOVOTING (Family Ownership × Frequency of the use of provisions protecting owners through voting rights)				0.20
FOSVOTING (Family Ownership Squared × Frequency of the use of provisions protecting owners through voting rights)				−0.01
FOSTATUS (Family Ownership × Frequency of the use of provisions protecting owners through sustaining control status)				−0.35 ***
FOSSTATUS (Family Ownership Squared × Frequency of the use of provisions protecting owners through sustaining control status)				0.01 ***
FONONCONTR (Family Ownership × Frequency of the use of provisions protecting noncontrolling owners)				−0.19

Table 3. *Cont.*

H1a-H5c with DV: FP1 (Firm Performance)	Model 1	Model 2	Model 3	Model 4
FOSNONCONTR (Family Ownership Squared × Frequency of the use of provisions protecting noncontrolling owners)				−0.04
FOPOSITION (Family Ownership × Frequency of the use of provisions protecting managers' positions)				0.05
FOSPOSITION (Family Ownership Squared × Frequency of the use of provisions protecting managers' positions)				0.04
Control Variables (First lagged)				
FOMONETARY (Family Ownership × Frequency of the use of provisions protecting managers monetarily)				0.55 ***
FOSMONETARY (Family Ownership Squared × Frequency of the use of provisions protecting managers monetarily)				−0.01 ***
FOLEGAL (Family Ownership × Frequency of the use of provisions protecting managers legally)				−0.28 ***
FOSLEGAL (Family Ownership Squared × Frequency of the use of provisions protecting managers legally)				0.01 ***
FMVOTING (Family Management × Frequency of the use of provisions protecting owners through voting rights)				−1.96 **
FMSVOTING (Family Management Squared × Frequency of the use of provisions protecting owners through voting rights)				0.59 *
FMSTATUS (Family Management × Frequency of the use of provisions protecting owners through sustaining control status)				0.05
FMSSTATUS (Family Management Squared × Frequency of the use of provisions protecting owners through sustaining control status)				0.02
FMNONCONTR (Family Management × Frequency of the use of provisions protecting noncontrolling owners)				4.21 ***
FMSNONCONTR (Family Management Squared × Frequency of the use of provisions protecting noncontrolling owners)				−0.84 ***
FMPOSITION (Family Management × Frequency of the use of provisions protecting managers' positions)				−0.03
FMSPOSITION (Family Management Squared × Frequency of the use of provisions protecting managers' positions)				−0.01
FMMONETARY (Family Management × Frequency of the use of provisions protecting managers monetarily)				−3.09 ***
FMSMONETARY (Family Management Squared × Frequency of the use of provisions protecting managers monetarily)				0.33 +
FMLEGAL (Family Management × Frequency of the use of provisions protecting managers legally)				1.71 ***
FMSLEGAL (Family Management Squared × Frequency of the use of provisions protecting managers legally)				−0.30 **
Log likelihood function	−843.70	−2902.08	−829.03	−2796.64

$^{+}$ $p < 0.10$; * $p < 0.05$; ** $p < 0.01$; *** $p < 0.001$.

To examine the endogeneity (*i.e.*, reverse causality), we used instrumental variables for both family ownership and family management. Stata 11 software is used to test family ownership and family management variables for endogeneity. Durbin-Wu-Hausman test is performed. Concerning the endogeneity of family ownership, GEN 1 (first generation's majority in management and board) and GEN2 1 (second generation's majority in management and board) instrumental variables are used. For family management variable, the instrumental variables were GEN 1 (first generation's majority in management and board), GEN2 1 (second or later generation's majority in management and board), and PROPORFM (proportion of family managers and directors). Partial F-test results indicate that the co-significance of the instrumental variables for family ownership are significant ($\chi^2 = 32.45$, $p = 0.00$). Partial F-test results also indicate that the co-significance of the instrumental variables for family management are significant ($\chi^2 = 405.69$, $p = 0.00$). Durbin-Wu-Hausman test tests the null hypotheses that family ownership and family management are exogenous. Hence, the results of Durbin-Wu-Hausman show that family ownership ($\chi^2 = 0.57$, $p = 0.45$) and family management ($\chi^2 = 1.13$, $p = 0.29$) variables can be considered as exogenous.

In panel data analyses, Model 1 is the base model where the set of control variables are entered. Manufacturing industry, firm size, other insiders' ownership, and firm risk were significant and service industry was marginally significant. The log likelihood function was −843.70. In Model 2, we entered the independent variables. The family ownership (FO) variable was positive and not significant ($\beta = 0.91$, ns). Family ownership squared (FOS) was negative and significant ($\beta = -0.00$, $p < 0.05$). Family management (FM) was significant ($\beta = 1.10$, $p < 0.05$) and family management squared (FMS) was marginally significant ($\beta = -0.18$, $p < 0.10$). The log likelihood function for the second model was −2902.08. Model 3 introduces the moderators. The log likelihood function for the third model was −829.03. The frequency of the use of provisions protecting managers monetarily was negative and significant ($\beta = -0.20$, $p < 0.05$).

Model 4 introduces the interactions. The log likelihood function was −2796.64. The beta coefficient of Family Ownership × Frequency of the use of Provisions Protecting Controlling Owners' Voting Rights (FO × VOTINGRIGHTS) is positive and not significant ($\beta = 0.20$, ns) and the beta coefficient of Family Ownership^2 × Frequency of the use of Provisions Protecting Controlling Owners' Voting Rights (FO^2 × VOTING) is negative and not significant ($\beta = -0.01$, ns). Therefore, Hypothesis 1a is not supported. The beta coefficient of Family Ownership × Frequency of the use of Provisions Protecting Controlling Owners' Status (FO × STATUS) is negative and significant ($\beta = -0.35$, $p < 0.001$) and the beta coefficient of Family Ownership^2 × Frequency of the use of Provisions Protecting Controlling Owners' Status (FO^2 × STATUS) is positive and significant ($\beta = 01$, $p < 0.001$). Hence, Hypothesis 1b is supported.

The beta coefficient of Family Management × Frequency of the use of Provisions Protecting Controlling Owners' Voting Rights (FM × VOTING) is negative and significant ($\beta = -1.96$, $p < 0.01$) and the beta coefficient of Family Management^2 × Frequency of the use of Provisions Protecting Controlling Owners' Voting Rights (FM^2 × VOTING) is positive and significant ($\beta = 0.59$, $p < 0.05$). Therefore, Hypothesis 2a is supported. The beta coefficient of Family Management × Frequency of the use of Provisions Protecting Controlling Owners' Status (FM × STATUS) is positive and not significant ($\beta = 0.05$, ns) and beta coefficient of Family Management^2 × Frequency of the use of Provisions Protecting Controlling Owners' Status (FM^2 × STATUS) is positive and not significant ($\beta = 0.02$, ns). Hence, Hypothesis 2b is not supported.

The beta coefficient of Family Ownership × Frequency of the use of Provisions Protecting Noncontrolling Owners (FO × NONCONTROLLING) is negative and not significant ($\beta = -0.19$, ns) and the beta coefficient of Family Ownership^2 × Frequency of the use of Provisions Protecting Noncontrolling Owners (FO^2 × NONCONTROLLING) is negative and not significant ($\beta = -0.00$, ns). Therefore, Hypothesis 3a is not supported. The beta coefficient of Family Management × Frequency of the use of Provisions Protecting Noncontrolling Owners (FM × NONCONTROLLING) is positive and significant ($\beta = 4.21$, $p < 0.001$) and the beta coefficient of Family Management^2 × Frequency of the use of Provisions Protecting Noncontrolling Owners (FM^2 × NONCONTROLLING) is negative and significant ($\beta = -0.84$, $p < 0.001$). Hence, Hypothesis 3b is supported.

The beta coefficient of Family Ownership × Frequency of the use of Provisions Protecting Managers' and Directors' Position (FO × POSITION) is positive and not significant ($\beta = 0.05$, ns) and the beta coefficient of Family Ownership^2 × Frequency of the use of Provisions Protecting Managers' and Directors' Position (FO^2 × POSITION) is positive and not significant ($\beta = 0.00$, ns). Hence, Hypothesis 4a is not supported. The beta coefficient of Family Ownership × Frequency of the use of Provisions Protecting Managers and Directors Monetarily (FO × MONETARY) is positive and significant ($\beta = 0.55$, $p < 0.001$) and the beta coefficient of Family Ownership^2 × Frequency of the use of Provisions Protecting Managers and Directors Monetarily (FO^2 × MONETARY) is negative and significant ($\beta = -0.01$, $p < 0.001$). However, the significant relationships are in the opposite direction than hypothesized. Therefore, Hypothesis 4b is not supported. The beta coefficient of Family Ownership × Frequency of the use of Provisions Protecting Managers and Directors Legally (FO × LEGAL) is negative and significant ($\beta = -0.28$, $p < 0.001$) and the beta coefficient of Family Ownership^2 × Frequency of the use of Provisions Protecting Managers and Directors Legally (FO^2 × LEGAL) is positive and significant ($\beta = 0.01$, $p < 0.001$). Hence, Hypothesis 4c is supported.

The beta coefficient of Family Management × Frequency of the use of Provisions Protecting Managers' and Directors' Position (FM × POSITION) is negative and not significant ($\beta = -0.03$, ns) and the beta coefficient of Family Management^2 × Frequency of the use of Provisions Protecting Managers' and Directors' Position (FM^2 × POSITION) is negative and not significant ($\beta = -0.01$, ns). Therefore, Hypothesis 5a is not supported. The beta coefficient of Family Management × Frequency of the use of Provisions Protecting Managers and Directors Monetarily (FM × MONETARY) is negative and significant ($\beta = -3.09$, $p < 0.001$) and the beta coefficient of Family Management^2 × Frequency of the use of Provisions Protecting Managers and Directors Monetarily (FM^2 × MONETARY) is positive and marginally significant ($\beta = 0.33$, $p < 0.10$). Hence, Hypothesis 5b is supported. The beta coefficient of Family Management × Frequency of the use of Provisions Protecting Managers and Directors Legally (FM × LEGAL) is positive and significant ($\beta = 1.71$, $p < 0.001$) and the beta coefficient of Family Management^2 × Frequency of the use of Provisions Protecting Managers and Directors Legally (FM^2 × LEGAL) is negative and significant ($\beta = -0.30$, $p < 0.01$). However, the significant relationships are in the opposite direction than hypothesized. Therefore, Hypothesis 5c is not supported.

Although not hypothesized, the results for the assumed inverted U-shaped relationships between family involvement (*i.e.*, family ownership and family management) and firm performance are the following: The beta coefficient of Family Ownership is positive and not significant ($\beta = 0.91$, ns) and the beta coefficient of Family Ownership^2 is negative and significant ($\beta = -0.00$, $p < 0.05$). The beta coefficient of Family Management is positive and significant ($\beta = 1.10$, $p < 0.05$) and the beta coefficient of Family Management^2 is negative and marginally significant ($\beta = -0.18$, $p < 0.05$). Therefore, the assumption of inverted U-shaped relationship between family management and firm performance is supported, whereas inverted U-shaped relationship between family ownership and firm performance is not supported (please see Table 4).

Table 4. Summary of Findings.

Hypotheses	Conditions That Will Demonstrate Support for the Hypotheses	Findings (Table 3)
H1a	Beta coefficient of Family Ownership × Frequency of the use of Provisions Protecting Controlling Owners' Voting Rights (FO × VOTINGRIGHTS) is negative and significant ($p < 0.05$) and beta coefficient of Family Ownership^2 × Frequency of the use of Provisions Protecting Controlling Owners' Voting Rights (FO^2 × VOTING) is positive and significant ($p < 0.05$).	Not supported
H1b	Beta coefficient of Family Ownership × Frequency of the use of Provisions Protecting Controlling Owners' Status (FO × STATUS) is negative and significant ($p < 0.05$) and beta coefficient of Family Ownership^2 × Frequency of the use of Provisions Protecting Controlling Owners' Status (FO^2 × STATUS) is positive and significant ($p < 0.05$).	Supported (Figure 1)
H2a	Beta coefficient of Family Management × Frequency of the use of Provisions Protecting Controlling Owners' Voting Rights (FM × VOTING) is negative and significant ($p < 0.05$) and beta coefficient of Family Management^2 × Frequency of the use of Provisions Protecting Controlling Owners' Voting Rights (FM^2 × VOTING) is positive and significant ($p < 0.05$).	Supported (Figure 2)
H2b	Beta coefficient of Family Management × Frequency of the use of Provisions Protecting Controlling Owners' Status (FM × STATUS) is negative and significant ($p < 0.05$) and beta coefficient of Family Management^2 × Frequency of the use of Provisions Protecting Controlling Owners' Status (FM^2 × STATUS) is positive and significant ($p < 0.05$).	Not supported
H3a	Beta coefficient of Family Ownership × Frequency of the use of Provisions Protecting Noncontrolling Owners (FO × NONCONTROLLING) is positive and significant ($p < 0.05$) and beta coefficient of Family Ownership^2 × Frequency of the use of Provisions Protecting Noncontrolling Owners (FO^2 × NONCONTROLLING) is negative and significant ($p < 0.05$).	Not supported

Table 4. *Cont.*

Hypotheses	Conditions That Will Demonstrate Support for the Hypotheses	Findings (Table 3)
H3b	Beta coefficient of Family Management × Frequency of the use of Provisions Protecting Noncontrolling Owners (FM × NONCONTROLLING) is positive and significant ($p < 0.05$) and beta coefficient of Family Management^2 × Frequency of the use of Provisions Protecting Noncontrolling Owners (FM^2 × NONCONTROLLING) is negative and significant ($p < 0.05$).	Supported (Figure 3)
H4a	Beta coefficient of Family Ownership × Frequency of the use of Provisions Protecting Managers' and Directors' Position (FO × POSITION) is negative and significant ($p < 0.05$) and beta coefficient of Family Ownership^2 × Frequency of the use of Provisions Protecting Managers' and Directors' Position (FO^2 × POSITION) is positive and significant ($p < 0.05$).	Not supported
H4b	Beta coefficient of Family Ownership × Frequency of the use of Provisions Protecting Managers and Directors Monetarily (FO × MONETARY) is negative and significant ($p < 0.05$) and beta coefficient of Family Ownership^2 × Frequency of the use of Provisions Protecting Managers and Directors Monetarily (FO^2 × MONETARY) is positive and significant ($p < 0.05$).	Not supported (Significant, but in the opposite direction) (Figure 4)
H4c	Beta coefficient of Family Ownership × Frequency of the use of Provisions Protecting Managers and Directors Legally (FO × LEGAL) is negative and significant ($p < 0.05$) and beta coefficient of Family Ownership^2 × Frequency of the use of Provisions Protecting Managers and Directors Legally (FO^2 × LEGAL) is positive and significant ($p < 0.05$).	Supported (Figure 5)
H5a	Beta coefficient of Family Management × Frequency of the use of Provisions Protecting Managers' and Directors' Position (FM × POSITION) is negative and significant ($p < 0.05$) and beta coefficient of Family Management^2 × Frequency of the use of Provisions Protecting Managers' and Directors' Position (FM^2 × POSITION) is positive and significant ($p < 0.05$).	Not supported
H5b	Beta coefficient of Family Management × Frequency of the use of Provisions Protecting Managers and Directors Monetarily (FM × MONETARY) is negative and significant ($p < 0.05$) and beta coefficient of Family Management^2 × Frequency of the use of Provisions Protecting Managers and Directors Monetarily (FM^2 × MONETARY) is positive and significant ($p < 0.05$).	Supported (Figure 6)
H5c	Beta coefficient of Family Management × Frequency of the use of Provisions Protecting Managers and Directors Legally (FM × LEGAL) is negative and significant ($p < 0.05$) and beta coefficient of Family Management^2 × Frequency of the use of Provisions Protecting Managers and Directors Legally (FM^2 × LEGAL) is positive and significant ($p < 0.05$).	Not supported (Significant, but in the opposite direction) (Figure 7)

The significant interactions can be seen in Figures 1–7.

The results are compared to the Pooled Model through OLS Regression. The results of OLS were compatible with the Tobit panel data analyses. Robustness tests also include the analyses with categorical moderators (*i.e.*, 1 = at least one provision is used in each provision group; 0 = none), the proportion of family managers and/or the board of directors (PFM), and other firm performance variables (*i.e.*, ROA, ROE, and ROI). The results of these analyses were consistent with the results presented above.

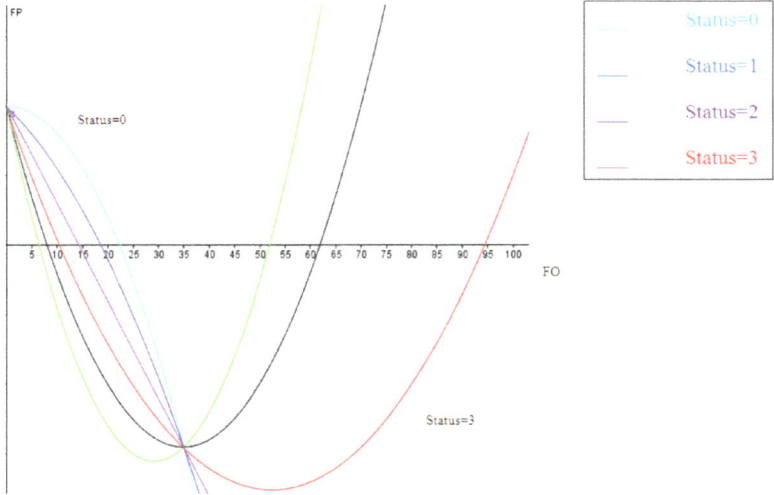

Figure 1. Significant Interactions between Family Ownership and Status Provision. The negative moderation effects of Status Provision changes the direction of inverted U-shaped relationship between Family Ownership and Firm Performance into a U-shape.

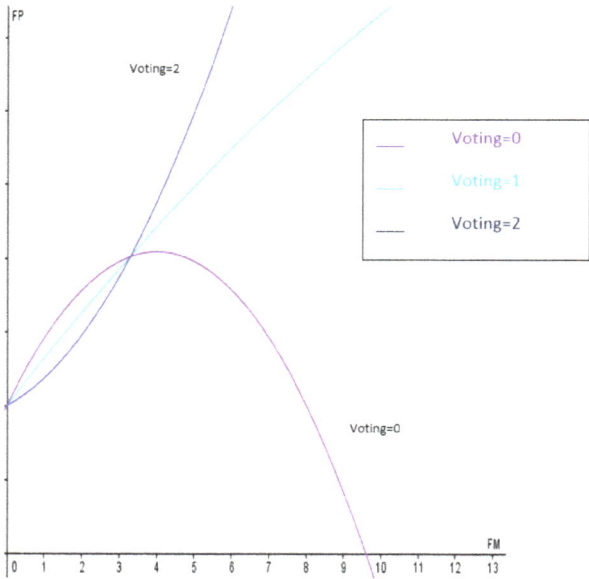

Figure 2. Significant Interactions between Family Management and Voting Provision. The negative moderation effects of Voting Provision changes the direction of inverted U-shaped relationship between Family Management and Firm Performance into a U-shape.

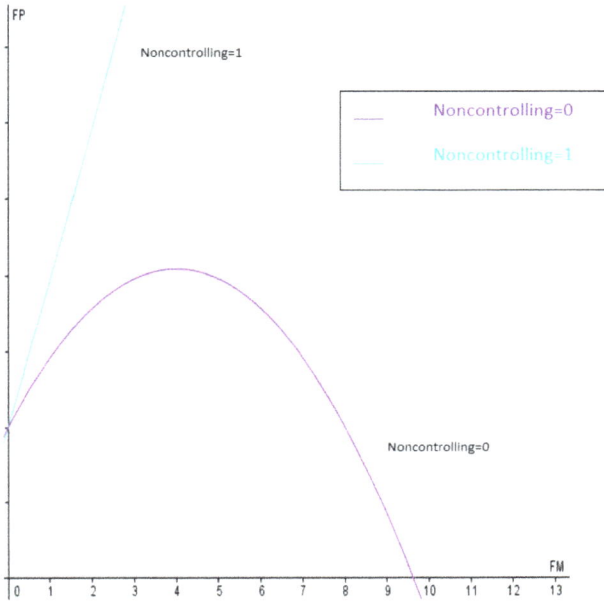

Figure 3. Significant Interactions between Family Management and Noncontrolling Provision. The positive moderation effects of Noncontrolling Provision makes the inverted U-shaped relationship between Family Management and Firm Performance steeper.

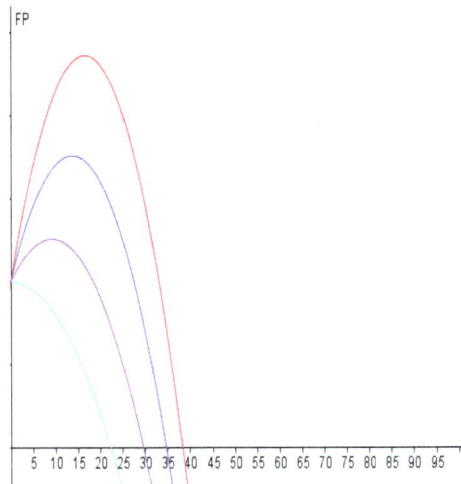

Figure 4. Significant Interactions between Family Ownership and Monetary Provision. Contrary to our hypothesis, the positive moderation effects of Monetary Provision make the inverted U-shaped relationship between Family Ownership and Firm Performance steeper.

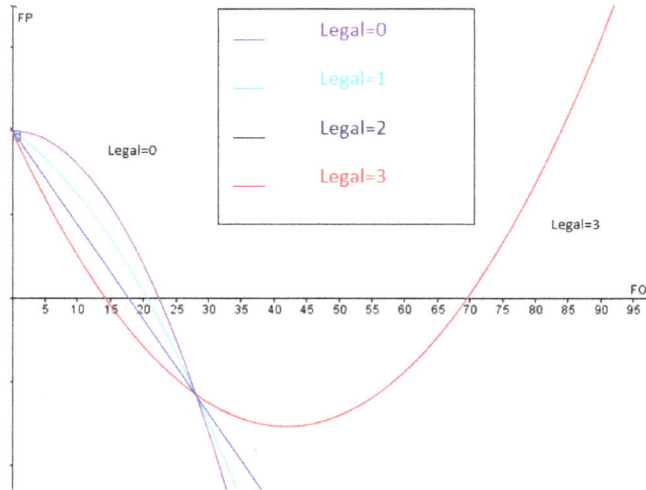

Figure 5. Significant Interactions between Family Ownership and Legal Provision. The negative moderation effects of Legal Provision changes the direction of inverted U-shaped relationship between Family Ownership and Firm Performance into a U-shape.

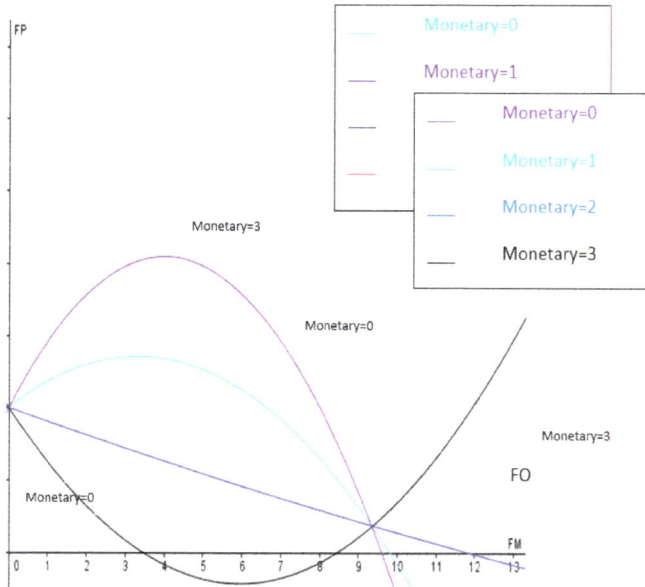

Figure 6. Significant Interactions between Family Management and Monetary Provision. The negative moderation effects of Monetary Provision changes the direction of inverted U-shaped relationship between Family Management and Firm Performance into a U-shape.

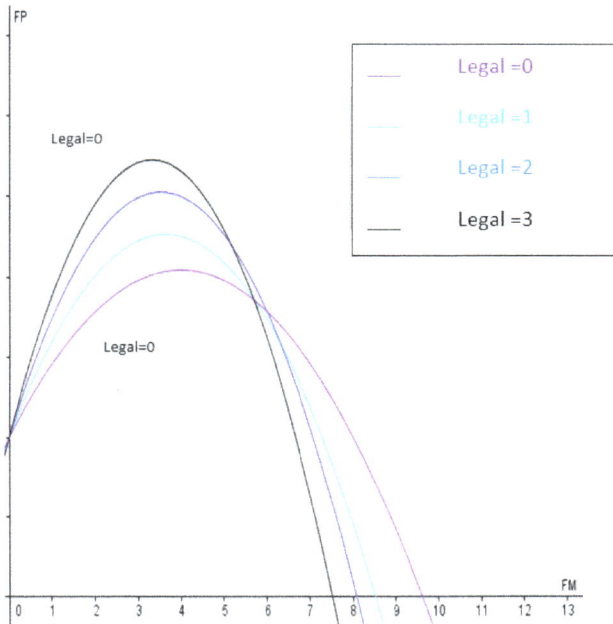

Figure 7. Significant Interactions between Family Management and Legal Provision. Contrary to our expectation, the positive moderation effects of Legal Provision makes the inverted U-shaped relationship between Family Management and Firm Performance steeper.

5. Discussion

Studies highlight the distinctive effects of family involvement (*i.e.*, ownership and management) on the behavior and performance of publicly traded firms (Anderson and Reeb [15,33], Claessens *et al.* [51], Villalonga and Amit [2,3]). However, to date, we do not know enough about how and why firm behavior and performance in family firms differ from those in nonfamily firms and among family firms themselves, and what the outcomes of the family involvement in the business are through the use of control enhancing governance mechanisms (Villalonga and Amit [2,3,21]).

To fill this gap, this paper suggests that the theory of the family firm will be advanced by the investigation of the link between family involvement components (*i.e.*, family ownership and family management), control enhancing governance provisions, and firm performance. Accordingly, this paper addresses how the use of different types of control enhancing mechanisms moderate the relationship between family involvement components and firm performance. We develop and test a model linking family involvement, control enhancing corporate governance mechanisms, and firm performance on a sample of 386 of the S&P 500 firms. The model in this paper is concerned with the moderation effects of the use of governance provisions on the relationship between family involvement and firm performance. It is expected that the frequency of the use of governance provisions will have a negative moderating influence on the relationship between family ownership and family management and firm performance.

The model is tested via panel data analyses. Findings support the hypotheses suggesting the moderation effects of (a) the use of provisions protecting owners' control status on the inverted U-shaped relationship between family ownership and firm performance (H1b); (b) the use of provisions protecting management legally on the inverted U-shaped relationship between family ownership and firm performance (H4c); (c) the use of provisions protecting controlling owners in terms of their voting rights on the inverted U-shaped relationship between family management and firm performance (H2a); (d) the use of provisions protecting noncontrolling owners on the inverted U-shaped relationship between family management and firm performance (H3b); and (e) the use of provisions protecting management monetarily will moderate the inverted U-shaped relationship between family management and firm performance (H5b). The results are consistent with the expected interplay between family involvement and the use of governance provisions in influencing firm performance.

The supported moderation effects of the frequency of the use of provisions protecting controlling owners in terms of their sustainability of controlling status on the inverted U-shaped relationship between family ownership and firm performance (H1b) appears to be negative. This may be because the higher use of provisions which secure sustainability of controlling owners' status can inflate family owners' power and authority, enabling them to engage in opportunistic behaviors. Family owners' equity rights at moderate levels enable them to effectively monitor and control, which can be beneficial to firm performance. However, enhanced power and authority through the use of provisions protecting controlling owners' status can weaken the positive effects of family ownership on firm performance since family owners may have the freedom to pursue family-centered noneconomic goals and enjoy the private benefits of control when their controlling status is secured. Particularly after an optimum level of family ownership, excessive power deriving from the combination of the higher levels of ownership and the use of provisions sustaining controlling owners' status can exacerbate principal-principal agency problems (Anderson and Reeb [15,33], Andres [34], Gomez-Mejia *et al.* [31], Shleifer and Vishny [39]) by allowing family owners to pursue family agendas primarily benefiting the family, which can be detrimental firm performance.

The hypothesized positive moderation effect of the frequency of the use of provisions protecting noncontrolling owners on the relationship between family management and firm performance (H3b) was also supported. Hence, the use of provisions protecting noncontrolling owners strengthens the positive effects of family management up to an optimum level and then weakens the negative effects after an optimum level is reached. The use of secret ballot provision assuring confidentiality in voting can facilitate noncontrolling shareholders' activism directed toward the replacement of managers and directors or the transfer of control to a hostile takeover bidder in case of underperformance. Particularly, the secrecy of voting, which gives noncontrolling owners' a larger voice in firm governance, can constitute an internal control mechanism by monitoring managers and directors' actions and allowing potentially beneficial takeovers to take place by weakening the family managers' resistance and prevention tactics. As a result, the threat of shareholder activism can be an internal monitoring mechanism and thereby discipline family managers, enhancing their positive impact on firm performance up to an optimum level of family management. Also, after an optimum level of family management is reached, this can weaken the negative effects of family management on firm performance, policing their expropriation and entrenchment attempts which can be triggered by their excessive power and authority.

The hypothesis suggesting the negative moderation effects of the use of provisions protecting controlling owners in terms of their voting rights on the relationship between family management and firm performance (H2a) was supported. Family managers' discretion to generate strategic ideas and their timely implementation can be beneficial to firm performance up to an optimum level of family management. However, the higher use of provisions, which create a discrepancy between controlling owners' cash flow and voting rights, can further enhance both family owners' and managers' power and authority. Controlling family's excessive discretionary power on strategic decisions and actions may weaken the positive effects of family management on firm performance since family management combined with the use of provisions enhancing controlling owners voting rights can enable family managers to focus primarily on the attainment of noneconomic goals that primarily benefit the family and to consume perks. Particularly after an optimum level of family management, the combined enhancement of voting rights of the controlling family and higher levels of family involvement in management and the board can increase family managers' ability to expropriate noncontrolling shareholder wealth and entrench themselves in management and board positions (Anderson and Reeb [15,33], Andres [34], Gomez-Mejia *et al.* [31], Shleifer and Vishny [39]), reducing firm performance.

The significant findings in the opposite direction may initially seem paradoxical since the use of provisions protecting managers and directors monetarily has positive moderation effect on the relationship between family ownership and firm performance (H4b), while having negative moderation effect on the relationship between family management and firm performance (H5b). When family members participate in the business through ownership only, monetary protection for managers and directors diminishes managerial risk bearing for nonfamily managers, enabling their taking more risk to engage in potentially fruitful projects which may be beneficial to firm performance. Family owners' effective monitoring can also limit nonfamily managers' opportunistic behaviors. Hence, combined effective monitoring of family owners and nonfamily managers' reduced risk bearing and increased risk taking may strengthen the positive effects of family ownership on firm performance and then weaken the negative effects of family ownership on firm performance. However, the combination of family management and the use of provisions protecting managers and directors monetarily can reduce the concern for monetary consequences of managerial wrongdoings and enable family managers and directors to engage in expropriation of noncontrolling shareholder wealth and managerial entrenchment activities, which can be detrimental to firm performance.

The other conflicting set of results is regarding the use of provisions protecting managers and directors legally. The use of such provisions has negative moderation effect on the relationship between family ownership and firm performance (H4c), while having positive moderation effect on the relationship between family management and firm performance (H5c). The reason for the positive interaction between those governance provisions and family management may be that when family members directly benefit from reduced legal risk bearing because of being managers as well as owners, they may be more likely to formulate and implement aggressive business strategies with potentially high returns. However, when legal protections are provided to managers, the family owners, who may not be managers, may veto the aggressive business strategies formulated by nonfamily managers, owing to a lack of trust or a concern for socioemotional wealth, even though they may yield high returns.

There were also several hypotheses (H1a, H2b, H3a, H4a, and H5a) that were not supported concerning the moderation effects of the frequency of the use of provisions protecting (a) controlling owners' voting rights; (b) noncontrolling owners; and (c) managers and directors' positions on the relationship between family ownership and firm performance and the moderation effects of the use of provisions protecting (a) controlling owners' status and (b) managers and directors' positions on the relationship between family management and firm performance.

The frequency of the use of provisions protecting controlling owners' voting rights have significant moderation effects on the relationship between family management and firm performance (H2a), whereas it has insignificant moderation effects on the relationship between family ownership and firm performance (H1a). Accordingly, the combined effects of family management and the enhancement of controlling owners' voting rights appear to be more influential in determining firm performance than the combination of family ownership and the enhancement of controlling owners' voting rights. This may be because family owners tend to have substantial voting rights naturally deriving from their equity rights. Hence, the use of provisions enhancing controlling owners' voting rights may not substantially affect the impact of family ownership on firm performance. However, the use of provisions enhancing controlling owners' voting rights combined with family management seem to have substantial impact on firm performance because family's participation in management and board combined with the controlling owners' elevated voting rights facilitate family influence over the business through multiple dimensions.

The lack of reinforcing effects of the frequency of the use of provisions protecting noncontrolling owners on the relationship between family ownership and firm performance (H3a) may be because of

Int. J. Financial Stud. **2015**, 3, 194–229

the noncontrolling owners' relatively low level of influence over the business compared to controlling owners even though provisions protecting noncontrolling owners may be in use. Also, the use of provisions protecting managers and directors' positions may not have significant influence on the effects of family ownership on firm performance (H4a) since any benefits or costs associated with those provisions may be mitigated by the monitoring abilities of family owners. Similarly, the use of provisions protecting managers and directors' positions (H5a) do not have significant moderation effects on the relationship between family management and firm performance. This may be because family managers and directors may be naturally expecting a relatively long tenure and higher levels of job security regardless of whether the provisions protecting their positions are in place or not. Hence, the use provisions protecting managers and directors' positions do not have substantial impact on the relationship between family management and firm performance. Finally, the use of provisions protecting controlling owners' status does not seem to influence the relationship between family management and firm performance (H2b). This may be due to family's already assuming its control over the business through participation in management and board regardless of the use of provisions protecting their controlling status.

Moreover, the assumed, but not hypothesized, inverted U-shaped relationship between family ownership and firm performance was not significant in this study, whereas the assumed, but not hypothesized, inverted U-shaped relationship between family management and firm performance was significant. This finding draws attention to the importance of family's involvement in management and board in determining firm performance, while ownership itself does not seem be sufficient to influence firm performance. On the one hand, this finding may be contrary to some studies suggesting that family ownership, rather than family management, is the key in differentiating family firms from nonfamily firms in other countries such as Germany and Chile (e.g., Klein [95], Silva and Majluf [96]). On the other hand, this finding is in line with Maury's [10] distinction between active (*i.e.*, family holds at least one of the top officer positions) and passive family control. The author also shows that active family control is associated with higher profitability compared to nonfamily firms, whereas passive family control does not influence profitability. Similarly, Andres [34] shows that family firms may perform better than nonfamily firms only when the founding family is still active either on the executive or the supervisory board in Germany. The author also demonstrates that if families are only large shareholders without board representation, their firm performance is not distinguishable from that of nonfamily firms. Westhead and Howorth [97] also illustrate that family management, rather than family ownership, is associated with performance in firms in the UK.

This paper contributes to the literature in several ways. First, it draws attention to the importance of family involvement within the context of corporations. Second, it adds to the understanding of how publicly traded family firms are heterogeneous in terms of the impact of the frequency of the use of different types of control enhancing governance mechanisms on the relationship between family involvement (*i.e.*, family ownership and family management) and firm performance, whereas studies mostly focus on the direct effects of family involvement or governance mechanisms on the firm performance (e.g., Anderson and Reeb [15], Andres [34]). This paper is one of the few attempts to use agency theory and family governance perspective to explain differences among family firms enlightening us regarding the heterogeneity among family firms. Third, this paper introduces the interplay between family involvement and the use of governance provisions as an explanation for the existence of principal-principal agency problems in publicly traded firms. Consequently, the contributions of this paper move us forward in the advancement of the theory of the family firm (Chrisman *et al.* [98], Conner [99]).

The limitations of this paper can also lead to a number of future research directions. First, as stated above, the regulatory context can affect the observed relationships and generalizability to the corporations around the world since the sample included S&P 500 firms headquartered in the U.S. Even though increased globalization tends to cause similarities in business conduct in world economies, different legal regimes (e.g., common *versus* civil law) in different countries can result in differences in corporate governance (Peng and Jiang [100]). For example, the legal system prevents pyramiding in the U.S., whereas it is permissible even in many developed countries in Asia and Europe (Peng and Jiang [100]). Since legal context may be influential on the findings of this paper, future studies can test or extend the model in other countries with different legal systems.

Similarly, we examine years 2001–2007. The findings may vary in other time periods (e.g., in 1990s) owing to the changes in the legal system. For example, the examined time periods in this paper involves the enactment and the aftermath of the Sarbanes-Oxley Act in 2002, also known as Investor Protection Act, as a reaction to corporate accounting scandals. This act enhanced the reliability of financial reporting, transparency, and accountability through increased internal controls and auditing (Coates [101]). Hence, future research can compare or contrast the findings of this paper to earlier periods than the periods examined in this paper. This can also illustrate whether legislation is influential on corporate governance.

Another limitation is that, in this paper, the seven categories of governance provisions that group the 24 provisions identified by Gompers *et al.* [11] according to the purposes of their usage by firms are formed by a judgment-based categorization (Perreault and Leigh [84]). Future research using different categorizations can provide further insights.

Aside from the future research directions suggested in the discussion of findings and limitations, there may be other factors that may affect the relationship between family involvement and performance in publicly traded family firms. The imminence of succession (Chua *et al.* [102]) is one of them. Furthermore, the effects of family involvement and control enhancing corporate governance mechanisms might vary in family firms depending upon diversification (Anderson and Reeb [17], Jones *et al.* [67]), entrepreneurial orientation (Dess and Lumpkin [103], Lumpkin and Dess [104,105]), corporate entrepreneurship (Dess *et al.* [106], Lumpkin *et al.* [107]), and life-cycle phases. All these contingencies suggest additional applications of corporate governance to the study of family businesses.

6. Conclusions

In conclusion, we hope that our paper will inform scholars, publicly traded family firms, and policy makers about the proper use of corporate governance mechanisms, which can help mitigate agency problems and maximizing shareholder value.

Author Contributions: Authors contributed equally to research and writing of the manuscript, deriving from the first author's dissertation.

Conflicts of Interest: The authors declare no conflict of interest.

References

1. Aguilera, R.V.; Crespi-Cladera, R. Firm family firms: Current debates of corporate governance in family firms. *J. Family Bus. Strategy* **2012**, *3*, 66–69. [CrossRef]
2. Villalonga, B.; Amit, R. How do family ownership, management, and control affect firm value? *J. Financ. Econ.* **2006**, *80*, 385–417. [CrossRef]
3. Villalonga, B.; Amit, R. Benefits and costs of control-enhancing mechanisms in U.S. family firms. Available online: http://isites.harvard.edu/fs/docs/icb.topic66847.files/Belen_Villalonga.pdf (accessed on 2 March 2015).
4. Chrisman, J.J.; Chua, J.H.; Litz, R. Comparing the agency costs of family and nonfamily firms: Conceptual issues and exploratory evidence. *Entrep. Theory Pract.* **2004**, *28*, 335–354. [CrossRef]
5. Neubauer, F.A.G. *Lank the Family Business: Its Governance for Sustainability*; Routledge: New York, NY, USA, 1998; Chapter 6; pp. 133–166.
6. Siebels, J.F.; zu Knyphausen-Aufseß, D. A review of theory in family business research: The implications for corporate governance. *Int. J. Manag. Rev.* **2012**, *14*, 280–304. [CrossRef]
7. Carney, M. Corporate governance and competitive advantage in family-controlled firms. *Entrep. Theory Pract.* **2005**, *29*, 249–266. [CrossRef]

8.   Miller, D.; Breton-Miller, I.L.; Lester, R.H. Family firm governance, strategic conformity, and performance: Institutional *vs.* strategic perspectives. *Org. Sci.* **2013**, *24*, 189–209. [CrossRef]

9.   Ali, A.; Chen, T.Y.; Radhakrishnan, S. Corporate disclosures by family firms. *J. Account. Econ.* **2007**, *44*, 238–286. [CrossRef]

10.   Maury, B. Family ownership and firm performance: Empirical evidence from Western European corporations. *J. Corp. Financ.* **2006**, *12*, 321–341. [CrossRef]

11.   Gompers, P.; Ishii, J.; Metrick, A. Corporate governance and equity prices. *Q. J. Econ.* **2003**, *118*, 107–155. [CrossRef]

12.   Daily, C.M.; Dalton, D.R.; Cannella, A.A. Corporate governance: Decades of dialogue and data. *Acad. Manag. Rev.* **2003**, *28*, 371–382.

13.   Daily, C.M.; Dalton, D.R.; Rajagopalan, N. Governance through ownership: Centuries of practice, decades of research. *Acad. Manag. J.* **2003**, *46*, 151–158. [CrossRef]

14.   Memili, E.; Misra, K.; Chrisman, J.J. Family involvement and the use of corporate governance provisions protecting controlling *vs.* noncontrolling owners. *J. Leadersh. Account. Ethics* **2012**, *9*, 11–27.

15.   Anderson, R.C.; Reeb, D.M. Founding-family ownership and firm performance: Evidence from the S&P 500. *J. Financ.* **2003**, *58*, 1301–1328.

16.   Anderson, R.C.; Reeb, D.M. *Who Monitors the Family?* Working Paper; American University: Washington, DC, USA, 2003.

17.   Anderson, R.C.; Reeb, D.M. Founding-family ownership, corporate diversification and firm leverage. *J. Law Econ.* **2003**, *46*, 653–684. [CrossRef]

18.   Miller, D.; le Breton-Miller, I.; Lester, R.H.; Cannella, A.A. Are family firms really superior performers? *J. Corporate Financ.* **2007**, *13*, 829–858. [CrossRef]

19.   Villalonga, B.; Amit, R. *Family Control of Firms and Industries*; Harvard Business School Publishing: Boston, MA, USA, 2009.

20.   Morck, R.; Steier, L. *The Global History of Corporate Governance: An Introduction*; Working Paper 11062; University of Chicago Press: Chicago, IL, USA, 2005.

21.   Villalonga, B. *Note on Valuing Control and Liquidity in Family and Closely Held Firms*; Harvard Business School Publishing: Boston, MA, USA, 2009.

22.   Dyer, W.G.; Whetten, D.A. Family firms and social responsibility: Preliminary evidence from the S&P 500. *Entrep. Theory Pract.* **2006**, *30*, 785–802.

23.   Chrisman, J.J.; Kellermanns, F.W.; Chan, K.C.; Liano, K. Intellectual foundations of current research in family business: An identification and review of 25 influential articles. *Family Bus. Rev.* **2010**, *23*, 9–26. [CrossRef]

24.   Gómez-Mejía, L.R.; Hynes, K.T.; Núñez-Nickel, M.; Moyano-Fuentes, H. Socioemotional wealth and business risk in family-controlled firms: Evidence from Spanish olive oil mills. *Adm. Sci. Q.* **2007**, *52*, 106–137.

25.   Chrisman, J.J.; Chua, J.H.; Pearson, A.W.; Barnett, T. Family involvement, family influence, and family-centered non-economic goals in small firms. *Entrep. Theory Pract.* **2012**, *36*, 267–293. [CrossRef]

26.   Crutchley, C.E.; Jensen, M.R.H.; Jahera, J.S.; Raymond, J.E. Agency problems and the simultaneity of financial decision making: The role of institutional ownership. *Int. Rev. Financ. Anal.* **1999**, *8*, 177–197. [CrossRef]

27.   Morck, R.; Shleifer, A.; Vishny, R.W. Management ownership and market valuation: An empirical analysis. *J. Financ. Econ.* **1988**, *20*, 293–315. [CrossRef]

28.   Memili, E. Control Enhancing Corporate Governance Mechanisms: Family *vs.* Nonfamily Publicly Traded Firms. Ph.D. Dissertation, Mississippi State University, Mississippi, MS, USA, August 2011.

29.   Fama, E.F.; Jensen, M.C. Agency problems and residual claims. *J. Law Econ.* **1983**, *26*, 327–349. [CrossRef]

30.   Jensen, M.C.; Meckling, W.H. Theory of the firm: Managerial behavior, agency costs, and economic organization. *J. Financ. Econ.* **1976**, *3*, 305–360. [CrossRef]

31.   Gómez-Mejía, L.R.; Núñez-Nickel, M.; Gutierrez, I. The role of family ties in agency contracts. *Acad. Manag. J.* **2001**, *44*, 81–95. [CrossRef]

32.   Morck, R.; Yeung, B. Agency problems in large family business groups. *Entrep. Theory Pract.* **2003**, *27*, 367–383. [CrossRef]

33.   Anderson, R.C.; Reeb, D.M. Board composition: Balancing family influence in S&P 500 firms. *Adm. Sci. Q.* **2004**, *49*, 209–237.

34.   Andres, C. Large shareholders ad firm performance: An empirical examination of founding-family ownership. *J. Corporate Financ.* **2008**, *14*, 431–445. [CrossRef]

35.   Johnson, S.; la Porta, R.; Lopez-de-Silanes, F.; Shleifer, A. Tunneling. *Am. Econ. Rev.* **2000**, *90*, 22–29. [CrossRef]

36. La Porta, R.; Lopez-De-Silanes, F.; Shleifer, A. Corporate ownership around the world. *J. Finance* **1999**, *54*, 471–517. [CrossRef]
37. Dharwadkar, R.; George, G.; Brandes, P. Privatization in emerging economies: An agency theory perspective. *Acad. Manag. Rev.* **2000**, *25*, 650–669.
38. Young, M.N.; Peng, M.W.; Ahlstrom, D.; Bruton, G.D.; Jiang, Y. Corporate governance in emerging economies: A Review of the principal-principal perspective. *J. Manag. Stud.* **2008**, *45*, 198–220. [CrossRef]
39. Shleifer, A.; Vishny, R.W. A survey of corporate governance. *J. Financ.* **1997**, *52*, 737–784. [CrossRef]
40. Mahoney, J.M.; Mahoney, J.T. An empirical investigation of the effect of corporate charter antitakeover amendments on stockholder wealth. *Strateg. Manag. J.* **1993**, *14*, 17–31. [CrossRef]
41. Mahoney, J.M.; Sundaramurthy, C.; Mahoney, J.T. The differential impact on stockholder wealth of various antitakeover provisions. *Manag. Decis. Econ.* **1996**, *17*, 531–549. [CrossRef]
42. Mahoney, J.M.; Sundaramurthy, C.; Mahoney, J.T. The effects of corporate antitakeover provisions on long-term investment: Empirical evidence. *Manag. Decis. Econ.* **1997**, *18*, 349–365. [CrossRef]
43. Cremers, K.J.M.; Nair, V.B. Governance mechanisms and equity prices. *J. Finance* **2005**, *60*, 2859–2894. [CrossRef]
44. Jensen, M.C.; Ruback, R.S. The market for corporate control: The scientific evidence. *J. Financ. Econ.* **1983**, *11*, 5–50. [CrossRef]
45. Berkovitch, E.; Narayanan, M.P. Motives for takeovers: An empirical investigation. *J. Finance. Quant. Anal.* **1993**, *28*, 347–363. [CrossRef]
46. Bebchuk, L.A. Why firms adopt antitakeover arrangements. *Univ. Penn. Law Rev.* **2003**, *152*, 713–753. [CrossRef]
47. Jensen, M.C. Takeovers: Their causes and consequences. *J. Econ. Perspect.* **1988**, *2*, 21–48. [CrossRef]
48. Gómez-Mejía, L.R.; Makri, M.; Kintana, M.L. Diversification decisions in family controlled firms. *J. Manag. Stud.* **2010**, *47*, 223–252. [CrossRef]
49. La Porta, R.; Lopez-De-Silanes, F.; Shleifer, A.; Vishny, R. Investor protection and corporate governance. *J. Financ. Econ.* **2000**, *58*, 3–27. [CrossRef]
50. Anderson, R.C.; Mansi, S.A.; Reeb, D.M. Founding family ownership and the agency cost of debt. *J. Financ. Econ.* **2003**, *68*, 263–285. [CrossRef]
51. Claessens, S.; Djankov, S.; Fan, J.P.H.; Lang, L.H.P. Disentangling the incentive and entrenchment effects of large shareholdings. *J. Financ.* **2002**, *57*, 2741–2771. [CrossRef]
52. Walsh, J.P.; Seward, J.K. On the efficiency of internal and external corporate control mechanisms. *Acad. Manag. Rev.* **1990**, *15*, 421–458.
53. Westhead, P.; Cowling, M.; Howorth, C. The development of family companies: Management and ownership imperatives. *Family Bus. Rev.* **2001**, *14*, 369–385. [CrossRef]
54. Miller, D.; le Breton-Miller, I. Family governance and firm performance: Agency, stewardship, and capabilities. *Family Bus. Rev.* **2006**, *19*, 73–88. [CrossRef]
55. Gilson, R.J.; Gordon, J.N. Doctrines and markets: Controlling shareholders. *Univ. Penn. Law Rev.* **2003**, *152*, 785–844. [CrossRef]
56. Villalonga, B.; Amit, R. How are U.S. family firms controlled? *Rev. Financ. Stud.* **2009**, *22*, 1–45. [CrossRef]
57. Ang, J.S.; Cole, R.A.; Lin, J.W. Agency costs and ownership structure. *J. Financ.* **2000**, *55*, 81–106. [CrossRef]
58. Berrone, P.; Cruz, C.; Gomez-Mejia, L.R.; Kintana, M.L. Socioemotional wealth and corporate responses to institutional pressures: Do family-controlled firms pollute less? *Adm. Sci. Q.* **2010**, *55*, 82–113. [CrossRef]
59. Chua, J.H.; Chrisman, J.J.; Sharma, P. Defining the family business by behavior. *Entrep. Theory Pract.* **1999**, *23*, 19–39.
60. Chrisman, J.J.; Chua, J.H.; Litz, R. A unified systems perspective of family firm performance: An extension and integration. *J. Bus. Ventur.* **2003**, *18*, 467–472. [CrossRef]
61. Wright, P.; Ferris, S.P.; Sarin, A.; Awasthi, V. Impact of corporate insider, blockholder, and institutional equity ownership on firm risk taking. *Acad. Manag. J.* **1996**, *39*, 441–463. [CrossRef]
62. Mishra, C.; McConaughy, D. Founding Family Control and Capital Structure. *Entrep. Theory Pract.* **1999**, *23*, 53–64.
63. Brecht, M.; Bolton, P.; Roell, A. Corporate Governance and Control. Available online: http://ssrn.com/abstract= 343461 (accessed on 5 March 2015).
64. Combs, J.G. Commentary: The servant, the parasite, and the enigma: A tale of three ownership structures and their affiliate directors. *Entrep. Theory Pract.* **2008**, *32*, 1027–1034. [CrossRef]
65. Demsetz, H.; Lehn, K. The structure of corporate ownership: Causes and consequences. *J. Polit. Econ.* **1985**, *93*, 1155–1177. [CrossRef]

66. Herman, E.S. *Corporate Control, Control Power*; Cambridge University Press: Cambridge, UK, 1981.
67. Jones, C.D.; Makri, M.; Gomez-Mejia, L.R. Affiliate directors and perceived risk bearing in publicly traded, family-controlled firms: The case of diversification. *Entrep. Theory Pract.* **2008**, *32*, 1007–1026. [CrossRef]
68. Kellermanns, F.W.; Eddleston, K.A. Feuding families: When conflict does a family good. *Entrep. Theory Pract.* **2004**, *28*, 209–228. [CrossRef]
69. Kellermanns, F.W.; Eddleston, K.A. A family perspective on when conflict benefits family firm performance. *J. Bus. Res.* **2007**, *60*, 1048–1057. [CrossRef]
70. Holmstrom, B.; Kaplan, S.N. Corporate governance and merger activity in the United States: Making sense of the 1980s and 1990s. *J. Econ. Perspect.* **2001**, *15*, 121–144. [CrossRef]
71. Davis, G.F. Agents without principles? The spread of the poison pill through the incorporate network. *Adm. Sci. Q.* **1991**, *36*, 583–613. [CrossRef]
72. Sundaramurthy, C. Corporate governance within the context of antitakeover provisions. *Strateg. Manag. J.* **1996**, *17*, 377–394. [CrossRef]
73. Gillan, S.L.; Starks, L.T. Corporate governance proposals and shareholder activism: The role of institutional investors. *J. Financ. Econ.* **2000**, *57*, 275–305. [CrossRef]
74. Gillan, S.L.; Hartzell, J.C.; Starks, L.T. Explaining corporate governance: Boards, bylaws, and charter provisions. Available online: http://ssrn.com/abstract=442740 (accessed on 2 February 2015).
75. Sciascia, S.; Mazzola, P. Family involvement in ownership and management: Exploring nonlinear effects on performance. *Family Bus. Rev.* **2008**, *21*, 331–345. [CrossRef]
76. Short, H.; Keasay, K. Managerial ownership and the performance of firms: Evidence from the UK. *J. Corporate Financ.* **1999**, *5*, 79–101. [CrossRef]
77. Morck, R.; Strangeland, D.A.; Yeung, B. *Inherited Wealth, Corporate Control and Economic Growth: The Canadian Disease?* Working Paper 6814; University of Chicago Press: Chicago, IL, USA, 1998.
78. Dyer, W.G. Examining the "family effect" on firm performance. *Family Bus. Rev.* **2006**, *19*, 253–273. [CrossRef]
79. Burkart, M.; Panunzi, F.; Shleifer, A. Family firms. *J. Financ.* **2003**, *58*, 2167–2201. [CrossRef]
80. Alchian, A.; Demsetz, H. Production, information costs, and economic organization. *Am. Econ. Rev.* **1972**, *62*, 777–795.
81. Short, J.C.; Payne, G.T.; Brigham, K.H.; Lumpkin, G.T.; Broberg, J.C. Family firms and entrepreneurial orientation in publicly traded firms: A comparative analysis the S&P 500. *Family Bus. Rev.* **2009**, *22*, 9–24.
82. Chung, K.H.; Pruitt, S.W. A simple approximation of Tobin's *q*. *Financ. Manag.* **1994**, *23*, 70–74. [CrossRef]
83. Carton, R.B.; Hofer, C.W. *Measuring Organizational Performance: Metrics for Entrepreneurship and Strategic Management Research*; Edward Elgar Publishing, Inc.: Northampton, MA, USA, 2006.
84. Perreault, W.D.; Leigh, L.E. Reliability of nominal data based on qualitative judgments. *J. Mark. Res.* **1989**, *26*, 135–148. [CrossRef]
85. Netemeyer, R.G.; Bearden, W.O.; Sharma, S. *Scaling Procedures: Issues and Applications*; Sage Publications: Thousand Oaks, CA, USA, 2003.
86. Hansen, G.; Wernerfelt, B. Determinants of firm performance: The relative importance of economic and organizational factors. *Strateg. Manag. J.* **1989**, *10*, 399–411. [CrossRef]
87. Dewar, R.D.; Dutton, J.E. The adoption of radical and incremental innovations: An empirical analysis. *Manag. Sci.* **1986**, *32*, 1422–1433. [CrossRef]
88. Schulze, W.S.; Lubatkin, M.H.; Dino, R.N. Exploring the agency consequences of ownership dispersion among inside directors at family firms. *Acad. Manag. J.* **2003**, *46*, 179–194. [CrossRef]
89. Decarolis, D.M.; Deeds, D.L. The impact of stocks and flows of organizational knowledge on firm performance: An empirical investigation of the biotechnology industry. *Strateg. Manag. J.* **1999**, *20*, 953–968. [CrossRef]
90. Graves, S.B.; Langowitz, N.S. Innovative productivity and returns to scale in the pharmaceutical industry. *Strateg. Manag. J.* **1993**, *14*, 593–605. [CrossRef]
91. Greene, H. *Econometric Analysis*, 7th ed.; Prentice Hall: New York, NY, USA, 2011; pp. 833–860.
92. Caselli, F.; Coleman, W.J. Cross-country technology diffusion: The case of computers. *Am. Econ. Rev.* **2001**, *91*, 328–335. [CrossRef]
93. Enders, W. *Applied Econometric Time Series*, 2nd ed.; John Wiley & Sons: Hoboken, NJ, USA, 2004; pp. 72–75.
94. Maddala, G.S. A perspective on the use of limited-dependent and qualitative variables models in accounting research. *Account. Rev.* **1991**, *66*, 788–807.
95. Klein, S.B. Family businesses in Germany: Significance and structure. *Family Bus. Rev.* **2000**, *13*, 157–182. [CrossRef]

96. Silva, F.; Majluf, N. Does family ownership shape performance outcomes? *J. Bus. Res.* **2008**, *61*, 609–614. [CrossRef]

97. Westhead, P.; Howorth, C. Ownership and management issues associated with family firm performance and company objectives. *Family Bus. Rev.* **2006**, *19*, 301–317. [CrossRef]

98. Chrisman, J.J.; Chua, J.H.; Sharma, P. Trends and directions in the development of a strategic management theory of the family firm. *Entrep. Theory Pract.* **2005**, *29*, 555–576. [CrossRef]

99. Conner, K.R. A historical comparison of resource-based theory and five schools of thought within industrial organization economics: Do we have a new theory of the firm? *J. Manag.* **1991**, *17*, 121–154. [CrossRef]

100. Peng, M.W.; Jiang, Y. Institutions behind family ownership and control in large firms. *J. Manag. Stud.* **2010**, *47*, 253–273. [CrossRef]

101. Coates, J.C. The goals and promise of the Sarbanes-Oxley Act. *J. Econ. Perspect.* **2007**, *21*, 91–116. [CrossRef]

102. Chua, J.H.; Chrisman, J.J.; Sharma, P. Succession and nonsuccession concerns of family firms and agency relationship with nonfamily managers. *Family Bus. Rev.* **2003**, *16*, 89–108. [CrossRef]

103. Dess, G.G.; Lumpkin, G.T. The role of entrepreneurial orientation in stimulating effective corporate entrepreneurship. *Acad. Manag. Exec.* **2005**, *19*, 147–156. [CrossRef]

104. Lumpkin, G.T.; Dess, G.G. Clarifying the entrepreneurial orientation construct and linking it to performance. *Acad. Manag. Rev.* **1996**, *21*, 135–172.

105. Lumpkin, G.T.; Dess, G.G. Linking two dimensions of entrepreneurial orientation to firm performance: The moderating role of environment and industry life cycle. *J. Bus. Ventur.* **2001**, *16*, 429–451. [CrossRef]

106. Dess, G.G.; Lumpkin, G.T.; McGee, J.E. Linking corporate entrepreneurship to strategy, structure, and process: Suggested research directions. *Entrep. Theory Pract.* **1999**, *23*, 85–102.

107. Lumpkin, G.T.; Wales, W.J.; Ensley, M.D. Assessing the Context for Corporate Entrepreneurship: The Role of Entrepreneurial Orientation. In *Praeger Perspectives on Entrepreneurship*; Habbershon, T., Rice, M., Eds.; Better World Books: Mishawaka, IN, USA, 2005; Volume 3, pp. 1–43.

International Journal of
Financial Studies

MDPI

Article

Effects of Family Ownership, Debt and Board Composition on Mexican Firms Performance

Juan Manuel San Martin-Reyna and Jorge A. Duran-Encalada *

Family Business Research Center, Universidad de las Americas Puebla, Ex hacienda Sta. Catarina Martir, 728320, San Andrés Cholula, Puebla, Mexico; juanm.sanmartin@udlap.mx
* Author to whom correspondence should be addressed; jorgea.duran@udlap.mx; Tel.: +52-2222292453.

Academic Editor: Esra Memili
Received: 1 May 2014; Accepted: 10 March 2015; Published: 19 March 2015

Abstract: This study examines the relationship between ownership structure and performance of public firms in Mexico, considering debt and the structure of the board of directors as contextual and institutional factors. This research seeks to explain the mixed results about the relationship of ownership and performance presented by other relevant studies in family and non-family businesses, mainly in emerging countries. The results confirm the positive association between family ownership concentration and performance, calculated by Tobin's Q, showing how the participation of inside shareholders on the board and a low debt level contribute to higher performance. However, the association of these variables with performance shows a contrasting effect in the case of family as compared to non-family businesses. The particular corporate legal context in Mexico could be highlighted as one of the main reasons for these results.

Keywords: ownership concentration; family business; corporate governance; market financial performance; Mexico

JEL Classification: G32

1. Introduction

It is widely acknowledged that property rights and ownership structure are crucial elements of the firm theory [1,2]. As ownership dispersion has become a feature of the modern corporation, the understanding of how this may be a source of internal conflict for the firm has been examined in the literature since the seminal work of Berle and Means [3]. There is a growing interest in the literature related to the analysis of how firms with ownership concentration, particularly in family groups, face these challenges, and the effects that particular ownership structures have on firm performance [4–11]. The importance of family firms in national economies is even more evident in emerging economies, where it has been measured in terms of contribution to gross domestic product, employment, and number of firms [12,13]. It has been shown that family businesses possess some features that lead to better performance when compared to non-family firms [14]. As in most developing countries, the majority of companies in Mexico are considered family firms [15]. However few studies refer specifically to Mexican family businesses, thus the importance for further investigation [2,15]. As Gedajlovic, Carney, Chrisman, and Kellermanns [6] discuss, it is important to further analyze this phenomenon in emerging countries, where some contextual and institutional factors may fill voids in particular institutional contexts where underdeveloped capital markets and weak corporate legal enforcement prevail.

Many studies have focused on comparing the performance of family *versus* non-family firms, however, this research is more focused on building upon the knowledge of factors that differ in family and non-family firms, and how they influence performance in both types of firms. Thus, the study focuses on debt and board structure and their effect on performance in family and non-family firms. Studying both family and non-family firms will permit the observation of how family firms choose to lessen agency problems by means of increasing leverage to reduce unrestricted funds for managers and the number of outside directors to reduce nepotism and entrenchment [16–19]. However, these same measures may lead to situations where family firms are not prepared to assume risks that affect their socioemotional wealth [18]. Observing the effects of leverage and board structure on non-family firm performance is an important comparison as, even though these companies also often have high ownership concentration in Mexico, they may tend to choose different strategies to reign in managers.

This research analyzes the relationship between ownership concentration in Mexican listed firms and performance. The study contributes to the literature by further observing contextual and institutional factors, which when added to the abovementioned relationship, are expected to have different repercussions on family and non-family firms. The sample is separated into family and non-family firms so as to demonstrate the different influences that debt and board structure have on firm performance.

The following section includes a review of the literature on ownership concentration and performance, and on debt and board structure as some of the most relevant factors that are associated with performance in family and non-family firms. Next, the methodology presents a description of the sample, data collected, variables defined, and the regression analysis conducted, followed by the presentation of the results. In the last section, discussion of results and conclusions are presented, highlighting the main contributions and limitations of this study as well as proposing some lines of further related research.

2. Literature Review

2.1. Ownership Concentration

Berle and Means [3] were the first authors to examine how ownership structure impacts decision making in the modern firm that is characterized by ownership dispersion. However, whereas Anglo-Saxon capital markets are characterized by high property dispersion, ownership concentration, mainly family groups, is still prevalent in other countries, especially in emerging economies [20]. This situation would be observed in the case of Mexico [11].

Many scholars have recognized that the lower supervision costs prompted by ownership concentration is an effective management control mechanism [21]. However, Morck and Yeung [20] argue that high ownership concentration may lead to agency problems as the owner-managers may act in the pursuit of their own interests. This phenomenon may be reflected by owner entrenchment, the use of pyramidal groups, as well as other types of actions that produce harmful effects for minority shareholders, including tunneling and propping [17]. Also, control by owners does not necessarily alleviate agency matters as some family dynamics may actually intensify them [22]. Strong family involvement in the firm may blur the division between a family perspective and its responsibility to other shareholders produced as a result of nepotism [16,19] and asymmetric altruism [23]. Thus, ownership concentration may be the cause of agency problems thus undermining firm performance.

Despite the problems associated with concentrating ownership, many studies have found that ownership affects substantially the interest structure of a company and has important consequences for the firm [13,24–26]. Mexico belongs to the group of countries with Roman style civil law systems, as opposed to Anglo-Saxon common law systems, which means that there is high ownership concentration and low protection for minority shareholders [8,24,27]. Mexican companies also tend to have pyramidal structures and thus concentrate ownership [24]. Demsetz [28–30] describes an association between the level of ownership concentration and the tolerance of risk of a company, where firms with higher volatility seek to reduce risk through higher concentration of ownership.

This relationship could be applied to firms in emerging markets, which tend to have higher volatility, and thus concentrate property to maintain control and minimize risk.

In the family business and financial performance meta-analysis conducted by Mazzi [8] considering mainly listed public companies in developed countries studies, finds that family firms outperform non-family firms. This situation tends to be altered whenever control rights exercised by the family exceeds their cash flow rights. Some studies undertaken in emerging countries, on the other hand, have shown a negative association between ownership concentration and financial performance, as the ones done in Chile by Espinosa [31], Shah, Butt, and Saeed [32,33] in South Asia, and Pervan, Pervan, and Todoric [34] in Croatia. Several studies, however, have rejected the presence of a significant relationship in this regard. For example, Sacristán, Gómez and Cabeza [35] examined different ownership structures in Spain and determined that there is not a particular structure that impacts firm performance significantly. Similarly, Goud [36] presents research of the 25 countries of the ex-Soviet Union and does not come to a solid conclusion concerning this relationship. Other studies have shown a non-linear relationship between ownership and performance. This is demonstrated by an inverse U-shaped form as ownership concentration moves from a low to a high concentration [37,38].

In general, a positive association between ownership structure and performance appears to prevail in most research for a longer range of family ownership concentration [8,21,35,39–41]. Thus, in a country such as Mexico in which there is poor shareholder protection, it is expected that ownership must be concentrated in order to organize company management and mitigate agency problems [11]. Thus, in this study one can expect that in the complete sample of firms, family and non-family, from the Mexican Stock Exchange, the following hypothesis can be proposed:

H1: A higher ownership concentration has a positive relationship with performance.

2.2. Effect of Other Factors on Performance

Consideration of the opposing views on the association between ownership concentration and performance begs the question of whether there are other factors that could contribute to these mixed results. The literature has argued for the existence of certain mediating factors and suggested that the relationship is much more complex. However, studies that have addressed these factors have only studied family firms, and usually study the effect these factors can have on incentives to mitigate agency problems. For example, authors have shown variations in that relationship when introducing mediating variables, as is the case when considering the generation in control [30,42,43], family management involvement [37,44,45], provision of incentives [46], and when distinguishing between lone-founder and family firms [43,47]. Thus, it is increasingly important to study the way in which these factors function in order to discover the nuances that make them successful for family firms and unsuccessful for non-family firms, and *vice versa*.

In Mexico, only a few studies exist on the issue regarding ownership structure and performance, much less the effect that the presence of other factors have on this relationship. Castrillo and San Martín [40] show that family ownership is a factor that works as a device for monitoring the management. Mexico is an interesting country in which to study these topics because it has a large ownership concentration tendency, for example, it is normal for a specification of a family firm to imply that the founding family holds 50 percent or more of the property [11]. Our study attempts to contribute to the literature by furthering research on the existence of other factors and how they affect performance in an environment with high ownership concentration.

2.2.1. Debt

There are some suggestions to address the topic of debt as a relevant factor for consideration [41, 48], and the benefits that indebtedness may bring to family and non-family firms have been explored in the literature. The impact of periodic payments that debt frequently provokes diminishes free-cash flow and may lead to lower discretional behavior by management [49]. This hypothesis arises from the Jensen's free cash flow argument where cash flow distribution is one of the main causes of agency problems. This flow may imply that resources surpass the amount required to fund all profitable investments as financial liabilities force management to direct these resources away from non-profitable investments opportunities [50]. Given that indebtedness implies recurrent disbursements over time, thus diminishing the unlimited funds for management, as some funding must be designated to repay debt, thus, restricting the discretionary behavior of management [49,51]. This reduction of unrestricted funds reduces agency costs, which is most common in widely-held firms, but leads to expropriation of minority stockholder interests [52]. This occurs more often in countries with low shareholder protection such as Mexico, which is characterized by high ownership concentration as previously discussed.

Family businesses are commonly hesitant to use debt as indebtedness reinforces financial risk [53], which relates in a positive way with bankruptcy risks and loss of firm control [54–56]. The dispersion of ownership in family firms has been proven to lead to less use of debt [57]. Carney, van Essen, Gedajlovic, and Heugens [58] also find that reliance on debt of first generation private family firms harms their performance, and in successive generation family firms become more averse to acquiring debt. Among the most important reasons for abstaining from debt is the effect it can have on diminishing family control [59], compromising long-term investments [60], and the possibility that debt can exacerbate family conflict [18]. In order to further research the effect these strategies have on Mexican family firms, this study attempts to examine performance in both family and non-family firms, introducing debt into the equation in order to observe differences between firms. Businesses in Mexico have higher family ownership concentration [11], and when combined with the aforementioned aversion to debt, the following hypotheses can be expected:

H2a: In family firms, the effect of debt on performance is negative.
H2b: In non-family firms, the effect of debt on performance is positive.

2.2.2. Board Structure

The board structure of a family firm can be an important tool that firms can use to monitor management and lower agency costs, as a clear association of more participation of insiders on the board with better performance which has been found in various studies conducted in developed countries [8,61–63]. Additionally, Bonilla, Sepulveda, and Carvajal [64] in Chile, and Wenyi [65] in Taiwan, find that family participation on the board leads to better performance and lower volatility in returns.

However, the benefits of external directors in broadly owned firms are recognized [23], as they are in the right position to oversee firm performance, enforce discipline, or even remove executives for inadequate or poor performance [66–68]. They also provide a critical appraisal of the firm's direction, strategy and business approaches, and broaden the boards' perspectives [69]. Furthermore, a 2010 study in Italy found that family presence on the board of directors affects performance negatively, and that the presence of independent directors affects performance positively [70], and another 2010 study found an inverted U-shaped association between the number of family members on the board and performance [71]. A recent study in Taiwan found that family firms with high ownership concentration and low family board representation had a higher performance than those with the opposite characteristics, *i.e.*, low levels of ownership concentration and high family board representation [72].

Even given the benefits of external directors, family firms are more resistant to accept them. First, outsiders in very few occasions are able to achieve a relevant representation of minority shareholders or non-family blockholders as they would do in companies with less concentrated ownership, also reducing their motivation to participate, as compared to family directors [73]. Secondly, even though their "unbiased" position can improve their capacity to provide counsel on some important matters, they have a restricted role with decisions that are connected to family members or family issues [74].

Therefore, external directors can be limited from collaborating effectively in a context where family ownership concentration is high [75].

Several studies on corporate governance have observed that independent or outside directors help firm performance and value in general [52,72]. In a study by Setia-Atmaja, Tanewski, and Skully [52], high ownership concentration and low family board representation was actually associated with a higher Tobin's Q. The latter study highlights the differences in corporate governance structure in family and non-family firms, suggesting that outside directors have a different impact on performance for the family *versus* non-family firms [52]. Furthermore, as is expected to be the case in Mexico, family firms have significantly lower board independence than their non-family counterparts [52], and this situation will be expected to have a different impact for the family firm. For example, Husted and Serrano [76] show that 53 percent of directors or senior executives of companies in Mexico are directors of other companies of the same group, or are family related to executives of the firms. This study proposes that these corporate governance practices impact family and non-family firms differently, as posed in the following hypotheses:

H3a: In family firms, the effect of insiders on the board structure on performance is positive.
H3b: In non-family firms, the effect of insiders on the board structure on performance is negative.

3. Methodology

The initial sample used in this study comprised all of the 142 firms listed on the Mexican Stock Exchange during the periods of 2005–2011. Those firms that did not provide sufficient information for comparison purposes in their financial statements were eliminated from the study. Also, financial institutions and nonprofit organizations were excluded as well given the difficulties for the estimation of Tobin's Q for financial institutions and non-comparable issues for the nonprofit organizations. The final sample consisted of 75 companies whose annual reports and financial information were collected from Economatica and Isi Emerging Markets. Finally, from the Mexican Stock Exchange website, information concerning industrial sectors was collected as well. The companies in the sample classified by industrial sector are shown in Table 1.

Table 1. Number and percent of family and non-family firms by sector.

Sector	Total
Materials	16
Industrial	21
Services and goods of consumer non-basic	14
Common consumer products	13
Health	4
Telecommunications services	7
Total	75

Source: Mexican Stock Exchange classification code, 2013.

The companies in the sample are basically medium to large companies compared with the average Mexican firm size, either in terms of assets, sales or employees. This could raise some caveats about a possible sample bias, notwithstanding, the Panel A of Table 2 descriptive statistics show that firm size (in terms of assets) is quite heterogeneous and highly dispersed around the mean value, so it is assumed that the results are not biased by size issues. The sample composition is quite industry-balanced, although there is a slight bias towards industrial and materials firms at the expense of health or telecommunications companies that can be explained by the heavier concentration of the former in the Mexican market.

Int. J. Financial Stud. **2015**, *3*, 56–74

Table 2. Descriptive data.

Panel A: Descriptive statistics for all firms				
Variables	Mean	Std. Dev.	Min	Max
Q	1.40	0.76	0.25	4.38
Famown	0.51	0.23	0.02	0.98
Lev	0.49	0.45	0.01	5.74
Ind	4.23	2.33	1	11
Sha	5.37	2.14	0	14
β	0.67	1.14	−5.89	7.20
Size	56,298.7	150,249	263	1,277,397

Panel B: Descriptive statistics by ownership structure								
	Family				Non-Family			
Variable	Mean	Std. Dev.	Min	Max	Mean	Std. Dev.	Min	Max
Q	1.36	0.73	0.25	4.38	1.54	0.82	0.62	4.23
Lev	0.41	0.20	0.02	0.92	0.46	0.21	0.01	1.21
Ind	4.4	2.34	0	9	6.14	2.94	2	14
Sha	5.14	2.17	0	11	3.69	2.23	0	9
β	0.66	1.12	−5.89	6.61	0.69	1.22	−5.28	7.20
Size	38,403	57,665	405	349,121	21,931	29,235	263	155,061

Panel A presents the descriptive statistics for market performance (Q), ownership concentration (*Famown*), number of independent directors (*Ind*) and shareholder directors (*Sha*) on the board, Leverage (*Lev*) is the total liability/total asset that is measured as the book value of debt divided by the book value of total assets, and control variable firm size (*Size*) is the total assets, which is measured as the book value of total assets (assets are in millions of pesos), and market risk is measured by the systematic risk (β). The sample period is the financial year 2005/2011. Panels B and C provide summary statistics for the data employed in the analysis segmented by ownership structure (family and non-family). The data set comprises 75 firms listed in the Mexican Stock Exchange for the period 2005–2011. Performance of the firm measured by Tobin's Q (Q) or the asset market-to-book ratio measures the performance of the firm. Family firms are companies where the founder or family member holds more than 40 percent ownership. The Panels A and B show the mean, standard deviation, minimum and maximum coefficients.

A key aspect of this study is the identification of family and non-family firms. Since the study focuses on ownership concentration, and family firms typically have more concentrated ownership, especially in non-Anglo-Saxon countries [72], it is important to identify the proper threshold of ownership that divides family and non-family firms in our sample in order to observe the effects of debt and board structure.

Mazzi, in her 2011 study [8] on 23 different research articles in different countries, states that owning families typically demonstrate a minimum control of 5, 10, or 20 percent, however, she later finds in her research that the median degree of family control among three-digit SIC industries is 50 percent when family firms are founder or founding family owned, and 51 percent when they are defined as individual or family controlled. La Porta, Lopez-de-Silanes, Schleifer, and Vishny [25,77], in a sample of large non-financial firms in 49 countries, find that the average ownership by the three largest shareholders is 46 percent. San-Martin and Duran [11] consider a firm a family firm as long as the family has 40 percent or more ownership of the company, as this percentage gives the family the ability to control the decisions and management of the company.

Since companies in general have a higher ownership concentration in Mexico, the choice of a higher starting concentration in order to properly divide the sample seems appropriate in this research, unlike other studies in which companies are classified as family companies when the owning family controls only 20 or 30 percent of the firm. Therefore, this study defines a family as one having an ownership concentration above 40 percent.

The percentage of ownership concentrated by the family was expressed as *Famown* and the Tobin'Q, or the asset market-to-book ratio, as Q. The remaining variables are leverage (*Lev*), which is measured as the book value of debt divided by the book value of total assets; and the board composition made of the number of independent (*Ind*) and insider or shareholder (*Sha*) directors. In addition, some control variables were included in order to examine some additional determinants of performance. Based on what has been done in previous works [31,78–80], the analysis considered size (*Size*), as represented by firm's total assets, the natural logarithm of size (*Lsize*), and market risk (β). As stated before, the sample combines 75 firms over seven years producing a 525 observations-panel data. Given the aim of the study, the panel data methodology seems to be the most accurate [39]. The fixed-effects term is unobservable, and hence becomes part of the random component in the estimated model. A pooling analysis of all the companies without noticing these peculiar characteristics could cause an omission bias and distort the results. The random error term εit controls both the error in the measurement of the variables and the omission of some relevant explanatory variables. The models can be expressed by the following equations, where *i* refers to the firms and *t* to the year ($i = 1, \ldots, 75$; $t = 1, \ldots, 7$):

$$Q_{it} = \theta_{it} + Famown_{it} + Lev_{it} + Ind_{it} + Sha_{it} + Lsize_{it} + \beta_{it} + \varepsilon_{it} \tag{1}$$

$$Q_{it} = \alpha_{it} + Lev_{it} + Lsize_{it} + \beta_{it} + \varepsilon_{it} \tag{2}$$

$$Q_{it} = \alpha_{it} + Ind_{it} + Lsize + \beta_{it} + \varepsilon_{it} \tag{3}$$

$$Q_{it} = \alpha_{it} + Sha_{it} + Lsize_{it} + \beta_{it} + \varepsilon_{it} \tag{4}$$

To provide robustness for the results, the percentage of ownership concentration to classify a company as a family or non-family firm was modified, using an ownership concentration level of 51 percent. It is important to mention that an attempt was made for an additional analysis using 35 percent as the ownership concentration level, but unfortunately, the Mexican market is characterized by high concentration across the board and at 35 percent of ownership concentration family firms represented 85 percent of the sample.

Also, to avoid the endogeneity problem in the relationship of family ownership and performance, the data was examined with the Generalized Method of Moments (GMM) that eliminates the possibility of second order serial correlation in the moments considered in the sample [81–83]. All regressors in the regression method are considered as exogenous except the lagged variable. The application of the Sargan test allows proving these conditions by avoiding incurring type I error, or accepting the null hypothesis. Thus, GMM provides mechanisms to limit errors over time, and to deal with heterocedasticity and simultaneity among the cases [31].

Finally, the effect of debt and board composition on performance was proved for first, second, and third or later generations of family firms, to examine if the results obtained for the whole sample of family firms vary. In this manner, the study tried to examine if the risk aversion and other motivations of family firms vary as the generation in control changes [57,58].

As shown in Table 2, on the one hand, family firms have a higher number of shareholders as board directors, and have more assets, while on the other hand, family firms have lower market performance, lower relative debt, fewer independent directors, and lower market risk.

4. Results

The results of the panel data estimation are displayed in Tables 3–5. These were estimated not only for the basic specification (Panels A and B of Table 4), but also segmenting the sample by alternative measure of ownership structure, with a level of ownership concentration in families to 51 percent, in order to assess robustness of the results (Table 5). The Hausman test reveals the importance of the fixed effect component, so that within-groups estimation method becomes necessary in order to deal with the constant unobservable heterogeneity.

Table 3. Results of estimation based on complete sample.

Variables	Coefficient	*t*-Statistic	*p*-Value
Famown	0.6026	1.71	0.088 ***
Lev	−0.2156	−1.88	0.061 ***
Ind	−0.4088	−1.22	0.221
Sha	0.6669	2.11	0.035 **
β	0.088	0.46	0.644
Lsize	0.0607	0.88	0.381
Constant	0.4179	0.57	0.566
Adjusted R^2	0.25		
Hausman test	32.57		0.000

Table shows estimated coefficients, *t*-statistics and *p*-value. Performance is the dependent variable and is measured using Tobin's Q ratios (*Q*) or the asset market-to book ratio. *Famown* represents the percentage of family ownership. Leverage (*Lev*) is total liability/total asset that is measured as the book value of debt divided by the book value of total assets. Board structure is *Ind* (number of independent directors on the board) and *Sha* (number of shareholder directors on the board), *Lsize* is log of total firm assets, used as a proxy for firm size and β is market risk. Hausman test allows testing fixed *versus* random effects hypothesis. Hausman test follows a χ^2 distribution. ** Significant at 0.05, *** Significant at 0.01.

According to Table 3, there is a positive significant statistical association of family ownership with Tobin's Q, which represents market performance, confirming the first hypothesis. Also, the participation of shareholders on the board is positively associated to performance in a significant way. The level of indebtedness is associated negatively to performance.

Further analysis observes the effect that these variables have on company performance or value creation after differentiating between family and non-family firms. The results are shown in Table 4.

Table 4 shows the effect that debt and board structure have on market performance considering family and non-family firms. Whereas lower levels of debt are associated in a significant way to higher market performance in family firms, higher levels of debt are related to superior performance in non-family businesses. Both results confirm hypotheses 2a and 2b.

Table 4. Results of estimations based on family and non-family sample (family holds more than 40 percent ownership).

Variables	Panel A: Family Firms				Panel B: Non-Family Firms			
	1	2	3	4	1	3	4	5
Lev	−0.210 (−1.94)**			−0.211 (−1.95)**	0.282 (2.72)**			0.211 (1.95)**
Ind		−0.188 (−1.80)*		−0.188 (−1.80)*		0.559 (2.06)**		0.562 (1.97)**
Sha			0.685 (1.94)**	0.608 (2.18)**			−0.120 (−2.20)**	−0.117 (−2.10)**
β	0.016 (0.80)	0.019 (0.91)	0.014 (0.67)	0.015 (0.74)	0.010 (0.25)	0.019 (0.47)	0.050 (0.21)	0.071 (0.79)
Lsize	0.115 (1.67)*	0.094 (1.37)	0.077 (1.13)	0.123 (1.76)*	0.123 (0.56)	0.188 (1.01)	0.236 (1.21)	0.138 (1.65)
Constant	0.327 (0.50)	0.712 (1.06)	0.460 (0.70)	0.920 (1.25)	0.812 (0.35)	0.442 (1.32)	0.452 (2.37)**	0.580 (1.35)
Adjusted R^2	0.14	0.22	0.19	0.15	0.13	0.18	0.17	0.19
Hausman test	20.17 (0.000)	23.10 (0.000)	31.42 (0.000)	36.49 (0.000)	15.58 (0.008)	22.09 (0.000)	29.31 (0.000)	24.78 (0.000)

Table shows estimated coefficients, *t*-statistics and *p*-value. The Panel A shows the results for family firms. Panel B reports the results for non-family firms. Performance is the dependent variable and is measured using Tobin's Q ratios (*Q*) or the asset market-to-book ratio. *Famown* represents the percentage of family ownership. Leverage (*Lev*) is total liability/total asset that is measured as the book value of debt divided by the book value of total assets. Board structure is *Ind* (number of independent director on the board) and *Sha* (number of shareholder director on the board), *Lsize* is log of total firm assets, used as a proxy for firm size and β is market risk. Hausman test allows testing fixed *versus* random effects hypothesis. Hausman test follows a χ^2 distribution. * Significant at 0.10, ** Significant at 0.05.

In the case of the structure of the board, the results show a significant positive relationship for inside directors and performance and a negative relationship for external board directors in family firms. Just the opposite is true for non-family firms, as performance is affected negatively by the presence of shareholders on the board and positively by independent director participation, thus hypotheses 3a and 3b are confirmed.

In all cases, market risk and firm size are positively associated with market performance, but only in the case of the family firm, size as measured as the amount of assets, shows a significant relationship.

The results of the regression analysis using 51 percent of family ownership as the threshold for defining family firms *versus* non-family firms are shown in Table 5.

The results shown in Table 5, using 51 percent for differentiating a family from a non-family firm, do not differ from the results in Table 4. This means that the results may apply for an extended range of ownership concentration.

Table 5. Results of estimations based on family and non-family sample (family holds more than 51 percent ownership).

Variables	Panel A: Family Firms				Panel B: Non-Family Firms			
	1	2	3	4	1	3	4	5
Lev	−0.067 (−1.78) *			−0.062 (−1.72) *	0.144 (1.92) **			0.234 (1.73) *
Ind		−0.109 (−1.94) **		−0.138 (−1.67) *		0.403 (1.73) *		0.685 (1.99) **
Sha			0.620 (1.68) *	0.684 (2.19) **			−0.203 (−1.72) *	−0.164 (−1.67) *
β	0.047 (2.09) **	0.059 (2.13) **	0.061 (2.18) **	0.060 (2.25) **	−0.056 (−1.15)	−0.030 (−0.83)	−0.027 (−0.73)	−0.061 (1.17)
Lsize	0.246 (3.59) ***	0.230 (3.19) ***	0.209 (2.83) ***	0.246 (3.58) ***	0.359 (2.14) **	0.279 (1.78) **	0.267 (1.70) *	0.138 (1.65)
Constant	0.934 (1.49)	0.909 (1.35)	0.861 (1.15)	0.961 (1.98) **	0.426 (2.49) **	0.567 (3.11) ***	0.359 (1.70) *	0.328 (1.91) **
Adjusted R²	0.16	0.18	0.15	0.21	0.13	0.14	0.16	0.21
Hausman test	22.36 (0.000)	23.42 (0.000)	21.53 (0.000)	39.12 (0.000)	15.29 (0.000)	21.19 (0.000)	28.71 (0.000)	29.34 (0.000)

Table shows estimated coefficients, *t*-statistics and *p*-value. The Panel A shows the results for family firms. Panel B reports the results for non-family firms. Q Performance is measured using Tobin's Q ratios (*Q*) or the asset market-to-book ratio. Leverage (*Lev*) is total liability/total asset that is measured as the book value of debt divided by the book value of total assets. Board structure is *Ind* (number of independent director on the board) and *Sha* (number of shareholder director on the board) and *Lsize* is log of total firm assets, used as a proxy for firm size and β is Market risk. Hausman test allows testing fixed *versus* random effects hypothesis. Hausman test follows a χ^2 distribution. * Significant at 0.10, ** Significant at 0.05, *** Significant at 0.01.

In order to deal with endogeneity, the results of the GMM model are shown in Table 6.

Table 6 shows that after controlling for endogeneity, and failing to reject the null hypothesis, results remain as already reported in previous regressions. This demonstrates the robustness of the results, reinforcing the hypotheses of this study.

The results of differentiating the effect of debt and board structure in first, second, and third or later generations of family firms are presented in Table 7.

The first and second generations of family firms show that higher performance associates with less debt, whereas in third or later generations, performance is linked to more debt. In the case of board structure, there is also a modification between the first two family firm generations and the third or later generations, as the association of independent directors with performance changes from negative to positive.

Table 6. Results of GMM Model based on family and non-family sample (family holds more than 51 percent ownership).

Variable	Panel A: Family Firms	Panel B: Non-Family Firms
Constant	0.598 (0.32)	0.351 (1.42)
Lev	−0.420 (−2.29) **	0.718 (1.96) **
Ind	−0.974 (−2.28) **	0.501 (2.02) **
Sha	0.297 (1.82) *	−0.246 (−2.02) **
β	0.074 (1.78) *	0.090 (1.42)
Lsize	0.190 (0.96)	0.117 (0.53)
m1	−6.21 ***	−5.34 ***
m2	−0.68	−0.71
Sargan test	9.13	8.53
Wald test	12.36 *	13.51 *

Table shows estimated coefficients, *t*-statistics and *p*-value. The Panel A shows the results for family firms. Panel B reports the results for non-family firms. Q Performance is measured using Tobin's Q ratios (Q) or the asset market-to-book ratio. Leverage (*Lev*) is total liability/total asset that is measured as the book value of debt divided by the book value of total assets. Board structure is *Ind* (number of independent director on the board) and *Sha* (number of shareholder director on the board) and *Lsize* is log of total firm assets, used as a proxy for firm size and β is Market risk. Sargan test allows testing serial correlation (m1 and m2). Sargan test validates the instruments and Wald test the joint significance of variables. * Significant at 0.10, ** Significant at 0.05, *** Significant at 0.01.

Table 7. Results of estimations based on generation family sample (first generation and second or more generations).

Variable	PGEN	SGEN	TGEN
Lev	−0.557 (2.53) ***	−0.168 (−1.80) *	0.221 (2.87) ***
Ind	−0.2937 (−2.16) **	−0.808 (−1.86) *	0.560 (1.81) *
Sha	0.8570 (3.47) ***	0.774 (1.91) **	−0.338 (−1.99) **
β	0.090 (0.27)	0.087 (0.20)	0.082 (0.19)
Lsize	0.109 (1.96) **	0.384 (2.15) **	0.256 (1.40)
Constant	0.313 (1.74) *	0.496 (1.39)	0.721 (0.48)
Hausman test	25.76 (0.000)	21.34 (0.000)	23.56 (0.000)

Table shows estimated coefficients, *t*-statistics and *p*-value. The Panel A shows the results for family firms. Panel B reports the results for non-family firms. Q Performance is measured using Tobin's Q ratios (Q) or the asset market-to-book ratio. Leverage (*Lev*) is total liability/total asset that is measured as the book value of debt divided by the book value of total assets. Board structure is *Ind* (number of independent director on the board) and *Sha* (number of shareholder director on the board) and *Lsize* is log of total firm assets, used as a proxy for firm size and β is Market risk. Hausman test allows testing fixed *versus* random effects hypothesis. Hausman test follows a χ^2 distribution. * Significant at 0.10, ** Significant at 0.05, *** Significant at 0.01.

5. Discussion and Conclusions

This study focuses on the role corporate governance plays in the relationship between ownership structure and performance. In particular, it deals with two mechanisms of corporate governance, externally, the level of debt in a firm, and internally, the structure of the firm's board.

From a theoretical point of view, the results of this study add to the relationship of ownership concentration and performance, indicating the reductions of agency costs given the weak corporate legal governance in Mexico. Thus, owners may assure by these means greater control of their firms.

Through the investigation of the level of debt and the composition of the board of directors, this study disentangles some findings that point to ambiguous or contradictory associations between family and non-family firms, and performance. The answers to the hypotheses that were formulated in this study lead to the conclusion that in both family and non-family cases, the financial leverage and the board structure act as reinforcing mechanisms in the achievement of better results.

The findings show that in family businesses, the avoidance of debt and the greater participation of dominant shareholders on the board act as regulatory mechanisms for better performance. Given the high concentration of property in family firms, debt is not seen as a necessary mechanism for reducing discretionary management behavior. This discretionary management behavior is limited by the control rights that owners exercise on discretionary funds. It is also likely that by reducing the level of debt, owners can reduce perception of the risk of financial bankruptcy and loss of control, strengthening the socioemotional goals maintained by a closer family group of owners. On the contrary, the dispersion of property may encourage owners to increase the level of debt as this mechanism would serve as a monitor to make better use of funds in profitable projects, leading to a better return on equity capital.

When there is a high concentration of property, the role of shareholders becomes more important for the firm. Majority shareholders are able to improve the firm's position by minimizing the risk of being distracted by the goals of fewer and less important minority shareholders. Apparently, according to the performance achieved by family businesses in this study, the presence of entrenchment or nepotism does not seem to be a common issue in these firms. Therefore, it may seem that stewardship in company management is best performed when owners in governance bodies maintain higher authority and discretion. The benefits that owners obtain by exercising their control rights on the board are effective in achieving better performance. In the opposite situation, when ownership is more dispersed, the role of independent directors on the board becomes more relevant. It can be argued that in the case of non-family businesses, independent directors are in a better position to provide more objective and informed advice than family shareholders. The higher dispersion of property may bias board decisions toward the dominant shareholder block, compromising a more comprehensive view of the firm. As other related studies have shown [11], in non-family firms, institutional investors, such as financial institutions, participate to a larger extent. This participation may increase the board's capabilities for monitoring free cash flow use in the firm, and also may serve as a mechanism to reduce risk aversion caused by macroeconomic volatile changes.

The association of debt and board structure with the generation in control shows that debt may become an effective mechanism, as there is dispersion in ownership and a consequent reduction of risk aversion in third and later generations [57]. The same arguments may apply to the growing number of independent directors on the board as their participation becomes more credible, acting as a more effective representation of minority shareholders [7,9]. This situation is explained by Schulze, Lubatkin, and Dino [57], who argue that the greater the ownership dispersion, and the smaller the average shareholding, the more likely their boards will favor growth, and, in the absence of the ability to issue equity or cut dividends, the more likely they will be to risk the use of debt to fund growth.

From a practical perspective, the differentiated effect of those factors may serve to fill the institutional voids mentioned by Gedajlovic *et al.* [6], mainly the weak protection allowed to minority investors in Mexico. As previously mentioned, the reinforcement effect of having a low debt and low participation of independent directors in family businesses, contributes to the association of family ownership with better performance, especially in a context where there is weak legal corporate shareholder protection, such as in emerging economies. By the same token, in the case of non-family businesses, the participation of independent or external directors on the board and a higher level of debt act as an effective device to achieve better performance.

However, the relatively lower average market performance of family firms as compared to non-family firms (see Table 2) may be affected by the strategies they follow in relation to indebtedness, which in some cases may cause underinvestment to support growth and profitability. Thus, in order to make better use of their potential, family firms are encouraged to create organizational structures and decision rules that facilitate intra-family communication; including the involvement of family members in the top management of the firm and professional advisors may help as well [37]. Additionally, it can be found that views and orientations of outsiders and owners can strengthen the firm's board. As Cannella, Jones, and Whiters [84] have shown, firms may seek directors with prior experience at firms with similar identities that are mainly *familial* or *entrepreneurial* in nature. For practical implications, recommendations can be directed to family owners to seek directors that have a close identity with the organization [85], and who have the experience and power to counsel an otherwise entrenched family leader [86].

We are aware of the limitations of this study, as the results may be only valid for Mexico and possibly for those countries in which there is a relatively high concentration of firm property. Also, we recognize that we have found an association between debt and board composition, and the results obtained in family and non-family firms, however, to show causality would require a longitudinal research design.

In spite of these considerations, the main contributions of this study include an important understanding of the relationship of debt and board structure, and also a simultaneous analysis of the effect of these variables in family and non-family businesses. With these findings, we seek to encourage similar research in other emerging economies to further explain the relationship between ownership concentration and performance.

Acknowledgments: The authors thank the reviewers and Howard Stanley Hart for their valuable suggestions to the content of this paper.

Author Contributions: All listed authors contributed equally to the research completed and writing of the paper.

Conflicts of Interest: The authors declare no conflicts of interest.

References

1. Coase, R. The nature of the firm. *Economica* **1937**, *4*, 386–405. [CrossRef]
2. Reyna, J.M.S.M.; Vázquez, R.D.; Valdés, A.L. Corporate governance, ownership structure and performance in Mexico. *Int. Bus. Res.* **2012**, *5*, 12–27. [CrossRef]
3. Berle, A.; Means, G. *The Modern Corporation and Private Property*; The MacMillan Company: New York, NY, USA, 1932.
4. Basco, R. The family's effect on family firm performance: A model testing the demographic and essence approaches. *J. Fam. Bus. Strategy* **2013**, *4*, 42–66. [CrossRef]
5. Block, J.; Jaskiewcz, P.; Miller, D. Ownership *versus* management effects on performance in family and founder companies: A Bayesian reconciliation. *J. Fam. Bus. Strategy* **2011**, *2*, 232–245. [CrossRef]
6. Gedajlovic, E.; Carney, M.; Chrisman, J.; Kellermanns, F. The adolescence of family firm research: Taking stock and planning for the future. *J. Manag.* **2012**, *38*, 1010–1037.
7. Le Breton-Miller, I.; Miller, D. Why do some family businesses out-compete? Governance, long-term orientations, and sustainable capacity. *Entrep. Theory Practice* **2006**, *30*, 731–746.
8. Mazzi, C. Family business and financial performance: Current state of knowledge and future research. *J. Fam. Bus. Strategy* **2011**, *2*, 166–181. [CrossRef]
9. Miller, D.; le Breton-Miller, I. Family governance and firm performance: Agency, stewardship, and capabilities. *Fam. Bus. Rev.* **2006**, *19*, 73–87. [CrossRef]
10. O'Boyle, E.; Pollack, J.; Rutherford, M. Exploring the relation between family involvement and firms' financial performance: A meta-analysis of main and moderator effects. *J. Bus. Ventur.* **2011**, *27*, 1–18. [CrossRef]

11. San Martin-Reyna, J.; Duran-Encalada, J. The relationship among family business, corporate governance and firm performance: Evidence from the Mexican stock exchange. *J. Fam. Bus. Strategy* **2012**, *3*, 106–117. [CrossRef]
12. Carney, M. Corporate governance and competitive advantage in family firms. *Entrep. Theory Pract.* **2005**, *29*, 249–265. [CrossRef]
13. Claessens, S.; Djankov, S.; Lang, L. The separation of ownership and control in East Asian corporations. *J. Financ. Econ.* **1999**, *58*, 81–112.
14. Whyte, M.K. The Chinese family and economic development: Obstacle or engine? *Dev. Cult. Chang.* **1996**, *45*, 1–30. [CrossRef]
15. Duran-Encalada, J.A.; San Martin-Reyna, J.M. Ownership structure, earnings management and investment opportunities set: Evidence from Mexican firms. *J. Entrep. Manag. Innov.* **2012**, *8*, 35–57. [CrossRef]
16. Burkart, M.; Pannunzi, F.; Schleifer, A. Family firms. *J. Financ.* **2003**, *58*, 2167–2202. [CrossRef]
17. Friedman, E.; Johnson, S.; Mitton, T. Propping and tunneling. *J. Comp. Econ.* **2003**, *31*, 732–750. [CrossRef]
18. Gomez-Mejia, L.R.; Cruz, C.; Berrone, P.; de Castro, J. The bind of ties: Socioemotional wealth preservation in family firms. *Acad. Manag. Ann.* **2011**, *5*, 653–707. [CrossRef]
19. Pérez-González, F. Inherited control and firm performance. *Am. Econ. Rev.* **2006**, *96*, 1550–1588. [CrossRef]
20. Morck, R.; Yeung, B. Agency problems in large family business groups. *Entrep. Theory Pract.* **2003**, *27*, 367–382. [CrossRef]
21. Schleifer, A.; Vishny, R. Large shareholders and corporate control. *J. Polit. Econ.* **1986**, *94*, 461–488. [CrossRef]
22. Hart, O. Corporate governance: Some theory and implications. *Econ. J.* **1995**, *105*, 678–689. [CrossRef]
23. Schulze, W.; Lubatkin, M.; Dino, R.; Buchholtz, A. Agency relationships in family firms: Theory and evidence. *Organ. Sci.* **2001**, *12*, 99–116. [CrossRef]
24. Castañeda, G. Governance of large corporations in Mexico and productivity implications. *Revista ABANTE* **2000**, *3*, 57–89.
25. La Porta, R.; Lopez-de-Silanes, F.; Shleifer, A.; Vishny., R. Agency problems and dividends policies around the world. *J. Financ.* **2000**, *55*, 1–33.
26. Schleifer, A.; Vishny, R. A survey of corporate governance. *J. Financ.* **1997**, *52*, 737–783. [CrossRef]
27. Harijono; Ariff, M.; Tanewski, G.A. The Impact of Family Control of Firms on Leverage: Australian Evidence. EFMA 2004, Basel Meetings Paper. Available online: http://dx.doi.org/10.2139/ssrn.487706 (accessed on 11 May 2013).
28. Demsetz, H. Information and efficiency: Another viewpoint. *J. Law Econ.* **1969**, *12*, 1–22. [CrossRef]
29. Demsetz, H. Corporate control, insider trading, and rates of return. *Am. Econ. Rev.* **1986**, *76*, 313–316.
30. Demsetz, H. The structure of ownership and the theory of the firm. *J. Law Econ.* **1983**, *26*, 375–390. [CrossRef]
31. Espinosa, C. Estructura de propiedad y desempeño de la firma: El caso chileno. *Academia Revista Latinoamericana de Administración* **2009**, *43*, 41–62.
32. Shah, S.; Butt, S.; Saeed, M. Ownership structure and performance of firms: Empirical evidence from an emerging market. *Afr. J. Bus. Manag.* **2011**, *5*, 515–523.
33. Kim, K.; Kitsabunnarat, P.; Nofsinger, J. Ownership and operating performance in emerging market: Evidence from Thai IPO firms. *J. Corp. Financ.* **2004**, *10*, 355–381. [CrossRef]
34. Pervan, M.; Pervan, I.; Todoric, M. Firm ownership and performance: Evidence form Croatian listed firms. *World Acad. Sci. Eng. Technol.* **2012**, *61*, 964–970.
35. Sacristán, M.; Gómez, S.; Cabeza, L. Large shareholders' combinations in family firms: Prevalence and performance effects. *J. Fam. Bus. Strategy* **2011**, *2*, 101–112. [CrossRef]
36. Goud, R.B., Jr. Ownership and Firm Performance: Evidence from 25 Countries Central and Easter Europe and the Former Soviet Union. Available online: http://econpapers.repec.org/paper/wpawuwpdc/0207002.htm (accessed on 10 January 2014).
37. De Massis, A.; Kotlar, J.; Campopiano, G.; Cassia, L. Dispersion of family ownership and the performance of small-to-medium size private family firms. *J. Fam. Bus. Strategy* **2013**, *4*, 166–175. [CrossRef]
38. Arosa, B.; Iturralde, T.; Maseda, A. Ownership structure and firm performance in non-listed firms: Evidence from Spain. *J. Fam. Bus. Strategy* **2010**, *1*, 88–96. [CrossRef]
39. Andrés-Alonso, P.; Azofra-Valenzuela, V.; Rodríguez-Sanz, J. Endeudamiento, oportunidades de crecimiento y estructura contractual: Un contraste empírico para el caso español. *Investigaciones Económicas* **2000**, *24*, 641–679.

40. Castrillo, L.A.; San Martín, J.M. La propiedad familiar como mecanismo de gobierno disciplinador de la dirección de empresas mexicanas: una evidencia empírica. *Contaduría y Administración* **2007**, *52*, 59–82.
41. Gallo, M.; Vilaseca, A. Finance in family business. *Fam. Bus. Rev.* **1996**, *9*, 287–305.
42. Bennedsen, M.; Pérez-González, F.; Wolfenzon, D. The governance of family firms. In *Corporate Governance: A Synthesis of Theory, Research, and Practice*; Baker, K.H., Anderson, R., Eds.; John Wiley: Hoboken, NJ, USA, 2010; pp. 371–390.
43. Miller, D.; le Breton-Miller, I.; Lester, R.; Cannella, A. Are family firms really superior performers? *J. Corp. Financ.* **2007**, *13*, 829–858. [CrossRef]
44. De Massis, A.; Kotlar, J.; Campopiano, G.; Cassia, L. The impact of family involvement on SMEs' performance: Theory and evidence. *J. Small Bus. Manag.* **2013**. [CrossRef]
45. Le Breton-Miller, I.; Miller, D.; Lester, R. Stewardship or agency? A social embeddedness reconciliation of conduct and performance in public family businesses. *Organ. Sci.* **2011**, *22*, 704–721. [CrossRef]
46. Chang, E.C.; Memili, E.; Chrisman, J.J.; Kellermanns, F.W.; Chua, J.H. Family social capital, venture preparedness, and start-up decisions: A study of Hispanic entrepreneurs in New England. *Fam. Bus. Rev.* **2009**, *22*, 279–292. [CrossRef]
47. García, R.; García, M. Board characteristics and firm performance in public founder- and non-founder-led family business. *J. Fam. Bus. Strategy* **2011**, *2*, 220–231. [CrossRef]
48. McConaughy, D.L.; Matthews, C.H.; Fialko, A.S. Founding family controlled firms: Performance, risk and value. *J. Small Bus. Manag.* **2001**, *39*, 31–49. [CrossRef]
49. Jensen, M. Agency cost of free cash flow, corporate finance, and takeovers. *Am. Econ. Rev.* **1986**, *76*, 323–329.
50. Alonso-Bonis, S.; Andrés-Alonso, P. Ownership structure and performance in large Spanish companies. Empirical evidence in the context of an endogenous relation. *Corp. Ownersh. Control* **2007**, *4*, 206–216.
51. Grossman, S.; Hart, O. Takeover bids, the free-rider problem and the theory of the corporation. *Bell J. Econ.* **1980**, *11*, 42–64. [CrossRef]
52. Setia-Atmaja, L.; Tanewski, G.A.; Skully, M. The role of dividends, debt and board structure in the governance of family controlled firms. *J. Bus. Financ. Account.* **2009**, *36*, 863–898. [CrossRef]
53. Nam, J.; Ottoo, R.E.; Thornton, J.H. The effects of managerial incentives to bear risk on corporate capital structure and R & D investment. *Financ. Rev.* **2003**, *38*, 77–101. [CrossRef]
54. Allouche, J.; Amann, B.; Jaussaud, J.; Kurashina, T. The impact of family control on the performance and financial characteristics of family *versus* nonfamily businesses in Japan: A matched-pair investigation. *Fam. Bus. Rev.* **2008**, *21*, 315–329. [CrossRef]
55. Gilson, S.C. Bankruptcy, boards, banks, and blockholders: Evidence on changes in corporate ownership and control when firms default. *J. Financ. Econ.* **1990**, *27*, 355–387. [CrossRef]
56. Mishra, C.S.; McConaughy, D.L. Founding family control and capital structure: The risk of loss of control and the aversion to debt. *Entrep. Theory Pract.* **1999**, *23*, 53–64.
57. Schulze, W.; Lubatkin, H.; Dino, R. Exploring the agency consequences of ownership dispersion among the directors of private family firms. *Acad. Manag. J.* **2003**, *46*, 179–194. [CrossRef]
58. Carney, M.; van Essen, M.; Gedajlovic, E.; Heugens, P. What do we know about private family firms? A meta-analytical review. *Entrep. Theory Pract.* **2013**. [CrossRef]
59. Anderson, R.; Reeb, D. Founding-family ownership, corporate diversification, and firm leverage. *J. Law Econ.* **2003**, *46*, 653–684. [CrossRef]
60. Smith, C.; Warner, J. On financial contracting: An analysis of bond covenants. *J. Financ. Econ.* **1979**, *7*, 117–161. [CrossRef]
61. Barontini, R.; Caprio, L. The effect of family control on firm value and performance: Evidence from continental Europe. *Eur. Financ. Manag.* **2006**, *12*, 689–723. [CrossRef]
62. Lee, J. Family firm performance: Further evidence. *Fam. Bus. Rev.* **2006**, *19*, 103–114. [CrossRef]
63. Miller, D.; le Breton-Miller, I.; Lester, R. Family and lone founder ownership and strategic behaviour: Social context, identity, and institutional logics. *J. Manag. Studies* **2011**, *48*, 1–25. [CrossRef]
64. Bonilla, C.A.; Sepulveda, J.; Carvajal, M. Family ownership and firm performance in Chile: A note on Martinez *et al.*'s evidence. *Fam. Bus. Rev.* **2010**, *23*, 148–154.
65. Wenyi, C. Family ownership and firm performance: Influence of family management, family control, and firm size. *Asia Pac. J. Manag.* **2011**, *28*, 833–851. [CrossRef]

66. Finkelstein, S.; D'Aveni, R.A. CEO duality as a double-edged sword: How boards of directors balance entrenchment avoidance and unity of command. *Acad. Manag. J.* **1994**, *37*, 1079–1108. [CrossRef]

67. Lin, L. The effectiveness of outside directors as corporate governance mechanism: Theories and evidence. *Northwestern Univ. Law Rev.* **1996**, *9*, 898–951.

68. Walsh, J.P.; Seward, J.K. On the efficiency of internal and external control mechanisms. *Acad. Manag. Rev.* **1990**, *15*, 421–458.

69. Finkelstein, S.; Hambrick, D.C. *Strategic Leadership: Top Executives and Their Effects on Organizations*; West Educational Publishing: St. Paul, MN, USA, 1996.

70. Giovannini, R. Corporate governance, family ownership and performance. *J. Manag. Gov.* **2010**, *14*, 145–166. [CrossRef]

71. Minichilli, A.; Corbetta, G.; MacMillan, I.C. Top management teams in family-controlled companies: 'Familiness,' 'faultiness,' and their impact on financial performance. *J. Manag. Studies* **2010**, *47*, 205–222. [CrossRef]

72. Yin-Hua, Y.; Tsun-Siou, L.; Tracie, W. Family control and corporate governance: Evidence from Taiwan. *Int. Rev. Financ.* **2001**, *2*, 21–48.

73. Alderfer, C.P. Understanding and consulting to family business boards. *Fam. Bus. Rev.* **1998**, *1*, 249–261. [CrossRef]

74. Nelsen, J.F.; Frishkoff, P.A. Boards of directors in family owned business. *Akron Bus. Econ. Rev.* **1991**, *23*, 88–96.

75. Rubenson, G.C.; Gupta, A.K. The initial succession: A contingency model of founder tenure. *Entrep. Theory Pract.* **1996**, *21*, 21–35.

76. Husted, B.; Serrano, C. Corporate governance in Mexico. *J. Bus. Ethics* **2001**, *37*, 337–348.

77. La Porta, R.; Lopez-de-Silanes, F.; Shleifer, A.; Vishny, R. Corporate ownership around the world. *J. Financ.* **1999**, *54*, 471–517. [CrossRef]

78. De Andres, P.; Azofra, V.; Lopez, F. Corporate boards in OECD countries: Size composition, functioning and effectiveness. *Corp. Gov. Int. Rev.* **2005**, *13*, 197–210. [CrossRef]

79. Wang, D. Founding family ownership and earnings quality. *J. Account. Res.* **2006**, *44*, 619–656. [CrossRef]

80. Warfield, T.; Wild, J.; Wild, K. Managerial ownership, accounting choices and informativeness of earnings. *J. Account. Econ.* **1995**, *16*, 61–91. [CrossRef]

81. Arellano, M.; Bond, S. Some test of specification for panel data: Monte Carlo evidence and an application to employment equations. *Rev. Eco. Studies* **1991**, *58*, 277–297. [CrossRef]

82. Liu, W.; Hsu, C. Corporate finance and growth of Taiwan's manufacturing firms. *Rev. Pac. Basin Financ. Mark. Policies* **2006**, *9*, 67–95. [CrossRef]

83. Al-Fayoumi, N.; Abuzayed, B.; Alexander, D. Ownership structure and earnings management in emerging markets: The case of Jordan. *Int. Res. J. Financ. Econ.* **2010**, *38*, 28–47.

84. Cannella, A., Jr.; Jones, C.; Whiters, M. Family *versus* lone-founder-controlled public corporations: Social identity theory and boards of directors. *Acad. Manag. J.* **2014**. [CrossRef]

85. Dutton, J.; Dukerich, J.; Harquail, C. Organizational images and member identification. *Adm. Sci. Q.* **1994**, *39*, 239–263. [CrossRef]

86. Anderson, R.; Reeb, D. Board composition: Balancing family influence in S&P 500 firms. *Adm. Sci. Q.* **2004**, *49*, 209–237.

International Journal of
Financial Studies

MDPI

Article

Incumbent Decisions about Succession Transitions in Family Firms: A Conceptual Model

Britta Boyd [1],*, Isabel C. Botero [2] and Tomasz A. Fediuk [3]

[1] Department for Border Region Studies, University of Southern Denmark, Alsion 2,
6400 Sønderborg, Denmark

[2] Department of Management, Gatton College of Business and Economics, University of Kentucky,
Lexington, KY 40506-0034, USA; Isabel.botero@uky.edu

[3] Fediuk Botero LLC, Lexington, KY 40515, USA; tafediuk@fedtero.com

* Author to whom correspondence should be addressed; bri@sam.sdu.dk;
Tel.: +45-(0)-6550-1756; Fax: +45-(0)-6550-1779.

External Editor: Esra Memili

Received: 30 April 2014; in revised form: 29 July 2014; Accepted: 24 October 2014; Published: 3 November 2014

Abstract: In the family business literature, succession research has focused on the family member as they enter the leadership role or on the different issues that affect the succession process. Although researchers have acknowledged that succession in family businesses is "punctuated" by decision making events, less attention has been given to understanding how incumbents make decisions about ownership and management transitions. In an effort to continue to understand the succession process it is important to understand how incumbents make decisions about the type of transitions they intend to engage in (*i.e.*, intra-family succession, out of family succession, or no succession). Building on the theory of planned behavior and the socioemotional wealth framework (SEW), this manuscript presents a conceptual framework to understand the factors that influence succession transitions and the role that contextual factors can play in this decision-making process. We present theory driven propositions and discuss the implications for understanding and evaluation of the succession process.

Keywords: decision-making; ownership transition; management transition; succession intent; succession in family firms; theory of reasoned action

1. Introduction

Succession has been one of the main areas of interest for family business scholars and practitioners. The reason for this is that only a small percentage of family firms are able to survive the transition to the next generation [1], and poor succession planning and management is often attributed as the main reason for this poor survival rate [2]. Although there are several integrative frameworks that explain the succession process in family firms [3–6] and there is research highlighting the factors that prevent intra-family succession [7], an aspect that is not well understood is how incumbents[1] make decisions about the type of succession they intend to engage in (*i.e.*, intra-family succession, out of family succession, or no succession). This decision-making process is important because the way that owners plan, manage and execute the succession of a firm is intrinsically linked to their decision about the type of transition they intend to engage in, can have an effect on how the succession process is evaluated, and the financial viability of the family and the business.

---

[1] Incumbents in our paper represents an individual who currently holds the management leadership position in a family firm, has majority of ownership in a business or represents those who have majority ownership in the family firm.

Int. J. Financial Stud. **2014**, *2*, 335–358

In the context of family firms, succession refers to the transfer of management and/or ownership from one family member to another [3,6]. Although research on succession has tried to understand the range of factors that are related to successful succession, there is not much understanding of determining what succession strategy founder/owners decide to engage in and why [8]. This gap in our understanding has affected the evaluation of what constitutes a successful succession and has promoted the assumption that in family firms exit strategies that have a non-family focus represent a failure for the family [9]. This assumption is inconsistent with empirical research that has found that the performance of family CEOs is affected by organizational size and concentration of ownership among family members such that firms with family CEOs perform better when the firm is smaller and the ownership is concentrated among family members [10]. Because of this, family business scholars have started to highlight the decision-making components of the succession process as an important source for understanding other exit alternatives. For example, De Massis and colleagues [7] suggest that the succession process is a "chain of causation" that begins with the decision of the incumbent or dominant coalition regarding the type of transition they hope to engage in based on an evaluation of the availability of successors to take over the business. Similarly, Royer and colleagues [5] suggest that before family firms begin the succession process they often analyze the costs and benefits of keeping the business in the family in comparison to finding other forms of succession (e.g., selling the business or having non-family management). These authors argue that in instances where intra-family succession becomes costly for the family business, owners will make different decisions of how to approach the succession process.

The work on transgenerational intent [11,12] (*i.e.*, the desire of organizational leaders to hand over control of the firm to their children) and transgenerational control intentions [13] (*i.e.*, intention to transfer the control of the business to the next generation) also suggests that the succession process begins with a decision-making event in which owners consider the benefits and costs of transferring management and control of the business to family and non-family successors. Finally, DeTienne and Chirico [14] recently present a conceptual model to explain how socioemotional wealth (SEW; *i.e.*, the nonfinancial aspects that motivate family business owners) affects the founder's decision to exit the family business. They argue that family firms with higher levels of SEW are more likely to select stewardship exits (*i.e.*, exit strategies that focus on keeping the family involved in the business either through ownership or through management).

When taken together, these studies suggest that before a succession can be planned/managed, the incumbent needs to make a decision regarding the type of transition to follow. Up to date, we have very little understanding of what factors play a role in making decisions about transitions, and how these factors affect the choices that incumbent make regarding transitions. This is problematic for two reasons. First, if researchers do not understand the complete succession process, including how incumbents make decisions about what type of succession they will follow, there might be key issues that are not being considered when studying the effectiveness of succession. Second, the incomplete understanding of the succession process can also limit the help that academic research can provide to practitioners (*i.e.*, consultants and family business owners). Thus, in an attempt to address the gap highlighted above, this paper presents a conceptual model that addresses two important research questions: (1) What factors play a role in the incumbent's decision to engage in a particular type of transition? And, (2) how do these factors influence the incumbent's decision of what transition to engage in? (See Figure 1).

Building on the theory of planned behavior [15], and the work on socioemotional wealth [16] we identify the contextual factors (*i.e.*, family, business, industry, and culture) that play a role in the incumbent's decision of what type of succession to engage in (*i.e.*, intra-family succession, non-family succession, or no succession). We also explore how contextual factors influence this decision making process based on the importance that the incumbent places on socioemotional wealth factors (*i.e.*, concern for the family and concern for the business). We believe that the conceptual model presented in this paper can provide some insights for academics and practitioners. For academics, our model can serve to understand what are factors that are understudied when exploring the different types of succession and why they occur. For practitioners, our model can provide some guidelines of aspects that need to be considered when helping family business owners make decisions about transitions, and how to plan and manage these transitions. In the following sections we summarize literature in the areas of family business, entrepreneurship and social psychology to present our theoretical model of how incumbents make decisions about succession transitions. We finish our paper by discussing the implications of our model and some ideas for future research.

Int. J. Financial Stud. **2014**, 2, 335–358

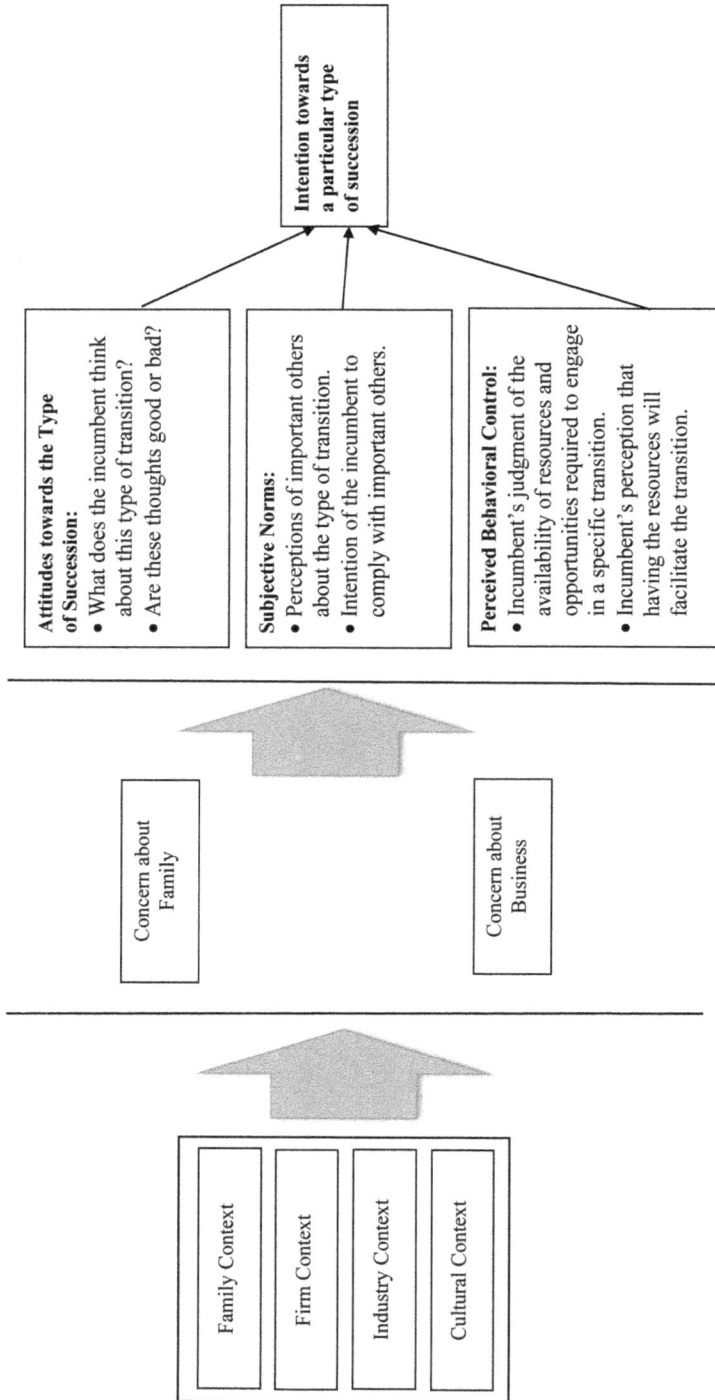

Figure 1. Incumbent decision making transitions model.

2. Literature Review: Succession in Family Firms

Family firms are organizations in which family involvement characterizes the management, control, and ownership of the business [17,18]. These types of firms represent a significant proportion of the world's organizations and a large percentage of GDP for multiple countries [19]. Because of this, in the last three decades there has been growing body of research dedicated to exploring the uniqueness of family firms, the challenges that they face, and the factors that affect their survival. One of the main concerns highlighted by previous work is the challenges family firms face when transitioning management and ownership of the firm from one generation to the next. Findings suggest that family firms are not very successful in this transition process because only a small percentage is able to survive [1]. This concern has led to a focus on intra-family succession as one of the major areas of interest for family business scholars and practitioners [4,20].

Although family business succession has been defined multiple ways, it includes the transfer of leadership and ownership from a senior to a junior generation [3,21]. Leadership succession encompasses the transition and transfer of the responsibility for the ongoing management of the family firm to a junior generation of the family or an outside member; while ownership succession includes the distribution of "shares or other measures of ownership" of the firm from senior to junior generations [8,22]. A great deal of family business research is dedicated to understanding the succession process, the problems in this process, and how these problems can be prevented or resolved [3,6,7,21]. This research has been summarized in several models that try to explain how succession occurs. Each of these model focuses on different aspects or actors of the succession process. For example, Longenecker and Schoen [23] and Churchill and Hatten [24] present succession models that focus on the on the successor as they move through stages of transitions. On the other hand, the work of Sharma and colleagues [6] focus on the interpersonal (e.g., acceptance of new roles, fit between successors career interests and the business, and trust in the successor) and decision-making and planning factors (e.g., agreement to continue in the business, the extent of planning for succession) that influence initial satisfaction with the succession process. In another work, Le Breton-Miller and colleagues [3] proposed an integrative model that explains what it takes for succession to succeed. This model indicates that succession is the sequence of four main stages: (1) establishing ground rules, (2) nurturing and developing a pool of potential successors, (3) selection, and (4) handoff to the chosen successor. They argue that there are four contexts that affect the succession process: industry, business, family and social. Finally, the model of De Massis and colleagues [6] suggests that the succession process is a "chain of causation" that begins with the dominant coalition's desire to engage in the succession process and the availability of a potential successor. These authors argue that the succession process begins with a decision-making event and ends when the incumbent relinquishes management and ownership control to the next generation (For a detailed review see the chapter by Long and Chrisman [4]).

There are several commonalities shared by these succession models. First, they all view succession as a long-term process and not a single event. This implies that can include several stages or steps. Second, these models imply that for succession to occur there needs to be both a desire from the dominant coalition [2] to pass the business on to others and the availability of a potential successor to take over the business. Third, these models suggest that the succession process is accentuated by several decision-making events [8] and culminates with the transition of leadership/management and ownership from one generation to another. And, fourth, there is the assumption that the success of the succession process is based on keeping the management of the business in the family.

---

[2] Similar to De Massis and colleagues (2008) [6] and Gersick and colleagues (1997) [25] we define the dominant coalition as a single individual (e.g., founder of a family business) or many individuals who have ownership and management control over the business.

Although decision-making events play an important role in the succession process, there is a gap in our understanding of how the incumbent and the dominant coalition in a family firm make decisions about transitions and the different factors that play a role in this decision-making process [7,8,14]. With this in mind, the focus of this paper was to develop a conceptual model to understand the factors that play a role in the incumbent's initial decision regarding the type of succession transition they would want to follow and how these factors affect decisions. We believe that this initial decision is important because it affects how owners approach other decisions in the succession process. In the following section we describe how we view the decision-making process about ownership and management transitions.

3. Making Decisions about Management Transitions

Before the succession process can be initiated, incumbents need to make decisions about what type of succession to engage in. Researchers that explore succession transitions in the family business context have explored it under the label of "exit strategy" of the founder [14]. DeTienne [26] defines exit strategy as the entrepreneur's decision to leave the firm that they decided to create. Given that in family firms owners might choose to leave the management of the firm while keeping ownership in the firm, we have decided to use the term succession transition to explain the decisions that incumbents make regarding who to transfer the leadership/management control in the family firm. Similar to other authors [26,27], we view succession transitions and exit planning as an important component of the entrepreneurial process, and focus on what DeTienne and Chirico [14] label as individual exit strategies or succession transitions at the individual level.

This paper considers three types of succession transitions: intra-family succession, non-family succession and no succession. Intra-family succession transition refers to the transfer of management to a family member that takes control of the family business when the incumbent decides to step down. Non-family succession transition represents the transfer of management to an individual who is not part of the family. In these situations, the family might transfer the leadership/management of the firm, but may not transfer the ownership to non-family managers. Thus, the non-family manager may be in this role until the family prepares someone to take over or may stay in this position for a long time. Finally, no-succession represents situations where the owner of the business decides to keep control of the firm at all costs, terminate the business or decides to sell the firm outside of the family.

Research in family business places great importance on the owner's intentions to keep the control of the business in the family is one of the most important concerns for family owners [17,28]. This intention to keep control in the family is associated to the family's commitment to the business [29], and serves as an indicator of the importance attached to family non-financial goals [30]. Thus, most of the research on succession in family firms has focused on intra-family succession as the primary transition strategy used by incumbents in family firms. An underlying assumption for focusing on intra-family succession is the belief that this type of succession is the one that will bring success to firm and will help preserve the family legacy throughout generations [9,14]. Empirical research has provided mixed results when evaluating whether family firms that are family managed outperform other types of organizations [10]. In their empirical study exploring the difference in performance between family firms managed by family CEOs and other CEOs, Miller and Colleagues [10] found that family firms that were managed by family CEOs were likely to outperform other organization when these firms where smaller and the ownership was highly concentrated among family members. In other conditions there were no differences in performance.

Given this empirical evidence, we believe that the focus on keeping the business in the family has led us to have less understanding regarding the consideration of other transition options and how family business owners make decisions about management transitions in general. This gap is important to address because it can expand the understanding of scholars and practitioners at least three different ways. First, it can provide a complete picture of the succession process that includes decision to engage in a type of succession transition, planning for the succession, executing the succession plan, and giving control to the next generation. Second, it can help scholars and practitioners articulate the meaning of the success of the succession process as one that is tied to the goals of the incumbent and the dominant coalition. And, third, it can help us understand how decision-making about transitions can influence other processes in the family and the business and how contextual factors can also influence decisions about transitions.

4. The Theory of Planned Behavior

The theory of planned behavior (TPB) provides a good conceptual framework to understand the factors that influence decisions about ownership and management transitions. The central premise of this theory is that decisions about behaviors are a logical sequence of cognitions [31]. Thus, individuals rationally make decisions about their actions using the information they have access to. This theoretical framework suggests that individual motivations to engage in a behavior (*i.e.*, behavioral intention) are the strongest predictors of behavior [15,32]. According to TPB behaviors are the result of a decision making process by which a person or group of people evaluate their intentions towards engaging in a behavior, the attitudes they have towards the behavior, how significant others evaluate that behavior, and their personal evaluations of how easy or difficult it is to perform a behavior [15,32]. In this theory, attitudes represent the affective responses that individuals hold towards a behavior [33] and are the summation of the beliefs held about the behavior and the evaluation of those beliefs [31]. Research suggests that before committing to a behavior, individuals first evaluate and prioritize their beliefs towards the behavior, and the stronger the belief towards the behavior the more likely the individual will be to develop intentions to perform it [33].

Although personal beliefs play an important role in determining intentions, individuals also rely on the beliefs of others. In TPB, subjective norms assess how valued social networks feel about the individual engaging in a behavior and the importance of these networks in influencing the individual [33]. Subjective norms can reflect the beliefs from valued social networks but can also represent general societal values and norms, as well as intrapersonal beliefs [34]. In this context social networks include family members, close friends, co-workers, and can also include members of a club, group, or ethnicity that are important to the individual. This theoretical approach argues that individuals make sense of others' beliefs by first assessing the expectations of others and then examining their personal motivations to comply with these expectations. Thus, TPB indicates that individuals will intend to engage in a behavior when their valued social networks have positive evaluations towards that behavior and the individual wants to comply with these important social networks. Finally, perceived behavioral control represents the individual's perception of how easy or difficult it will be to perform a behavior [35]. The assessment of the individual's control is based on two factors: control beliefs (*i.e.*, beliefs regarding the presence or absence of the resources/opportunities necessary to perform a behavior) and perceived power (*i.e.*, evaluation of whether having the knowledge about the resources and opportunities will help perform the behavior).

In the context of family firms, TPB has been used to explore the effects of paternalistic leadership on perceptions of successors [36], the determinants of career choice intentions for individuals with a family business background [37,38], the effects of prior family business exposure on entrepreneurial intent [39], financial decision-making in family firms [40], family member involvement in the firm [41], and the predictors for engaging in environmental management practices [42]. Most of these studies used TPB as a framework to understand how people make decisions about engaging in a behavior. Thus, we wanted to apply this decision-making framework to the context of succession transitions in family firms. When applied to making decisions about transitions in family firms, TPB would indicate that the type of succession that an incumbent intends to engage in is dependent on the attitudes that the incumbent has about a type of succession, what important others think about this type of succession, and the individual perception of how easy or difficult it would be to engage in that type of succession.

5. Socioemotional Wealth (SEW)

Family firms are unique in that they combine two important subsystems as part of the firm: the family and the business [43]. Because of this unique composition, an owner's decision of what type of succession to engage in will be greatly influenced by their considerations of the family and the business. Family business researchers indicate that family firms are unique because they can derive value from the economic success of the business and from non-economic affect related issues such as the perpetuation of the family legacy, the visibility of the firm or the perpetuation of family values through the business [44]. This is known as the socioemotional wealth framework (SEW). SEW represents the non-economic and emotional value that owners associate with a family firm and helps achieve the family affective (e.g., identity, influence, and perpetuation of the family dynasty [45]). Thus, SEW plays an important role when making strategic decisions about a family firm.

Family firms vary in the extent to which they focus on financial and non-financial goals [46]. Thus, we argue that concern about the family and the business are important when making decisions about succession transitions. Concern about the family represents the degree of importance that the incumbent gives to the family. This is consistent with the ideas of high SEW. That is, incumbents that are high on concern for the family believe that family dynamics, family resources, the family legacy, the survivability of the family, and/or rivalries/conflict between family members are important factors to consider when making decisions about transitions. On the other hand, concern about the business describes the degree of importance that the incumbent places on the business. In this process the owners determine how a transition decision will impact the survivability of the business, the attitudes of non-family workforce, profitability, ability to manage the business, competition, innovation, and perceptions of legitimacy of the organization. Thus, we believe that the SEW is a useful framework to understand the factors that play a role in making decisions about transitions and why these factors impact this decision-making process.

6. Conceptual Model to Understand Transition Decisions

Although considerations about the family and the business play a central role in the decision-making of family business owners, there are contextual factors that can affect how the owner evaluates their concerns about the family and the business. Previous research provides some ideas of the different contexts that need to be assessed to be able to make a decision about the succession process. Le Breton-Miller and colleagues [3] suggest that to fully understand the succession process in family firms there are four contexts that need to be considered: the family, the business, the industry, and the cultural context. We believe that these contexts also play an important role in scanning the environment to be able to weigh the considerations about the family and the business when making decisions about what type of succession to follow in the family firm.

As viewed in this paper, the type of succession transition that a family firm decides to engage in is the result of a decision-making process that an owner/incumbent goes through to determine the future of how their business will be governed and/or managed (*i.e.*, will business leadership/management of the firm be transferred to others inside the family? to non-family managers? Or will the business be sold out of the family?). We argue that the intention towards a particular type of succession transition is the result of an evaluation process by the owner of a firm that has several stages (See Figure 1). In the first stage, the family business owner evaluates four components of their environment (*i.e.*, the family, the business, the industry, and the social/cultural contexts) to determine the effects that the particular type of succession could have on the family and on the business. In the second stage, the owner uses their evaluation of the contextual factors to determine what considerations they have about the family and the business. Once they have collected enough information, the family business owner will weigh their concerns for the family and their concerns for the business to evaluate their attitudes towards the three different types of succession (*i.e.*, intra-family succession, non-family succession, or no succession), the beliefs of important others regarding the different types of succession, and they perceptions about how easy or difficult it will be for them to achieve each type of succession transition.

Int. J. Financial Stud. **2014**, *2*, 335–358

The combination of these opinions will determine which type of transition the owners intend to engage in.

There are a few boundary conditions that are important to consider when interpreting our model. First, this model is based on the assumption that family business owners go through a decision process that is primarily rational. That is, even though there are affective considerations when making decisions about transitions, an incumbent is capable of evaluating different features of the family, the business, and the context to better understand the strengths and weaknesses of their firm and their family regarding each type of transition. Second, we also assume that business owners are able to weigh the positives and negatives of the decision they make. That is, we assume an incumbent is able to predict the consequences that a decision can have for a family and a business. Third, we believe that decisions about succession transitions differ from the decision of when to start the succession process (*i.e.*, succession planning and management) and who to choose as a successor. Thus, the reader should be cognizant that this paper only focuses on the decision of what type of succession to engage in and not when the succession should occur or who would be the best successor for a firm. Fourth, this model is interested in leadership/management transitions in family firms. Thus, our ideas may not apply when evaluating ownership transitions in the family firm. Finally, we focus on the incumbent or the family business owner, and assume that their decision to transition out of the leadership of the family firm is voluntary and intentional. Thus, this model would not apply to transitions that result from death or hostile takeover. With this in mind, the following sections explain the different factors that are evaluated and how they affect decisions about succession transitions.

7. Contextual Factors Influencing Evaluations of Succession Transitions

Previous research on family firm succession provides some ideas of the different contexts that need to be assessed to evaluate the transitions available during a succession. Le Breton-Miller and colleagues [3] suggest that to fully understand the succession process in family firms there are four contexts that need to be considered: family, business, industry, and social/cultural (see Table 1). We believe that these contexts play an important role when the incumbent is scanning the environment to make their decisions about transitions. We argue that incumbents need to understand and evaluate these four contexts to determine the concerns they have for the family and the business if they decide to engage in the succession process.

The evaluation and understanding of the family context includes gaining knowledge in at least three areas: family dynamics, availability and willingness of a successor, and family influence and commitment to the business. Family dynamics represents the evaluation of factors such as family harmony (*i.e.*, how well do family members get along), level of collaboration of family members, quality of the relationship between family members, the level of trust between family members, and the quality communication in the family. Previous research exploring the succession process has found that family dynamics play a critical role in the success of a succession process [3]. In particular, family environments that are characterized by collaboration, accommodation, harmony and positive sibling relationships are more likely to be successful during the succession process [6,47,48]. The availability and willingness of a successor is the second aspect of the family context that needs to be evaluated. Before an owner can decide what type of succession they want to engage in, they need to know whether they have qualified individuals that can take over the business, what is the motivation of the possible successors, what is their leadership preparation, what is the knowledge that they have about the business, and what are the abilities that they could bring into the business. Previous research has suggested that all of these factors are important in determining the success of the succession process [3,10]. Thus, it is not only the availability of a successor, but the willingness and the preparation that this successor has that can impact the concerns of an owner for the succession process and its effects on the family and the business.

The third and final component of the family context is the level of influence and commitment that the family has with the business. Lansberg and Astrachan [49] found that the family's commitment to the business and the relationship quality with the successor have a positive effect on succession planning and training. Some aspects that need to be considered when looking at commitment are the financial support that the family provides to the business, the availability of a family council and a family protocol/constitution, and the number of family members that are owners or work for the family firm [3]. All of these factors should influence the family-business interaction to help the owner assess the viability of a successful succession process. We believe that the evaluation of the family context will play an important role in the owner's assessment of considerations about the family and the business that they need to evaluate. This information is important because it helps the owner evaluate the readiness of the family with regard to the succession process and how this can impact the business. The family information helps the owner assess the strengths and weaknesses they currently have if they were to engage in the succession process.

The business/firm context is the second aspect that will influence the considerations that owner's have about the family and the business when thinking about the succession process. When evaluating the business context, owners consider information in several areas. First, the owners evaluate the general economic/financial state of the business, which includes information about the current business strategy, how this strategy is being applied, the current financial state of the business, the viability of the business in the future, and the potential for future economic and financial success. By considering this information the family business owner is able to ascertain what the current and future economic viability of the business is. Economic viability will be important because it will determine what type of succession the owners are willing and able to engage in [40,50]. The second type of business information to consider would be organizational size. Organizational size can be represented as the number of employees a firm has or by the sales that it produces every year. The work of Miller and colleagues [10] suggests that firm size is an important indicator of administrative complexity and places cognitive limitation on those who are responsible for managing the firm. They argue that in larger organizations there are more complex control and monitoring systems that require more formalized managerial skills and the mastery of management practices that are required by the future manager of the firm. Thus, understanding the complexity brought about by organizational size is important when making decisions about transitions.

The third type of information in the business context is concentration and dispersion of ownership between family members. Given that family firms are likely to provide the economic means to the family, a family business manager is likely to be vigilant and caring of the company, specially when it is smaller and ownership is concentrated between a few family members [10]. When ownership is more diffused between family members (*i.e.*, there are generations of family members involved) there is a higher likelihood of fractions in the business ownership that cause family CEOs to be a liability [51]. Thus, the incumbent needs to understand these issues to figure out what transition strategy will work best with the firm and the business. The final component of the business context is the culture of the organization. This includes understanding the values of the business, the commitment of family and non-family employees to the success of the business, the level of diversity present in the business, the general climate of the organization, and the level of adaptability that the people in the business have to deal with changes in the industry and changes in the business. We believe that these three areas of information about the business will help the owner create a picture about the strengths and weaknesses in the family firm to determine what type of succession transition is best for the firm, what needs to be done for succession to occur, and how the choice to engage in a succession process can affect the family and the business.

The industry context represents the evaluation and understanding of information about an industry that is critical in planning how to successfully lead a firm. This context is important because it determines the qualities required for the successor of a firm and can help the incumbent determine whether the family has a potential successor or can develop a potential successor. Although there has not been a lot of research articulating which characteristics of an industry may influence the selection of a successor to a firm, the work from Royer and colleagues [5] suggests that the type of knowledge required in an industry can affect whether a family member or an outsider is a better fit as a successor in a firm. These authors suggest that family insiders are better as successors in conditions where there is higher relevance for experiential family business specific knowledge and when the family insider is better qualified than outsider regarding general and technical industry specific knowledge. Other information about the industry that may be important for an owner to determine what type of succession to engage in includes where the industry is heading, how is the industry changing, how is the industry growing, and what are the challenges of the industry is facing? All of this information can help owners determine what type of succession process a firm can handle and how this decision will affect both the family and business subsystems.

Table 1. Research on the different contextual factors that influence succession decisions.

Context	Variables	Sources
Family	Family dynamics Availability and willingness of a successor Family influence Commitment to the business	Le Breton-Miller *et al.* [3]; Morris *et al.* [47]; Potts *et al.* [48]; Sharma *et al.* [6]; Habbershon & Pistrui [52]; Lansberg and Astrachan [49]
Firm	General economic state Financial considerations Governance and ownership structure Culture of the organization	Le Breton-Miller *et al.* [3]; Potts *et al.* [47]; Sharma *et al.* [6]; Koropp *et al.* [40]; Molly *et al.* [53]
Industry	Type of industry Industry growth Challenges Taxation	Royer *et al.* [5]; Le Breton-Miller *et al.* [6]; Greens Analyseinstitut [54]
Culture	Cultural influences Social norms, ethics and religion Laws	Lee *et al.* [55]; Goto [56]; Royer *et al.* [6]; Le Breton-Miller *et al.* [3]; Birley [57]; Birley, Ng and Godfrey [58]; Yan and Sorensen [59]

The final context that we consider in this paper is the cultural context. The cultural context involves the evaluation and understanding of information that pertains to culture, social norms, ethics, and laws that can affect the succession process. There is not much research in this area, but the limited international projects that have explored family firms in different cultures suggest that culture can affect the succession process. For example, Royer and colleagues [5] argue that Japanese family firms may have a longer life span because they have a higher concern for long-term orientation and they have a preference for internal successor [56]. Thus, the Japanese culture promotes the idea of transforming individuals into family insiders to enable an internal succession to occur [55]. Yan and Sorenson [59] investigated the effect Confucian values on family business succession and stressed the importance of examining values across cultures to identify underlying intent or principles in a certain culture. Similarly, the work of Birley and colleagues [57,58] indicates that culture affects an owner's attitude towards involving the family in the business. Given this, we believe that the cultural context also plays an important role in deciding what type of succession to engage in. In particular, we think family business owners assess information about the context (*i.e.*, laws, cultural expectations and norms) to determine the strengths and weaknesses that they have for a type of succession to occur.

When making decisions about transitions, the incumbent's familiarity with these four contextual areas provides them with a general understanding of the environment in which a transition will take place. Thus, knowledge about these contextual factors will help incumbent's assess the cost and benefits for the family and for the business of any decision. Building on this line of thought, we suggest the following proposition:

> P1: Before making decision about succession transitions, incumbents should evaluate the family, firm, industry and cultural contexts in which the firm operates to be able to assess what type of succession transition they are capable of engaging in.

8. Importance Given to the Family and the Business

One of the characteristics that differentiate family firms from other types of organizations is the importance given to non-economic aspects of the business. Researchers suggest that the value given to non-economic aspects of the firm affects the decisions and behaviors that family managers and owners follow in their business [60]. This is not to say that family business owners ignore the importance of business or financial aspects of the firm [46]. Thus, we believe that when evaluating decisions about transitions it is important to separate two areas of the family firm: the family, and the business. In our model we describe concern about the family as the importance that the incumbent gives to family aspects in the business. This includes the future of the family, the preservation of family harmony, and the preservation of the family legacy inside the family and inside the business. We believe that the concern that an incumbent has about the family will play a role in the attitudes they develop towards a type of transition, how they interpret the subjective norms about a transition, and their evaluation of how difficult or easy it will be for them engage in a specific type of transition. For example, when an incumbent has high concern for the family and the preservation of the family legacy, they will have a tendency to develop stronger positive attitudes towards family-transitions in comparison to non-family or no transition. On the other hand, when an incumbent has low concern for the family, they will be more likely to have positive attitudes towards non-family transitions. A similar issue may play out when evaluating subjective norms. That is, when an incumbent has high concern for family, they will be likely to consider and comply with the evaluations of family members when making decisions about transitions; while when the have low concern for family the incumbent may value and comply with the opinions of friends or employees as important others. Thus, building on this idea we propose the following:

> P2: The incumbent's concern about the family will affect their attitudes, subjective norms, and perceived behavioral control when evaluating the type of succession transition to engage in.

Concern about the business describes the importance that an incumbent gives to the company as a whole. This can include the importance given to the preservation of the business, the financial performance of the business, responsibility towards non-family employees in the business, and the potential future of the business. The importance given to the business will also affect the attitudes that incumbents have towards transitions, the interpretation of subjective norms and the perceived personal control. For example, incumbents who believe in the importance of the business will pay close attention to the effects that a transition may have on a business. Thus, incumbents will have positive attitudes towards transitions that will help the business survive and achieve future success. The importance given to the business will also affect whose opinions the incumbent values. In the case when there is a high concern for the business, the incumbent will be likely to value and comply with the opinions of important employees and important individuals in the business. Building on this rationale with advance the following proposition:

> P3: The incumbent's concern about the family will affect their attitudes, subjective norms, and perceived behavioral control when evaluating the type of succession transition to engage in.

Table 2 shows how the incumbent can combine the evaluation of these two important aspects of the family business when making decisions about transitions. In this case, incumbents would be likely to engage in intra-family succession when there is a high concern for family and high concern for business. Intra-family succession could also be an option when the owner perceives that there are positive considerations for the family from taking over the business and there might be some costs for the business. Under these conditions the incumbent believes that the benefits for the family can outweigh the costs for the business. Non-family succession is likely to be an option under two conditions. First, when an owner believes that choosing a family successor might bring a serious disruption into the family (*i.e.*, negative family consideration) and they believe that the business is in a positive state. Under these conditions costs for the family may persuade the business owner to think about involving an outsider in the management of the firm. The second situation would be when the owner does not see that the future successor is ready to take over the business (e.g., she/he is too young, or does not have enough education/knowledge about the business at this point). Under these circumstances owners will be likely to consider non-family succession to have enough time to prepare the next family successor. Finally, a family business owner will consider no succession or selling the business when the costs for the family and for the business are very steep. In these situations they might believe that selling the business or not engaging in succession may be the best choice for the business and the firm to survive.

Table 2. Considerations towards family and business and their effects on decisions about succession.

		Concern about Family	
		Low	High
Concern about the business	**High**	Owners in this quadrant believe that the business has a future and that succession should occur. They also believe that for the family it would be costly to engage in a succession process given the current personnel they have. Because of this, they will be likely to decide towards a non-family succession.	Owners in this quadrant view the benefits for the family and for the business of engaging in succession. Because of this, they will be the most likely to engage in intra-family succession.
	Low	Owners in this quadrant perceive that a succession will have important costs for both the family and the business. Thus, they will be more likely to sell the business, or to avoid thinking about the succession process.	Owners in this quadrant perceive the benefits for the family from engaging in the succession process, but also see the costs that this process can bring to the business. Thus, they will be interested in engaging in succession only when they have a family member to be the successor.

From our point of view, there are additional factors that also paly a role when making decisions about transitions. As mentioned earlier the evaluation of the four contextual aspects in which the business operates is essential when determining the type of succession transition to engage in. Thus, in the following section we combine importance of family and business with the understanding of contextual factors to explain how they influence incumbent decisions about transitions.

9. Deciding the Type of Succession Transition to Engage in

Building on the theory of planned behavior, we have argued that an owner's intent to engage in a particular type of succession is the result of their attitudes towards that particular type of succession, subjective norms and perceived behavioral control. This theory suggests that an incumbent will engage in a particular type of succession when they have positive attitudes toward that type of transition, when important others (*i.e.*, with whom they want to comply) also think positively about this transition as being positive, and when incumbents perceive that they have the capabilities and resources to go through with the transition. Thus, we argue that an incumbent's decision of what type of succession to engage in will depend on the attitudes that they hold towards the transition, the subjective norms and incumbent perceptions of how easy or difficult it will be to engage in that transition. Given this we advance the following proposition:

> P4: An incumbents intention to engage in a particular type of transition will be positively related to their attitudes towards that transition, the positive evaluations of important others, and the belief that they have the resources and capabilities to engage in that transition.

There are important factors to consider when using this theoretical framework to understand how people make decisions about behavior. The first consideration is that individuals may place different weight on the importance they give to attitudes, subjective norms, and perceived behavioral control when making decisions. This means that while for some incumbents they attitudes they hold about the transition may be weighted higher than subjective norms of perceived behavioral control, others may value the opinion of others more, or their perceptions about how easy or difficult it might be to engage in a behavior. Meta-analytic research conducted in this area has found that although individuals may differ in the weigh they give to these three components, attitudes has the strongest relationship with behavioral intentions [33]. A second consideration comes from the belief that the three factors that predict behavior intention (*i.e.*, attitudes, subjective norms, and perceived behavioral control) can influence one another. Empirical research up does not support this idea. Thus, in this paper we assume that these three factors are independent of each other. A final consideration refers to the role of emotions in the decision-making process. Although TPB is rational model, attachment and interdependencies of an emotional nature can play a role in the beliefs and evaluation of those beliefs.

In this model we argue that the combination of contextual factors with the concern the incumbent has about family and business influences their attitudes, subjective norms and perceived behavioral control towards type of succession transition. As seen in Table 3, we argue that there are different contextual factors that combined need to be considered in conjunction with the importance of family and business to determine the valence of the three components that will influence the incumbent's choice of a succession strategy. Incumbents will be likely to select intra-family succession under the following condition:

- They have high concern for family.
- A family successor is willing and able to take the business over.
- The family is committed to the business.
- The business has viability in the future.
- The industry also has a positive outlook in the future.
- The incumbent has a long-term orientation focus.
- Tax and state laws provide benefits for keeping the business in the family.
- The family supports and is committed to the business.

And, the incumbent perceives that they have the resources and capabilities to teach the successor about the business.

Table 3. Identifying decisions about succession transitions.

Incumbent's Perception/Evaluation	Intra-Family Transition	Non-family Transition	No Transition
Family Context			
Family dynamics	Non-destructive conflict	Non-destructive or destructive conflict	Non-destructive or destructive conflict
Availability and willingness of successor	Yes	Successor is willing and not currently available	No
Family commitment to business	Yes	Yes	No
Business Context			
Financial state of business	Good or with future potential	Good or with future potential	Good or with future potential/not positive
Organizational size	Smaller	Small/large	Small/large
Concentration of Ownership	Concentrated among some family members	Concentrated or dispersed among family members	Concentrated/dispersed among family members
Viability of the business	Has potential	Has potential	Has potential/no viability
Organizational culture	Positive culture that shows commitment	Positive culture that shows commitment	Positive culture that shows commitment
Industry Context			
State of industry	Good	Good	Good/decline
Future opportunities	Good	Good	Good/no opportunities
Type of knowledge necessary for success	Industry specific and family business specific	Industry specific and not family specific	Industry specific and not family specific
Cultural Context			
Social norms	Long-term orientation and importance of keeping it in the family	Long-term orientation	Short-term orientation
Law	Considerations estate and labor laws of country	Considerations estate and labor laws of country	Considerations estate and labor laws of country
Concern for family	High	Low/high	Low/high
Concern for business	Low/high	High	Low/high

There are two sets of factors that may influence the incumbent's choice to engage in non-family succession transitions. On one side, it may be that the incumbent decides to transition out of the business because although the family is supportive and willing to be involved in the business they might not have a successor ready to take over the business. That is, the successor may be too young, may not have the education, or may be beginning their career in the company. Under these conditions, the incumbent may feel that the best way to keep the business in the family and prepare the successor is by having an outsider manage the business while the successor learns about his/her role. The second set of factors that may lead an incumbent to develop positive attitudes towards a non-family transition are:

- The incumbent may perceive that there is too much destructive conflict in the family that can be enhanced by selecting a family transition in this case showing high concern for the business.
- The incumbent has high concern for the business and does not perceive that a family member can do justice to the business.
- There may not be a family successor that is willing and able to take over the business.
- The incumbent may perceive that the family is not committed to the business.
- The business and the industry are perceived as having potential and viability in the future.
- The incumbent is long-term oriented.

Finally, the factors that are likely to enhance the incumbent's consideration of the no transition option are the following:

- The incumbent perceives that the family is not committed to the business, that there is no successor that is willing or able to take over the business, and that there is destructive conflict in the family context.
- The incumbent perceives that there are problems with the future viability of the business.
- The industry might be in decline and there are no opportunities for the business in the future.
- The incumbent might be short term oriented.
- Estate and tax laws might prevent the business from transitioning to family or non-family stakeholders.

10. Discussion

The purpose of this paper was to conceptually explore the factors that influence a successors decision about what type of succession transition an incumbent chooses and how they play a role in this decision. We view the succession transition as the culmination of a decision-making process. In this process the incumbent evaluates contextual factors (*i.e.*, industry, firm, family, and cultural) to gather information about the strengths and weaknesses a firm and a family have before entering the succession process. The incumbent also evaluates the importance that they place in the family and in the business. Following this the incumbent combines their evaluation of the context with the importance of family and business to determine their attitudes, subjective norms and perceived behavioral control regarding each type of transition. Thus, our model builds on the theory of planned behavior and the SEW framework to understand decision-making choices about succession transitions.

Similar to others [3,7,8], we argue that the succession process is full of decision-making events that we still do not understand very well. Thus, our model provides a conceptual representation of how initial decisions about transitions are likely to occur. We believe that there are at least two reasons for why this paper is important. First, to enhance our understanding of succession we also need to better comprehend the decision-making events that are part of the succession, and how owners make the decisions involved in these events. Understanding both of these ideas can help family business be successful during the succession process. Second, understanding that owners may have the intent to engage in different types of succession may also help better define what is a successful succession process. In this case success may entail that a family business owner achieves the type of succession that they intended initially. Viewing the success of succession process can help us re-evaluate when and why family business successions fail.

11. Implications of Our Succession Intent Model

From our point of view, our model can have several important implications for theory. First, thinking about succession intent as a dependent variable can be useful in understanding why succession occurs and why it is successful. Although previous research has suggested that one of the characteristics of family firms is their intent to engage in succession processes inside of the family, we do not understand when do family business owners have these intentions, how this decision comes about and how it can affect other parts of the succession process. Therefore, studying succession intent as a dependent variable can shed light on how family business owners think about this process. A second theoretical implication of our study comes from understanding decision about transition intent separate from succession timing (*i.e.*, when should the succession occur?) or the successor choice (*i.e.*, who should be the successor of the firm?). By separating these three processes researchers can better understand the intricacies of the succession process and how incumbents might approach each of these events differently. Finally, our approach contributes to recent work that has explored other succession options besides intra-family succession [14]. The continuation of this work is helping clarify the previous belief of what represents a successful transition [9]. In particular, our project suggests that in family firms, non-family transition strategies could also represent a benefit to the family and the business.

Our model also has important implications for practice. First, it can help family business consultants guide family business owners in their evaluation of whether succession should occur, and what type of succession they should engage in. We believe that our model provides interesting factors to consider when making decisions about a firm. A second implication that this model can have is the idea of how a family owner weighs their decision by considering both the impact to the family and the impact to the business. From our understanding of the literature, family business researchers tend to focus on the concerns for family sometimes ignoring the concerns that owners may have for the business or other contextual factors. Finally, this paper also has important implications for understanding other decisions during the succession process. For example, the work of Koropp and colleagues [50] suggests that transactions costs during a succession process can affect how succession occurs. Thus, financial resources can impact the decisions of what type of succession to engage in. At the same time, they also indicate that the succession process can have an impact on the financial structure of the business and the financial opportunities of the family. Given this, we believe that we need to further understand this decision-making process.

12. Ideas for Future Research

Research in the last decade has moved to understanding issues such as transgenerational intent, transgenerational control intention and family firm exit strategies. This project complements that line of research by suggesting the factors that can influence the intent to engage in different types of succession and by identifying different types of transitions or exit strategies that family business incumbents can engage in. Given this, it would be useful to begin testing the model presented in this paper with family business owners to ascertain how incumbents evaluate their concerns about the family and about the business in their decision making process. It would be useful to begin testing this model by conducting in-depth interviews with owners who are thinking about the succession process or have recently begun this process in their firms. In depth interviews can help better understand the intricacies of the decision making process.

Another way to obtain similar information can be by interviewing family business consultants about their experience when helping during the succession process. Given that consultants are very likely to facilitate the succession process they can also have important insights of how family business owners make decisions about whether to engage in the succession process. Finally, survey research could also be developed to test this model. Researchers can work with family business centers, institutes or associations to obtain a population that can answer questions about how they think about the succession process and whether their company should engage in this process or not.

At the same time, it would be interesting to explore incumbent's transition choices by comparing incumbents based on their country of origin. It may be that comparing respondents from Japan and Denmark, for example, could give insights on how family businesses behave in different cultures.

13. Conclusions

This paper presents a model of the factors used in the process of determining succession intent. We argue that family business incumbents evaluate contextual factors and then use this information based on the strength and weaknesses they perceive their family firm has. At the same time, owners weigh their concern for the family and concern for the business and use the information about strengths and weaknesses to determine their intent to engage in the succession process. We believe that owners will be more likely to engage in the succession process when they perceive that the business is viable for the future and there are family members who are willing and able to take over the business.

Acknowledgments: We thank the reviewers for their valuable feedback for making this paper better.

Author Contributions: All authors came up with the idea and wrote the paper together. All authors contributed equally to this work.

Conflicts of Interest: The authors declare no conflict of interest.

References

1. Ward, J.L. *Keeping the Family Business Healthy: How to Plan for Continuity Growth, Profitability and Family Leadership*; Palgrave Macmillan: Marietta, GA, USA, 2004.
2. Miller, D.; Steier, L.P.; le Breton-Miller, I. Lost in time: Intergenerational succession, change and failure in family firms. *J. Bus. Ventur.* **2003**, *18*, 513–531. [CrossRef]
3. Le Breton-Miller, I.; Miller, D.; Steier, L.P. Toward an integrative model of FOB succession. *Entrep. Theory Pract.* **2004**, *28*, 305–328.
4. Long, R.G.; Chrisman, J.C. Management succession in family business. In *The Sage Handbook of Family Business*; Melin, L., Nordqvist, M., Sharma, P., Eds.; Sage Publications: London, UK, 2014; pp. 371–387.
5. Royer, S.; Simons, R.; Boyd, B.; Rafferty, A. Promoting family: A contingency model of family business succession. *Fam. Bus. Rev.* **2008**, *21*, 15–30. [CrossRef]
6. Sharma, P.; Chrisman, J.J.; Pablo, A.L.; Chua, J.H. Determinants of initial satisfaction with the succession process in family firms: A conceptual model. *Entrep. Theory Pract.* **2001**, *25*, 17–35.
7. De Massis, A.; Chua, J.H.; Chrisman, J.J. Factors preventing intra-family succession. *Fam. Bus. Rev.* **2008**, *21*, 183–199.
8. Blumentritt, T.; Mathews, T.; Marchisio, G. Game theory and family business succession. *Fam. Bus. Rev.* **2013**, *26*, 51–67. [CrossRef]
9. Zellweger, T.; Nason, R.; Nordqvist, M. From longevity of the firm to transgenerational entrepreneurship of families: Introducing family entrepreneurial orientation. *Fam. Bus. Rev.* **2012**, *25*, 136–155. [CrossRef]
10. Miller, D.; Minichilli, A.; Corbetta, G. Is family leadership always beneficial? *Strateg. Manag. J.* **2013**, *34*, 553–571.
11. Gedajlovic, E.; Carney, M.; Chrisman, J.J.; Kellermanns, F.W. The adolescence of family firm research: Taking stock and planning for the future. *J. Manag.* **2012**, *38*, 1010–1047.
12. Zellweger, T.M.; Kellermanns, F.W.; Chrisman, J.J.; Chua, J.H. Family control and family firm valuation by family CEOs: The importance of intentions for transgenerational control. *Organ. Sci.* **2012**, *23*, 851–868. [CrossRef]
13. Chua, J.H.; Chrisman, J.J.; Chang, E.P.C. Are family firms born or made? An exploratory investigation. *Fam. Bus. Rev.* **2004**, *17*, 37–54. [CrossRef]
14. DeTienne, D.R.; Chirico, F. Exit strategies in family firms: How socioemotional wealth drives the threshold of performance. *Entrep. Theory Pract.* **2013**, *37*, 1297–1318. [CrossRef]
15. Ajzen, I. From intentions to actions: A theory of planned behavior. In *Action-Control: From Cognition to Behavior*; Kuhl, J., Beckman, J., Eds.; Springer: Heidelberg, Germany, 1985; pp. 11–39.
16. Gomez-Mejia, L.R.; Haynes, K.T.; Nunez-Nickel, M.; Jacobson, K.J.L.; Moyano-Fuentes, J. Socio-emotional wealth and business risks in family-controlled firms: Evidence from Spanish olive oil mills. *Adm. Sci. Q.* **2007**, *52*, 106–137.
17. Chua, J.H.; Chrisman, J.J.; Sharma, P. Defining the family business by behavior. *Entrep. Theory Pract.* **1999**, *23*, 19–39.
18. Klein, S.B.; Astrachan, J.H.; Smyrnios, K.X. The F-PEC scale of family influence: Construction, validation, and further implication for theory. *Entrep. Theory Pract.* **2005**, *29*, 321–339. [CrossRef]
19. International Family Enterprise Research Academy (IFERA). Family businesses dominate. *Fam. Bus. Rev.* **2003**, *16*, 235–240.
20. Handler, W. Succession in family firms. *Entrep. Theory Pract.* **1990**, *15*, 37–51.
21. Sharma, P.; Chrisman, J.J.; Chua, J.H. Predictors of satisfaction with the succession in family firms. *J. Bus. Ventur.* **2003**, *18*, 667–687. [CrossRef]
22. Eddleston, K.A.; Kellermanns, F.W.; Floyd, S.W.; Crittenden, V.L.; Crittenden, W.F. Planning for growth: Life stage differences in family firms. *Entrep. Theory Pract.* **2013**, *37*, 1177–1202. [CrossRef]
23. Longenecker, J.G.; Schoen, J.E. Management succession in family business. *J. Small Bus. Manag.* **1978**, *16*, 1–6.
24. Churchill, N.; Hatten, K. Non-market based transfers of wealth and power: A research framework for family business. *Am. J. Small Bus.* **1987**, *11*, 51–64.

25. Gersick, K.; Davis, J.; McCollom Hampton, M.; Lansberg, I. *Generation to Generation: Life Cycles of the Family Business*; Harvard Business School Press: Boston, MA, USA, 1997.

26. DeTienne, D.R. Entrepreneurial exit as a critical component of the entrepreneurial process: Theoretical development. *J. Bus. Ventur.* **2010**, *25*, 203–215. [CrossRef]

27. DeTienne, D.R.; Cardon, M. Impact of founder experience on exit intentions. *Small Bus. Econ.* **2012**, *38*, 351–374. [CrossRef]

28. Chua, J.H.; Chrisman, J.J.; Sharma, P. Succession and nonsuccession concerns of family firms and agency relationship with nonfamily managers. *Fam. Bus. Rev.* **2003**, *16*, 89–107. [CrossRef]

29. Holt, D.T.; Rutherford, M.W.; Kuratko, D.F. Advancing the field of family business research: Further testing the measurement properties of the F-PEC. *Fam. Bus. Rev.* **2010**, *23*, 76–88. [CrossRef]

30. Chrisman, J.J.; Chua, J.H.; Pearson, A.W.; Barnett, T. Comparing the agency costs of family and nonfamily firms: Conceptual issues and exploratory evidence. *Entrep. Theory Pract.* **2010**, *28*, 335–354. [CrossRef]

31. Fishbein, M.; Ajzen, I. *Belief, Attitude, Intention, and Behavior: An Introduction to Theory and Research*; Addison-Wesley: Reading, MA, USA, 1975.

32. Ajzen, I. The Theory of Planned Behavior. Organizational Behavior and Human Decision Processes. Available online: http://www.nottingham.ac.uk/~ntzcl1/literature/tpb/azjen2.pdf (accessed on 15 September 2014).

33. Hale, J.R.; Householder, B.J.; Greene, K.L. The theory of reasoned action. In *The Persuasion Handbook: Developments in Theory and Practice*; Dillard, J.P., Pfau, M.W., Eds.; Sage Publications: Thousand Oaks, CA, USA, 2002; pp. 259–286.

34. Park, H.S.; Smith, S.W. Distinctiveness and influence of subjective norms, personal descriptive and injunctive norms, and societal descriptive and injunctive norms on behavioral intent: A case of two behaviors critical to organ donation. *Hum. Commun. Res.* **2007**, *33*, 194–218. [CrossRef]

35. Eagly, A.H.; Chaiken, S. *The Psychology of Attitudes*; Harcourt Brace: Fort Worth, TX, USA, 1993.

36. Mussolino, D.; Calabrò, A. Paternalistic leadership in family firms: Types and impacts for intergenerational succession. *J. Fam. Bus. Strategy* **2014**, *5*, 197–210. [CrossRef]

37. Schröder, E.; Schmitt-Rodermund, E.; Arnaud, N. Career choice intentions of adolescents with a family business background. *Fam. Bus. Rev.* **2011**, *24*, 305–321. [CrossRef]

38. Zellweger, T.; Sieger, P.; Halter, F. Should I stay or should I go? Career choice intentions for students with family business background. *J. Bus. Ventur.* **2011**, *26*, 521–536. [CrossRef]

39. Carr, J.C.; Sequeira, J.M. Prior business exposure as intergenerational influence and entrepreneurial intent: A theory of planned behavior approach. *J. Bus. Res.* **2007**, *60*, 1090–1098. [CrossRef]

40. Koropp, C.; Kellermanns, F.W.; Grichnik, D.; Stanley, L. Financial decision-making in family firms: An adaptation of the theory of planned behavior. *Fam. Bus. Rev.* **2014**, *27*, 1–21.

41. Kellermanns, F.W.; Eddleston, K.A.; Barnett, T.; Pearson, A. An exploratory study of family member characteristics and involvement: Effects of entrepreneurial behavior in the family firm. *Fam. Bus. Rev.* **2008**, *21*, 1–14. [CrossRef]

42. Uhlaner, L.M.; Berent-Braun, M.M.; Jeurissen, R.J.M.; de Witt, G. Beyond size: Predicting engagement in environmental management practices of Dutch SMEs. *J. Bus. Ethics* **2012**, *109*, 411–429. [CrossRef]

43. Tagiuri, R.; Davis, J.A. On the goals of successful family companies. *Fam. Bus. Rev.* **1992**, *5*, 43–62. [CrossRef]

44. Cruz, C.; Firfiray, S.; Gomez-Mejia, L.R. Socioemotional wealth and human resource management in family-controlled firms. In *Research in Personnel and Human Resource Management*; Joshi, A., Liao, H., Martocchio, J.J., Eds.; Emerald Publishing Group: Bingley, UK, 2011; Volume 30, pp. 159–217.

45. Kellermans, F.W.; Eddleston, K.A.; Zellweger, T.M. Extending the socioemotional wealth perspective: A look at the dark side. *Entrep. Theory Pract.* **2012**, *36*, 1175–1182. [CrossRef]

46. Berrone, P.; Cruz, C.; Gomez-Mejia, L.R. Socio-emotional wealth in family firms: Theoretical dimensions, assessment approaches, and agenda for future research. *Fam. Bus. Rev.* **2012**, *25*, 258–279. [CrossRef]

47. Morris, M.H.; Williams, R.O.; Allen, J.A.; Avila, R.A. Correlates of success in family transitions. *J. Bus. Ventur.* **1997**, *12*, 385–401. [CrossRef]

48. Potts, T.L.; Schoen, J.E.; Engel Loeb, M.; Hulme, F.S. Effective retirement for family business owner managers: Perspectives of financial planners—Part 2. *J. Financ. Planning* **2001**, *14*, 86–96.

49. Lansberg, I.; Astrachan, J.H. Influence of family relations on succession planning and training: The importance of mediating factors. *Fam. Bus. Rev.* **1994**, *7*, 39–59. [CrossRef]

50. Koropp, C.; Grichnik, D.; Gygax, A.F. Succession financing in family firms. *Small Bus. Econom.* **2013**, *41*, 315–334. [CrossRef]

51. Lubatkin, M.H.; Schulze, W.S.; Ling, Y.; Dino, R.N. The effects of parental altruism on the governance of family managed firms. *J. Organ. Behav.* **2005**, *26*, 313–330. [CrossRef]

52. Habbershon, T.G.; Pistrui, J. Enterprising families domain: Family-influenced ownership groups in pursuit of transgenerational wealth. *Fam. Bus. Rev.* **2002**, *15*, 223–237. [CrossRef]

53. Molly, V.; Laveren, E.; Deloof, M. Family business succession and its impact on financial structure and performance. *Fam. Bus. Rev.* **2010**, *23*, 131–147. [CrossRef]

54. Greens Analyseinstitut. *I Familiens eje en Undersøgelse af de Familieejede Virksomheder I*; Børsen: Copenhagen, Danmark, 2008.

55. Lee, K.S.; Lim, G.M.; Lim, W.S. Family business succession: Appropriation risk and choice of successor. *Acad. Manag. Rev.* **2003**, *28*, 657–666.

56. Goto, T. Longevity of Japanese family firms. In *The Handbook of Research on Family Business*; Poutziouris, P.Z., Smyrnios, K.X., Klein, S.B., Eds.; Edward Elgar: Cheltenham, UK, 2006; pp. 517–536.

57. Birley, S.; Ng, D.; Godfrey, A. The family and the business. *Long Range Planning* **1999**, *32*, 598–608. [CrossRef]

58. Birley, S. Owner-Manager attitudes to family and business issues: A 16 country study. *Entrep. Theory Pract.* **2001**, *26*, 63–76.

59. Yan, J.; Sorensen, R. The effect of Confucian values on succession in family business. *Fam. Bus. Rev.* **2006**, *19*, 235–250. [CrossRef]

60. Cennamo, C.; Berrone, P.; Cruz, C.; Gomez-Mejia, L.R. Socio-emotional wealth and proactive stakeholder engagement: Why family-controlled firms care more about their stakeholders. *Entrep. Theory Pract.* **2012**, *36*, 1153–1173. [CrossRef]

International Journal of
Financial Studies

MDPI

Article

Capital Asset Pricing Model Testing at Warsaw Stock Exchange: Are Family Businesses the Remedy for Economic Recessions?

Jacek Lipiec

Collegium of Business Administration, Warsaw School of Economics, 02-554 Warsaw, Poland;
jlipiec@sgh.waw.pl; Tel.: +48-(22)-564-8671

Received: 16 April 2014; in revised form: 8 July 2014; Accepted: 11 July 2014; Published: 22 July 2014

Abstract: In this article, we test the capital asset pricing model (CAPM) on the Warsaw Stock Exchange (WSE) by measuring the performance of two portfolios composed of construction firms: family-controlled and nonfamily controlled. These portfolios were selected from the WIG-Construction (WIG—Warszawski Indeks Giełdowy—Warsaw Stock Exchange Index). The performance of both portfolios was measured in the period from 2006 to 2012 with respect to three sub-periods: (1) pre-crisis period: 2006–2007; (2) crisis period: 2008–2009; and (3) post-crisis period: 2010–2012. This division was constructed in this way to find out how family firms performed in crisis times in relation to nonfamily firms. In addition, the construction portfolio was chosen due to its sensitivity to recessions. When an economy faces a downturn, construction firms are among the first to be exposed to risk. The performance was measured by using the capital asset pricing model with statistical inference. We find that public family firms significantly outperformed non-family peers in the crisis times.

Keywords: CAPM; beta; portfolio return; Polish family firms; Warsaw Stock Exchange

JEL Classification: D21, G12

1. Introduction

The most recent U.S. domestic housing subprime crisis in 2007–2008 predominantly impacted the construction sector. Its negative consequences spread out to the rest of the U.S. economy and eventually expanded worldwide (International Labour Organization [1]). According to The Organisation for Economic Co-operation and Development (OECD) data, almost all countries tracked by the OECD reported a fall in GDP of 2.1 percentage points in the first quarter of 2009 and a rise in unemployment of 2.4 percentage points in May, 2009 (OECD [2]). This was the largest decline reported by the OECD since 1960, which predominantly affected the construction and automobile sectors. In the U.S., this impact was more devastating and led to an almost tripling of the unemployment rate, which reached 20.6% in 2010 (Current Population Survey (CPS) [3]). In response, the U.S. launched the American Recovery and Reinvestment Act of 2009. This crisis also had a very deep and negative impact on EU countries and the Euro area, where the construction sector accounted for 6.0% of EU GDP in 2010. The deepest decline of −8.5% in the EU-27 and −7.9% in the Euro area hit in 2009 (see Table 1).

Table 1. Annual growth, index of production for construction, EU-27 and Euro area, 2000–2010 (^{1}) (% growth; comparison with the previous year).

		2000	2001	2002	2003	2004	2005	2006	2007	2008	2009	2010
	Total construction	4.0	0.5	1.1	1.8	0.8	1.9	3.6	2.0	−3.8	−8.5	−4.1
EU-27	Building	5.2	0.4	0.7	2.7	1.8	2.2	4.3	1.9	−4.3	−10.9	−3.4
	Civil engineering	0.2	1.1	1.7	−1.5	−3.2	1.9	−1.2	2.9	−1.4	2.3	−7.1
	Total construction	4.1	0.6	0.4	0.9	0.0	2.2	3.7	1.3	−5.5	−7.9	−7.7
EA-17	Building	5.3	0.4	−0.1	1.6	0.8	2.6	4.7	1.2	−6.1	−10.1	−6.7
	Civil engineering	1.4	0.8	0.5	−0.8	−2.1	2.7	−1.8	2.1	−4.2	0.6	−12.0

(^{1}) Estimates; working day adjusted series. Source: Eurostat.

Only one EU country reported positive growth in the construction sector during the crisis period: Poland with a growth of 10.2% in 2008 and 4.5% in the following year (see Table 2).

Table 2. Annual growth, index of production for total construction, 2000–2010 (^{1}) (% growth; comparison with the previous year).

	Weight in 2005 (% of EU-27)	2000	2001	2002	2003	2004	2005	2006	2007	2008	2009	2010
EU-27	100.0	4.0	0.5	1.1	1.8	0.8	1.9	3.6	2.0	−3.8	−8.5	−4.1
EA-17	71.3	4.1	0.6	0.4	0.9	0.0	2.2	3.7	1.3	−5.5	−7.9	−7.7
Belgium	2.0	:	−2.4	−2.6	−0.2	2.9	0.6	3.3	1.5	−0.4	−3.3	−2.1
Bulgaria	0.1	:	13.4	3.8	4.6	35.3	31.7	24.8	26.8	12.6	−14.2	−17.9
Czech Republic	0.8	0.8	10.3	2.9	9.5	8.6	5.2	6.4	6.8	−0.3	−0.6	−7.3
Denmark	1.7	1.7	−6.7	−1.2	2.1	−0.2	3.1	3.8	−4.2	−5.7	−10.8	−8.4
Germany	11.1	−3.5	−7.6	−4.3	−4.2	−5.3	−5.3	6.3	2.9	−0.7	0.1	0.2
Estonia	0.1	18.6	4.2	22.6	6.1	12.5	22.4	26.9	13.5	−13.3	−29.8	−12.4
Ireland	2.8	:	3.4	2.0	5.7	25.3	10.0	3.8	−13.5	−29.2	−36.9	−30.1
Greece	1.1	:	6.6	39.1	−5.7	−15.9	−38.7	3.6	14.3	7.7	−17.5	−31.6
Spain	18.8	10.7	3.0	0.6	7.2	2.3	10.9	2.2	−4.3	−16.3	−11.3	−20.2
France	12.5	6.0	1.2	−2.3	−0.8	−1.2	2.7	4.2	2.3	−3.7	−5.9	−3.4
Italy	11.5	6.2	6.2	5.1	2.8	1.6	1.3	3.9	6.4	−1.1	−11.5	−3.4
Cyprus	0.3	:	3.7	3.2	6.5	4.4	2.9	4.1	6.8	2.3	−10.6	−8.0
Latvia	0.1	7.2	6.2	12.1	13.1	13.1	15.5	13.3	13.6	−3.1	−34.9	−23.4
Lithuania	0.2	−18.1	7.4	21.7	27.8	6.8	9.9	21.7	22.2	4.0	−48.5	−7.7
Luxembourg	0.3	:	4.2	1.9	0.9	−1.1	−0.9	2.6	2.6	−1.8	0.8	0.1
Hungary	0.5	7.7	9.3	18.0	2.7	4.3	15.7	−0.7	−14.0	−5.2	−4.4	−10.4
Malta	0.0	:	−4.0	23.4	−5.7	8.0	18.5	4.4	7.2	6.6	−7.9	0.2
Netherlands	4.9	:	1.9	−3.1	−4.9	−2.6	3.2	2.3	5.6	3.2	−3.0	−11.0
Austria	2.2	−0.6	−0.6	0.5	12.3	5.0	4.9	5.9	3.9	−0.9	−1.6	−4.3
Poland	1.7	1.2	−10.9	−10.1	−7.2	−1.9	9.2	15.6	16.3	10.2	4.5	3.7
Portugal	1.8	:	4.7	−1.1	−8.6	−4.4	−4.5	−6.3	−4.0	−1.2	−6.6	−8.5
Romania	0.4	:	11.5	4.5	3.2	1.4	6.6	15.6	33.1	26.7	−15.2	−13.4
Slovenia	0.2	2.9	−10.5	7.5	9.6	0.7	2.0	15.7	18.5	15.5	−20.9	−16.9
Slovakia	0.2	0.2	0.7	4.1	5.7	5.9	14.5	15.4	5.5	11.5	−11.2	−4.3
Finland	1.3	8.0	−0.1	1.4	4.2	4.4	5.2	7.8	10.2	4.1	−13.2	11.9
Sweden	2.1	4.4	5.4	0.3	0.0	0.1	3.0	8.0	6.2	4.2	−3.5	5.9
United Kingdom	21.2	4.2	1.1	4.6	5.6	3.5	−0.5	1.4	2.3	−1.3	−11.6	7.3
Norway	-	−2.1	1.2	−0.1	2.1	7.4	8.9	6.0	5.8	1.1	−8.3	−0.1
Switzerland	-	2.7	−2.7	0.9	0.1	3.1	2.6	2.0	1.2	2.4	1.4	1.9
Montenegro	-	:	5.3	0.3	−8.5	−5.8	7.6	46.1	−1.7	20.7	−19.3	−0.6
Croatia	-	−8.9	3.7	13.0	22.3	1.6	−0.2	9.3	2.6	11.8	−6.9	−15.9
FYR of Macedonia	-	:	:	:	:	:	:	−12.3	7.5	25.5	13.7	15.2
Turkey	-	:	:	:	:	:	:	18.4	5.5	−7.6	−16.3	17.5

(^{1}) Estimates; working day adjusted series. Source: Eurostat.

Due to its market vulnerability, the construction sector may be used as a litmus test for company performance and in a particular crises resistance.

It seems interesting to measure the behavior of family firms exposed to crises. Some researchers argue that during periods of economic meltdown, family businesses exposed to increased risk situations may perform differently than non-family business by prioritizing the security of family over firm interests (Lee [4]; Van Gils *et al.* [5]; Rosenblatt [6]). In opposition to this opinion, some

Int. J. Financial Stud. **2014**, *2*, 266–279

researchers have found that family firms may withstand crisis exposure, because of having strong family and stakeholder relations (Sirmon *et al.* [7]; Corbetta and Salvato [8]; Anderson and Reeb [9]). These contradictory views call for further research of the behavior of family firms in crises.

The objective of this paper is to measure the performance of construction companies listed on the Warsaw Stock Exchange with respect to two portfolios: family- and non-family controlled. The performance of these portfolios was measures in three sub-periods: (1) pre-crisis period: 2006–2007; (2) crisis period: 2008–2009; (3) post-crisis period: 2010–2012. The capital asset pricing model was used to conclude whether family-controlled firms underperformed or outperformed their non-family peers in terms of expected returns and risk.

Since the seminal findings of Sharpe [10], Lintner [11] and Mossin [12], CAPM has gained the immense interest of researchers. Some questioned, while others supported, the positive and linear relation between the risk and return of securities that CAPM predicted. In addition, over the past few decades, researchers have tried to relax CAPM assumptions and apply this model in a wide array of contexts. The cross-sectional behavior of asset returns has been researched voluminously in U.S., though with limited interest in Poland (Lyn and Zychowicz [13]; Kompa and Matuszewska [14]; Witkowska [15]; Gębka [16]; Kowalewski *et al.* [17]; or Waszczuk [18]).

Risk and return are two basic and important financial indicators for investors. In general, investors expect more returns for taking more risk. This linear relationship is reflected in the CAPM model and is still perceived as being powerful. Its components as beta or as systematic risk allow the prediction of rates on returns of securities portfolios.

This paper is structured as follows: The next section provides the theoretical background of CAPM with an outline of its evolution and supportive and contradictory views. In the methodological part, we present portfolio construction, address the public family firms and test data retrieved from the Warsaw Stock Exchange. The final section discusses the results and limitations.

2. Theoretical Background

The capital asset pricing model was developed almost simultaneously by Sharpe [10], Lintner [11] and Mossin [12] based on Harry Markovitz's modern portfolio theory [19]. This model assumes the mean variance as the investment allocation predictor to one-period utility maximizing investors. Five decades later, this model and its variants are still widely used in finance to explain and predict the performance of asset portfolios, the cost of capital and the relation between asset risk and expected return, among others things. In particular, this theory assumes that investors should be rewarded by higher asset returns for taking higher risks. In essence, CAPM assumes two types of risk: systematic (non-diversifiable), which is related to the market, and specific and diversifiable (or unsystematic), which are related to individual securities that may be diversified. Unsystematic risk may be minimalized by effectively diversifying and increasing the portfolio size. On the other hand, systematic risk relates to the overall movement of the market or economy and cannot be diversified. As a consequence, CAPM helps investors in measuring a security risk with respect to the market. Testing CAPM over the long term, researchers have replicated this model in many contexts and countries and are still divided regarding its viability. Some find supportive and some contradictory evidence against CAPM.

Jensen *et al.* [20] proved the validity of CAPM on the New York Stock Exchange by testing linearity in a cross-section of expected monthly excess returns and betas on ten portfolios between 1931 and 1965. Fama and McBeth [21] found a positive linear relationship between average returns and the beta of assets on the NYSE between 1926 and 1968. Isakov [22], in his examination of the Swiss stock market between 1983 and 1991, proved the viability of CAPM. Zhang and Wihlborg [23] tested a monthly time series of equity prices by analyzing 753 firms quoted in six European emerging stock markets: Cyprus, Czech Republic, Greece, Hungary, Russia and Turkey between 1995 and 2002. They found a positive correlation between beta and returns for domestic CAPM. Litzenberger and Ramaswamy [24] found a positive relationship between dividend yield and stock return for the 1936–1977 period.

Durack *et al.* [25] found supportive evidence for the CAPM model by testing Australian companies. Köseoğlu and Mercangöz [26] proved the validity of the zero beta capital asset pricing model by analyzing stocks within the ISE 100 on the Istanbul Stock Exchange.

However there is another stream of research against CAPM. Ibbotson and Sinquefield [27] revised the CAPM formula by ruling out beta and arguing that returns are better explained by the size of company and its book to market ratio. Roll [28] proved CAPM misspecification as the result of not finding an adequate measure of market portfolio. Banz [29] challenged CAPM by analyzing NYSE stocks between 1936 and 1975 and found that small firms had higher risk adjusted returns than larger firms. He argued that the size effect had existed for at least forty decades, which stood against the CAPM model. However, he argued that this effect was not linear and not stable; thus, the conclusions may not be supportive. Fama and French [30] analyzed a hundred portfolios on NYSE, AMEX and NASDAQ between July 1963, and December 1990. Their findings proved that size mattered, but not the relationship between beta and returns. Michailidis *et al.* [31] tested weekly stock returns of 100 firms listed in Greece between January 1998, and December 2002, and arrived at conclusions that higher risk is correlated with higher return, but the reverse correlation does not hold. Adedokun and Olakojo [32] arrived at the same results by testing monthly stock returns from a hundred Nigerian firms between January 2008, and December,2009. Hasan *et al.* [33] tested CAPM for the Bangladesh stock market and found out that this model does not prove its validity.

Mixed results of testing CAPM encouraged researchers to adjust this model by other variables than just using beta to explain returns. Merton [34] introduced intertemporal beta to differentiate investor and market beta. In the first case, investors bear greater risk (cash flow) than the market overall (discount beta equal to the variance of the market return), which should be reflected in higher returns. Breeden [35] proposed adjusting Merton's beta by the consumption aggregate in a single equation. Basu [36] argued that the relationship between price-earnings ratios is stronger than CAPM predicts. Bhandari [37] found a positive relationship between debt to equity and expected stock returns. This relation holds true, even with different controlling variables, such as firm size, beta and the January effect. In addition, the relationship holds, even without the January effect, though it is weaker. Some researchers found that leverage and the book-to-market ratio better explain higher asset returns than CAPM (Rosenberg *et al.*, [38]; Chan *et al.* [39]). In addition, Chan *et al.* [39] measured the relation between stock returns and four variables: earnings yield, size, book to market ratio and cash flow yield in Japan. They found that all four of these variables correlate with market return, out of which, the book to market ratio and cash flow yield correlate the most with returns. In line with these vast contributions, Fama and French [40] revised their model by analyzing the two variables of size and book-to-market ratio in addition to excess market return. Javid and Ahmad [41] argued that conditional co-skewness explains non-normality in stock prices. Akbari and Mohammadi [42] found no relation between beta and the leverage ratios of 115 firms quoted at the Tehran Stock Market between 2005 and 2012.

There is very limited interest in research testing CAPM on family firms. Zellweger [43] pointed out the revision of CAPM to address the time horizon inherent in family firms. Zellweger argues that by extending the time horizon for investments, the marginal risk of an investment is reduced.

Some research studies have focused on testing CAPM on the Warsaw Stock Exchange. Lyn and Zychowicz [13] found book to market and dividend yield ratios in some Eastern European markets to be predictors of returns over six to 12 months. Kompa and Matuszewska [14] researched returns of five companies with the highest percentage shares listed under the Warsaw Stock Exchange Index 20 that characterize the largest and the most liquid companies. Witkowska [15] analyzed five portfolios composed of securities between 2002 and 2005 and found proof for the viability of the CAPM on the WSE. Gębka [16] found, for example, cross-autocorrelation between size and volume in portfolio returns during the 1996–2000 period. Waszczuk [18] showed that momentum trading may not be taken into account to generate profits beyond a one-month holding period between 2002 and 2011. In addition, she found proof for applying size and value strategies; however, their relevance varies over time. Almost none of the analyses of quoted Polish securities focused on measuring the performance of family firms. The only study that addressed family firms was performed by Kowalewski *et al.* [17]. They analyzed public family firms and found a relationship between the share of ownership and firm performance by analyzing 217 Polish companies from 1997 to 2005.

This study aims at contributing to the field of CAPM testing by analyzing securities of family-controlled *vs.* non-family peers, in particular measuring their performance in the crisis period.

3. Methodology

3.1. Definition

Chua *et al.* [44] analyzed the literature on the definition of family businesses, where they referred to Alcorn's definition of a public family firm as follows: "if part of the stock is publicly owned, the family must also operate the business". This rests in line with the principles of the Wallenbergs, the owners of the group of family businesses termed as the Wallenberg sphere. The Wallenbergs use the term "active ownership" to express family engagement in the businesses (Lindgren *et al.* [45]). This does not rely on quantification of ownership shares, but rather, controlling firms both in formal and informal ways. The minimum degree of active ownership means taking an active part in management tasks in the sense of influencing managerial and supervisory functions. Jaskiewicz *et al.* [46] define family businesses by numbers, *i.e.*, having "family ownership of more than 25%, as well as family control and management participation". Blondel *et al.* [47] analyzed family firms quoted on the Partis Stock Exchange defined as: "a business where one or several individuals or families are identified as the major ultimate owner or owners". Leach and Bogod [48] classified a firm "as family controlled when at least 25% of shares are in the hands of family shareholders (provided the other 75% shareholding is distributed across smaller minority shareholders) and the business has experienced generational change". Villalonga and Amit [49] examine their research findings and assume a family firm with "a minimum control threshold of 20% of the votes, being the largest shareholder or voteholder, having family officers or directors, or being in second or later generation". Sraer and Thesmar [50] followed the definition of Villalonga and Amit [49] to measure the performance of public family firms in France. Miller *et al.* [51] stress the importance of family involvement in the ownership from the time perspective. They define "a family firm as one in which multiple members of the same family are involved as major owners or managers, either contemporaneously or over time". We follow the definition of Villalonga and Amit [49].

3.2. Data Description

We analyzed monthly weighted portfolio returns consisting of 24 public construction firms that belong to the Warsaw Stock Exchange Construction Index (WIG-Construction) (see Tables 3 and 4).

Table 3. WIG-Construction portfolio in PLN (family-controlled firms in italics).

Company	Market Cap		Family	
	Market Cap	%	Shares %	Votes %
Budimex	1,303,762,250	36.62%	-	-
Elektrobudowa	498,435,000	14.00%	-	-
Trakcja PRKII	322,712,640	9.06%	-	-
Mostostal Zabrze	190,973,650	5.36%	-	-
Erbud	163,726,800	4.60%	-	-
Polimex-Mostostal	134,416,620	3.78%	-	-
Ulma-Construccion Polska	121,458,400	3.41%	-	-
Instal Kraków	117,900,450	3.31%	-	-
Unibep	*101,347,200*	*2.85%*	*26.98% *17.83%*	*26.98% 17.83%*
P.A. Nova	*94,367,000*	*2.65%*	*18.19% 9.13%*	*20.80% 10.88%*
Prochem	66,588,900	1.87%	-	-
Mirbud	*63,918,020*	*1.80%*	*43.19%*	*43.19%;*
Herkules	*62,118,000*	*1.74%*	*18.99%*	*18.99%; 93.31% ***
Elektrotim	61,625,740	1.73%	-	-
ZUE	*58,560,000*	*1.64%*	*72.75% 0.01%*	*72.75% 0.01%*
Projprzem	50,534,820	1.42%	-	-
Mostostal Warszawa	39,325,140	1.10%	-	-
Centrum Nowoczesnych Technologii	34,203,650	0.96%	-	-
Tesgas	*20,029,750*	*0.56%*	*40.58%*	*55.66%*
Mostostal Płock	14,261,400	0.40%	-	-
Energoaparatura	13,069,400	0.37%	-	-
Bipromet	12,009,900	0.34%	-	-
Mostostal Export	7,941,450	0.22%	-	-
Awbud	7,413,450	0.21%	-	-
Non-family cap	3,160,359,660	88.76%	-	-
Family-controlled cap	400,339,970	11.24%	-	-
TOTAL CAP	3,560,699,630	100.00%	-	-

* Two owning families; ** % in the Extraordinary General Meeting. Source: Warsaw Stock Exchange [52].

Table 4. WIG-Construction companies by expected returns and betas (not adjusted for size).

Company	2006–2007		2008–2009		2010–2011	
	Expected Return	Beta	Expected Return	Beta	Expected Return	Beta
Budimex	0.04	1.12	0.00	0.48	0.01	1.34
Elektrobudowa	0.08	1.23	−0.01	0.38	−0.02	0.88
Trakcja PRKII	-	-	−0.01	0.59	−0.06	2.12
Mostostal Zabrze	0.11	2.11	−0.01	1.31	−0.04	2.16
Erbud	0.03	0.51	0.00	1.16	−0.04	0.82
Polimex-Mostostal	0.02	1.45	−0.03	1.17	−0.03	1.50
Ulma-Construccion Polska	0.11	0.70	−0.02	1.40	−0.01	0.31
Instal Kraków	0.07	0.98	0.00	1.00	−0.01	0.85
Unibep	-	-	*0.30*	*1.19*	*0.01*	*0.48*
P.A. Nova	*0.01*	*0.31*	*0.28*	*0.71*	*0.01*	*1.04*
Prochem	0.02	1.17	−0.01	1.36	−0.01	1.64
Mirbud	-	-	*0.19*	*0.61*	*−0.01*	*0.59*
Herkules	*0.09*	*3.04*	*0.18*	*1.40*	*−0.06*	*1.40*
Elektrotim	−0.07	1.20	0.00	0.38	−0.02	1.39
ZUE	-	-	-	-	*−0.07*	*−0.05*
Projprzem	0.05	2.09	−0.03	0.69	−0.02	1.18
Mostostal Warszawa	0.09	0.73	0.01	0.52	−0.04	1.31
Centrum Nowoczesnych Technologii	0.18	3.30	0.00	1.40	0.02	0.18
Tesgas	-	-	*0.06*	*0.02*	*−0.03*	*0.78*
Mostostal Płock	0.08	1.69	−0.01	0.99	−0.04	1.81
Energoaparatura	0.05	1.90	−0.01	0.65	−0.03	1.21
Bipromet	-	-	−0.02	0.39	0.01	−0.09
Mostostal Export	0.08	3.59	−0.02	0.53	−0.01	1.36
Awbud	0.10	2.76	−0.04	0.58	0.01	0.74

Source: own computations based on the Warsaw Stock Exchange data [52].

Int. J. Financial Stud. **2014**, *2*, 266–279

Next, these firms were separated to form two sub-portfolios: family-controlled firms (6 firms) and nonfamily-controlled peers (18 firms). The firm size was used as weight in the portfolio formation. We calculated beta estimates and portfolio expected returns followed by Blume [53], Friend and Blume [54] and Black *et al.* [55]:

$$\beta_{constr} \equiv \sum_{i=1}^{N} x_{ip}\beta_i \; ; \; E(R_{constr}) = \sum_{i=1}^{N} x_{iconstr} E(R_i)$$

(1)

where $x_{iconstr}$ denotes weights $i = 1,2, \dots , N$ for assets in the construction portfolio (*constr*), $E(R_{constr})$ expected return on the construction portfolio and $E(R_i)$ expected return on security i.

The financial data for both of these types of portfolios were analyzed from 2006 to 2012 and divided into three sub-periods: (1) before the crisis: 2006–2007; (2) in crisis: 2008–2009; and (3) after the crisis 2010–2012 (see Table 5).

Table 5. Portfolio population.

	Before The Crisis	In Crisis	After The Crisis
Portfolio formation period	2006–2007	2008–2009	2010–2012
No. of family firms	2	5	6
No. of nonfamily firms	16	18	18

3.3. Methodology and Results

The CAPM model assumes a linear dependency between expected return on any asset with the expected return on the market portfolio. Jagannathan and McGratten [56] reflected that CAPM explains differences in the risk premium across assets, which helps investors make decisions. The risk is equivalent with beta. The slope of the CAPM line expresses the market risk premium, while the intercept represents the risk-free rate. Black *et al.* [55] and Fama and MacBeth [21] proposed a two-pass methodology to test the viability of CAPM. The first pass estimates portfolio betas, while the second pass regresses average returns based on the first-pass estimated portfolio betas. Sharpe [10], Lintner [11] and Mossin [12] provided the formula that explains the excess return of assets by risk premium:

$$E(R_i) = R_f + (E(R_m) - R_f)$$

(2)

where $E(R_i)$ is the expected return on security i, R_f the return of the risk-free security, β_i the systematic risk of the security i calculated as $Cov(R_i,R_m)/Var(R_m)$ and $E(R_m)$ the expected return on the market portfolio.

Jensen [20] concludes that the correlation between beta and expected returns requires a time-series regression formulated as follows:

$$R_i - R_f = \alpha_i + \beta_i(R_m - R_f) + \varepsilon_i$$

(3)

Jensen's alpha defines the pricing error (abnormal performance). When alpha increases, the reliability of return estimates may deteriorate. Jensen's alpha shall equal zero to hold the CAPM model. We followed Formulas (4) and (5) to measure the performance of construction portfolios on the Warsaw Stock Exchange. We calculated the total risk as the variance of returns:

$$\sigma^2_{constr} = \sum_{i=1}^{N} x_{iconstr} + \left(\sum_{i=1}^{N} x_{iconstr}\beta_i \right)^2 \sigma_m^2$$

(4)

and unsystematic risk as the transformation of the Equation (4):

$$\sigma_{\varepsilon i}^2 = \sigma_{constr}^2 - \beta_i^2 \sigma_m^2$$

(5)

We used the Warsaw Stock Exchange Index as the proxy for the construction market portfolio and the reference rates (minimum money market intervention rate) published by the National Bank of Poland as the proxy for the risk-free rate. Then, we tested stock returns for the normal distribution by using the Jarque–Bera test. The Jarque–Bera test relies on the third and fourth momentum and follows $\chi2$ distribution with two degrees of freedom:

$$Jarque\text{-}Bera = \frac{n}{6}\left[S^2 + \frac{(K-3)^2}{4}\right]$$

(6)

where S is the skewness, K the kurtosis and n the number of observations. The null hypothesis of returns following the normal distribution was tested at a p-value of 95%. The results are presented in Table 6.

Table 6. Tests of two construction portfolios on the Warsaw Stock Exchange (WSE): non-family controlled firms (NFF) and family-controlled firms (FF).

	2006–2007		2008–2009		2010–2012	
	NFF	FF	NFF	FF	NFF	FF
Expected Return	5.35%	4.13%	−0.76%	23.56%	−1.56%	−1.72%
Variance	0.093	0.071	0.022	0.031	0.011	0.010
Standard Deviation	0.306	0.267	0.150	0.175	0.107	0.103
Coefficient of variation	5.719	6.467	−19.816	0.742	−6.816	−5.963
Beta	1.223	1.392	0.680	0.921	1.305	0.711
Systematic Risk	0.005	0.006	0.004	0.007	0.004	0.001
Specific Risk	0.089	0.065	0.018	0.023	0.008	0.009
Specific Risk/Variance	0.948	0.912	0.819	0.757	0.661	0.892
Jensen's alpha	0.032	0.018	−0.008	0.237	−0.018	−0.020
Skewness	6.142	1.231	0.438	−0.623	0.175	0.212
Kurtosis	72.109	0.471	2.210	5.022	2.206	1.722
Jarque–Bera	3284.634	1.039	1.043	1.175	0.564	0.453

The Jarque–Bera test proved that the normal distribution has to be rejected for the period from 2006 to 2007 ($\chi^2_{0.05;2} > 5.991$). However, the normal distribution test may not be rejected for all remaining portfolios between 2008 and 2012 ($\chi^2_{0.05;2} \leq 5.991$), and therefore, the CAPM model may be used to explain the relationship between the market returns and risk of construction portfolios. Before the crisis, both portfolios reported positive returns, and non-family firms outperformed family-controlled ones by 1.22%. The returns were opposite in the crisis period, when family firms significantly outperformed non-family peers. In addition, the latter firms reported negative returns in the crisis. The data shows that tolerance for risk has declined since the crisis hit. This behavior seems to be rational, as invoked by the reaction to the global recession. In addition, public construction companies exhibited high proportions of specific, rather than systematic, risk. In periods before and after the crisis, all construction portfolios were oversensitive with respect to the market ($\beta > 1$). During the crisis, both portfolios were less sensitive to the market ($\beta < 1$). When the crisis hit, all public construction companies were overvalued, except for family-controlled ones, which were undervalued.

4. Conclusions

This research focused on testing the validity of CAPM on the Warsaw Stock Exchange across two portfolios of family- and non-family-controlled companies. These portfolios were constructed on the basis of the complete data retrieved from the Warsaw Stock Exchange. As a consequence, we made calculations on the whole population (not sample) data. In this respect, even the small amount of data does not exclude an inference. These two portfolios were then adjusted for the size, *i.e.*, market capitalization, to avoid the dominance of large companies in the population.

The assumption of normal distribution may not be rejected according to the Jarque–Bera test for the period from 2008 to 2012; therefore, the relation between return and risk holds in the case of the WSE. However, for the period from 2006 to 2007, the Jarque–Bera yielded outlying numbers; therefore, we did not draw conclusions.

By assuming that market portfolios were efficient, returns of family construction companies significantly outperformed their nonfamily peers in the latest crisis. Investors who invested in family-controlled portfolios during that time might have expected exceptional returns of 23.56%. In addition, these securities were undervalued, which does not prove CAPM invalidity. As Jensen argued [55], "deficiencies as measurement and model specification error due to proxies for variables do not reject CAPM".

Although the capital asset pricing model was substantially developed since its inception (see Theoretical Background), we decided to prove its validity as developed by Sharpe [10], Lintner [11] and Mossin [12], because of scant testing in the case of family firms. However it would be tempting to move beyond this version of CAPM to get more insight into the performance of family firms on stock exchanges.

This research was limited to public companies. In addition to the extraordinary returns of family-controlled firms, the results suggest that a vast amount of risk is specific for all construction portfolios. It would be interesting to find out the sources of this risk. As mentioned in the Introduction, Poland was the only EU country in which the construction industry withstood the crisis and reported positive returns. However, as this research is limited to public companies, it would be interesting to analyze in-depth factors that allowed family-controlled firms operating in the construction sector to outperform their non-family peers. In addition, this paper used the capital asset pricing model to explain the performance of two portfolios that used a family-ownership as the distinction factor. The outperformance of the family-owned firms during the crisis may be either attributed to family-ownership or non-family-related factors and being the result of portfolio composition. This issue also needs to be further analyzed, *i.e.*, by conducting a qualitative research.

Conflicts of Interest: The author declares no conflict of interest.

References

1. International Labour Office, Governing Body. *The Current Global Economic Crisis: Sectoral Aspects*; International Labour Office, Governing Body: Geneva, Switzerland, 2009; pp. 1–13.
2. Organisation for Economic Co-operation and Development (OECD). Responding to the Economic Crisis. Fostering Industrial Restructuring and Renewal. Available online: http://www.oecd.org/industry/ind/43387209.pdf (accessed on 30 January 2014).
3. Current Population Survey (CPS). United States Census Bureau. Available online: https://www.census.gov/cps/ (accessed on 30 January 2014).
4. Lee, J. Family firm performance: Further evidence. *Fam. Bus. Rev.* **2006**, *19*, 103–114.
5. Van Gils, A.; Voordeckers, W.; van den Heuvel, J. Environmental uncertainty and strategic behavior in Belgian family firms. *Eur. Manag. J.* **2004**, *22*, 588–595. [CrossRef]
6. Rosenblatt, P.C. The interplay of family system and business system in family farms during economic recession. *Fam. Bus. Rev.* **1991**, *4*, 45–57.
7. Sirmon, D.; Arregle, J.; Hitt, M.; Webb, J. The role of family influence in firms' strategic responses to threat of imitation. *Entrep. Theory Pract.* **2008**, *32*, 979–998. [CrossRef]
8. Corbetta, G.; Salvato, C. Self-serving or self-actualizing? Models of man and agency costs in different types of family firms: A commentary on comparing the agency costs of family and non-family firms: Conceptual issues and exploratory evidence. *Entrep. Theory Pract.* **2004**, *28*, 355–362. [CrossRef]
9. Anderson, R.; Reeb, D.M. Founding-Family Ownership and Firm Performance: Evidence from the S&P 500. *J. Financ.* **2003**, *58*, 1301–1327. [CrossRef]
10. Sharpe, W.F. Capital Asset Prices: A Theory of Market Equilibrium under conditions of risk. *J. Financ.* **1964**, *19*, 425–442.

11. Lintner, J. The Valuation of Risk Assets and the Selection of Risky Investments in Stock Portfolios and Capital Budgets. *Rev. Econ. Stat.* **1965**, *47*, 13–25. [CrossRef]

12. Mossin, J. Equilibrium in a capital Asset Market. *Econometrica* **1966**, *34*, 768–783. [CrossRef]

13. Lyn, E.O.; Zychowicz, E.J. Predicting Stock Returns in the Developing Markets of Eastern Europe. *J. Invest.* **2004**, *13*, 63–71. [CrossRef]

14. Kompa, K.; Matuszewska, A.M. Rates of Return Analysis: Examples from the Warsaw Stock Exchange. *Int. Adv. Econ. Res.* **2007**, *13*, 111–112. [CrossRef]

15. Witkowska, D.M. Portfolio Analysis: Example for the Warsaw Stock Exchange. *Int. Adv. Econ. Res.* **2007**, *13*, 247–248.

16. Gębka, B. Volume- and size-related lead–lag effects in stock returns and volatility: An empirical investigation of the Warsaw Stock Exchange. *Int. Rev. Financ. Anal.* **2008**, *17*, 134–155. [CrossRef]

17. Kowalewski, O.; Talavera, O.; Stetsyuk, I. Influence of Family Involvement in Management and Ownership on Firm Performance: Evidence from Poland. *Fam. Bus. Rev.* **2010**, *23*, 23–45.

18. Waszczuk, A. Do Local or Global Risk Factors Explain the Size, Value and Momentum Trading Payoffs on the Warsaw Stock Exchange? *Appl. Financ. Econ.* **2013**, *23*, 1497–1508. [CrossRef]

19. Markowitz, H.M. Portfolio Selection. *J. Financ.* **1952**, *7*, 77–91.

20. Jensen, M.C. The performance of mutual funds in the period 1945–1964. *J. Financ.* **1968**, *23*, 389–416.

21. Fama, E.F.; MacBeth, J.D. Risk, Return, and Equilibrium: Empirical Tests. *J. Polit. Econ.* **1973**, *81*, 607–636.

22. Isakov, D. Is beta still alive? Conclusive evidence from the Swiss stock market. *Eur. J. Financ.* **1999**, *5*, 202–212. [CrossRef]

23. Zhang, J.; Wihlborg, C. Unconditional and conditional CAPM: Evidence from European emerging markets. Available online: http://snee.org/filer/papers/266.pdf (accessed on 30 January 2014).

24. Litzenberger, R.H.; Ramaswamy, K. The Effects of Dividends on Common Stock Prices Tax Effects or Information Effects? *J. Financ.* **1982**, *37*, 429–443.

25. Durack, N.; Durand, R.B.; Maller, R.A. A best choice among asset pricing models? The Conditional Capital Asset Pricing Model in Australia. *Account. Financ.* **2004**, *44*, 139–162.

26. Köseoğlu, S.D.; Mercangöz, B.A. Testing the Validity of Standard and Zero Beta Capital Asset Pricing Model in Istanbul Stock Exchange. *Int. J. Bus. Humanit. Technol.* **2013**, *3*, 58–67.

27. Ibbotson, R.; Sinquefield, R. Stocks, Bonds, Bills and Inflation: Year-by-Year Historical Returns (1926–1974). *J. Bus.* **1976**, *49*, 11–47.

28. Roll, R. A Critique of the Asset Pricing Theory's Tests. *J. Financ. Econ.* **1977**, *4*, 129–176. [CrossRef]

29. Banz, R.W. The relationship between return and market value of common stocks. *J. Financ. Econ.* **1981**, *9*, 3–18. [CrossRef]

30. Fama, E.F.; French, K.R. The Cross-Section of Expected Stock Returns. *J. Financ.* **1992**, *47*, 427–465.

31. Michailidis, G.; Tsopoglou, S.; Papanastasiou, D.; Mariola, E. Testing the Capital Asset Pricing Model (CAPM): The Case of the Emerging Greek Securities Market. *Int. Res. J. Financ. Econ.* **2006**, *4*, 78–91.

32. Adedokun, A.J.; Olakojo, S.A. Test of Capital Asset Pricing Model: Evidence from Nigerian Stock Exchange. *J. Econ. Theory* **2012**, *6*, 121–127.

33. Hasan, Z.; Kamil, A.A.; Baten, A. Analyzing and estimating portfolio performance of Bangladesh stock market. *Am. J. Appl. Sci.* **2013**, *10*, 139–146. [CrossRef]

34. Merton, R.C. An intertemporal capital asset pricing model. *Econometrica* **1973**, *41*, 867–887. [CrossRef]

35. Breeden, D.T. An intertemporal asset pricing model with stochastic consumption and investment opportunities. *J. Financ. Econ.* **1979**, *7*, 265–296. [CrossRef]

36. Basu, S. Investment Performance of Common Stocks in Relation to Their Price-Earnings Ratios: A Test of the Efficient Market Hypothesis. *J. Financ.* **1977**, *32*, 663–682. [CrossRef]

37. Bhandari, L. Debt/Equity Ratio and Expected Common Stock Returns: Empirical Evidence. *J. Financ.* **1988**, *2*, 507–528. [CrossRef]

38. Rosenberg, B.; Reid, K.; Lanstein, R. Persuasive evidence of market inefficiency. *J. Portf. Manag.* **1985**, *11*, 9–16. [CrossRef]

39. Chan, L.; Hamao, Y.; Lakonishok, J. Fundamentals and Stock Returns in Japan. *J. Financ.* **1991**, *46*, 1739–1764.

40. Fama, E.F.; French, K.R. Common Risk Factors in the Returns on Stocks and Bonds. *J. Financ. Econ.* **1993**, *33*, 3–56. [CrossRef]

41. Javid, A.Y.; Ahmad, E. *Test of Multi-moment Capital Asset Pricing Model: Evidence from Karachi Stock Exchange*; Pakistan Institute of Development Economics Working Paper 2008:49; Pakistan Institute of Development Economics: Islamabad, Pakistan, 2008.
42. Akbari, P.; Mohammadi, E. A Study of the Effects of Leverages Ratio on Systematic Risk based on the Capital Asset Pricing Model Among Accepted Companies in Tehran Stock Market. *J. Educ. Manag. Stud.* **2013**, *3*, 271–277.
43. Zellweger, T. Time Horizon, Costs of Equity Capital, and Generic Investment Strategies of Firms. *Fam. Bus. Rev.* **2007**, *20*, 1–15. [CrossRef]
44. Chua, J.H.; Chrisman, J.J.; Sharma, P. Defining the Family Business by Behavior. *Entrep. Theory Pract.* **1999**, *23*, 19–39.
45. Lindgren, H.; Fritz, S. Aktivt Ägande. Investor under Växlande Konjunkturer. In *Scandinavian Economic History Review*; Routledge: Abingdon, UK, 1996. (in Swedish)
46. Jaskiewicz, P.; Gonzalez, V.M.; Menendez, S.; Schiereck, D. Long-run IPO Performance Analysis of German and Spanish Family-owned businesses. *Fam. Bus. Rev.* **2005**, *18*, 179–202. [CrossRef]
47. Blondel, C.; Rowell, N.; van der Heyden, L. Prevalence of Patrimonial Firms on Paris Stock Exchange: Analysis of the Top 250 Companies in 1993 and 1998. Available online: http://www.insead.edu/facultyresearch/research/doc.cfm?did=990 (accessed on 30 January 2014).
48. Leach, P.; Bogod, T. *The BDO-Stoy Hayward Guide to the Family Business*; Kogan Page: London, UK, 1999.
49. Villalonga, B.; Amit, R. How do family ownership, control and management affect firm value? *J. Financ. Econ.* **2006**, *80*, 385–417. [CrossRef]
50. Sraer, D.; Thesmar, D. Performance and Behavior of Family Firms: Evidence from the French Stock Market. Available online: http://papers.ssrn.com/sol3/papers.cfm?abstract_id=925415 (accessed on 20 December 2013).
51. Miller, D.; Le Breton-Miller, I.; Lester, R.H.; Cannella, A.A., Jr. Are Family Firms Really Superior Performers. *J. Corp. Financ.* **2007**, *5*, 829–858.
52. Warsaw Stock Exchange. Available online: http://www.gpw.pl (accessed on 20 December 2013).
53. Blume, M.E. Portfolio Theory: A Step Toward Its Practical Application. *J. Bus.* **1970**, *43*, 152–173.
54. Friend, I.; Blume, M. Measurement of Portfolio Performance under Uncertainty. *Am. Econ. Rev.* **1970**, *60*, 607–636.
55. Black, F.; Jensen, M.C.; Scholes, M. The Capital Asset Pricing Model: Some Empirical Tests. In *Studies in the Theory of Capital Markets*; Jensen, M.C., Ed.; Praeger: New York, NY, USA, 1972; pp. 79–121.
56. Jagannathan, R.; McGrattan, E.R. The CAPM debate. *Fed. Reserv. Bank Minneap. Q. Rev.* **1995**, *19*, 2–17.

International Journal of
Financial Studies

MDPI

Article

The Corporate Social Responsibility of Family Businesses: An International Approach

Gérard Hirigoyen and Thierry Poulain-Rehm *

Institute of Research into Management of Organisations (IRGO), University Department of Business
Administration, PUSG, University of Bordeaux, 35 Avenue Abadie, 33100 Bordeaux, France;
gerard.hirigoyen@u-bordeaux4.fr
* Author to whom correspondence should be addressed; tpr@u-bordeaux4.fr;
  Tel.: +33-556-009-720; Fax: +33-556-009-729.

Received: 4 May 2014; in revised form: 19 June 2014; Accepted: 23 June 2014; Published: 9 July 2014

Abstract: This study analyzes the links between listed family businesses and social responsibility. On
the theoretical level, it establishes a relationship between socioemotional wealth, proactive stakeholder
engagement, and the social responsibility of family businesses. On a practical level, our results
(obtained from a sample of 363 companies) show that family businesses do not differ from non-family
businesses in many dimensions of social responsibility. Moreover, family businesses have statistically
significant lower ratings for four sub-dimensions of "corporate governance", namely "balance
of power and effectiveness of the Board", "audit and control mechanisms", "engagement with
shareholders and shareholder structure", and "executive compensation".

Keywords: family business; corporate governance; human resources; social responsibility; stakeholders

JEL Classification: G30

1. Introduction

Milton Friedmans provocative statement, "The Social Responsibility of Business is to Increase its
Profits" (Friedman, 1970 [1]) is an explicit reminder of the problem and assumed purpose of Corporate
Social Responsibility (CSR) at a time when, encouraged by various intergovernmental, international
and regional agencies [1], many companies are seeking to develop a form of social responsibility [2].
As long ago as 1953, Bowen [3] thought it mandatory for companies to meet the expectations of society.
Bowens concern was clearly to maximize social welfare rather than company profitability. Since then,
numerous definitions of CSR have been proposed, including Jones (1980) [4], Wartick and Cochran
(1985) [5], Wood (1991) [6], Blair (1996) [7], and McWilliams and Siegel (2001) [8]. In particular, Blair [7]
defines a socially responsible firm as one that takes conscious decisions and reduces profits to benefit
other stakeholders.

Although many empirical studies have sought to link social responsibility and financial
performance (Margolis and Walsh, 2003 [9]; Makni *et al.*, 2009 [10]), few have focused specifically
on family businesses (De la Cruz Déniz Déniz and Cabrera-Suarez, 2005 [11]; Dyer and Whetten,

---

[1] For example, the Organisation for Economic Co-operation and Development (OECD) Guidelines for Multinational
Enterprises (written in 1976 and revised in 2000), which provide voluntary principles and standards for companies;
the Global Reporting Initiative (GRI), launched in 1997 by the United Nations Environment Programme (UNEP), which seeks
to establish guidelines and standardize norms for social and environmental reporting; the European Unions Green
Paper (published in 2001 and again in 2007) to promote a European framework for Corporate Social Responsibility;
and certifications, standards and labels such as the Social Accountability 8000 Standard or ISO 14001, which aim to measure
the impact of corporate activity on the environment.

2006 [12]; Bingham *et al.*, 2011 [13]), despite the fact that family businesses are a key part of the economic fabric, and their contribution to GDP is significant (Sharma *et al.*, 1996 [14]; Neubauer and Lank, 1998 [15]; La Porta *et al.*, 1999 [16]; Faccio and Lang, 2002 [17]; Morck and Yeung, 2004 [18]; Anderson and Reeb,003 [19]; PricewaterhouseCoopers, 2012 [20]). Fundamental questions related to our understanding of family businesses, their performance, functioning and relationships with stakeholders remain unanswered or have been only partially addressed. Do family businesses have a higher level of social responsibility than non-family firms, and if so, what are the underlying explanatory factors? In which areas do family businesses engage in CSR? Can a hierarchy be established? What does CSR translate into for the various stakeholders in the family business and what is its impact on the relationships between the family business and its stakeholders?

Here, we investigate whether family businesses have a higher level of CSR than non-family businesses. We adopt a broad concept of social responsibility, which takes into account multiple dimensions and the company's diverse stakeholders (human resources, shareholders, the community, the environment, suppliers, and clients). To improve the external validity of the results, we take an international approach, which is based upon a sample of companies representing different geographical areas. Our research makes both a theoretical and empirical contribution.

At the theoretical level, we establish a relationship between socioemotional wealth (SEW), proactive stakeholder engagement (PSE), and the social responsibility of family businesses. Recent literature explains the PSE of family businesses in terms of the creation and preservation of socioemotional wealth (Gomez-Mejia *et al.*, 2012 [21]; Berrone *et al.*, 2012 [22]; Cennamo *et al.*, 2012 [23], Miller *et al.*, 2012 [24]). For example, Gomez-Mejia *et al.* (2007) [25] explain empirical differences between family and non-family firms as an extension of the behavioral agency model, which postulates that choices made by a company depend on the reference point of its senior managers (Wiseman and Gomez-Mejia, 1998 [26]). In family businesses, the concept of SEW constitutes this reference point. For example, [22] claim that SEW is the dominant paradigm in the family business; they argue that it is the most important differentiator of the family firm as a unique entity, and explains their distinctive behavior. When there is a risk that it may be lost, or conversely, an opportunity to strengthen it, the family makes decisions that are not dictated by economic logic. The approach provides an integrated conceptual framework to explain the greater social responsibility of family businesses. The creation of SEW explains higher levels of PSE in both normative and instrumental terms: normative, because the family aims to be considered as a responsible actor; instrumental because gains in social legitimacy and enhanced reputation promote organizational efficiency and sustainability. On the empirical level, our concept of CSR integrates human and social dimensions, and adds other dimensions related to the quality of governance, business behavior, respect for stakeholders, and the environment.

The study implements an international comparative approach based on a sample of listed companies representing three geographic zones: Europe, North America, and the Asia-Pacific region. Our sample is taken from a database developed by the social rating agency Vigeo, and is based on a longitudinal analysis of data from 2001 to 2010.

The article is organized as follows: Section 2 presents the theoretical framework and hypotheses. Section 3 outlines the methodology. Section 4 presents the results and Section 5 offers a discussion of these results.

2. Theoretical Framework

2.1. CSR and Proactive Stakeholder Engagement

Many definitions of CSR exist in the literature. Although this has led some authors to argue that it is an elusive concept (Lee, 1987 [27]), which is poorly defined (Preston and Post, 1975 [28]), most consider it to refer to actions taken by businesses to improve societal, social and environmental conditions ([6,9]; Aguilera *et al.*, 2007 [29]; Waddock, 2004 [30]). Given the lack of theoretical integration (Post, 1978 [31]; DeFillipi, 1982 [32]), CSR is increasingly analyzed in terms of the relationship between companies and their stakeholders, *i.e.*, "any group or individual who can affect or is affected by the achievement of the organizations objectives" (Freeman, 1984 [33]).

Stakeholder theory sees businesses as nodes in complex relationships with their stakeholders. Consequently, many authors (e.g., Longo *et al.*, 2005 [34], Abreu *et al.*, 2005 [35], Uhlaner *et al.*, 2004 [36] or Papasolomou *et al.*, 2005 [37]) have favored this approach. More innovative research is based on "proactive stakeholder engagement" (PSE), which is defined as the willingness of businesses to anticipate the needs of their stakeholders and develop practices that meet these needs ([23]; Sharma, 2000 [38]).

Mitchell *et al.* (1997) [39] provide a deeper insight into the identification of stakeholders and their influence. They distinguish three stakeholder attributes: power (the ability of those who hold it to bring about the results they want), legitimacy (ethical, moral, and social demands) and urgency (the extent to which stakeholders accept delays in responding to their demands and criticality, *i.e.*, the importance of the demand or the relationship). Based on these attributes, they identify seven stakeholder classes and establish a typology that orients the priorities of senior managers towards either stakeholders with the greatest number of attributes (definitive), or those with a combination of attributes requiring special attention (dominant).

In later work they define the concept of "stakeholder salience", which determines the priority that managers give to meeting the demands of stakeholders, and apply it to the particular case of family businesses (Mitchell *et al.*, 2011 [40]). They argue that such companies are characterized by the intersection of two institutions (the family and the business), and that the managerial response to stakeholder demands is more complex. In particular, power, legitimacy and urgency are specific to the business. Power is more normative than utilitarian. Legitimacy, which in the general managerial context is socially constructed, is based on ideas of inheritance. Finally, although in general, time considerations and the importance of stakeholders demands are somewhat independent in the management of an emergency, in family businesses they are linked by family ties and specific goals. Family firms pursue non-economic objectives (Chrisman *et al.*, 2005 [41]) that create SEW [25]. These objectives are rooted in relationships between family members (Pearson *et al.*, 2008 [42]) and are unique to the business. Given the traditional goals of profitability and growth, they may be mutually reinforcing, conflict, or be independent of each other (Gomez-Mejia *et al.*, 2010 [43]; Zellweger and Nason, 2008 [44]). Finally, the desire to preserve SEW usually prevails over economic considerations.

2.2. Proactive Stakeholder Engagement (PSE) and Socioemotional Wealth (SEW)

Recent literature explains the PSE of family businesses in terms of the creation and preservation of SEW [21–24], which goes beyond simple financial objectives. The approach provides an integrated framework to explain the higher levels of social responsibility found in family businesses.

The concept of SEW was first proposed by [25] to explain empirical differences between family and non-family firms in certain areas, notably risk-taking. It extends the behavioral agency model [26], which postulates that choices made by the firm depend on the reference point of senior managers, who seek to preserve their investment. The authors of [25] apply this to the family business and argue that the reference point of family shareholder-managers is to maintain SEW, which explains why family business takes decisions that do not follow a completely economic logic. Berrone *et al.* (2010) [45] support the idea that family firms are more susceptible to institutional pressures exerted by the environment—all the more so as risk is offset by gains in social legitimacy. The authors of [23] claim that the creation of SEW and higher levels of PSE can be explained using both normative and instrumental arguments.

Normative arguments consider that PSE strategies are driven by the familys desire to be seen as a responsible citizen [12]. Kets de Vries (1977) [46], Schein (1983) [47], and Dyer (1986) [48] point out that the founders of family businesses see it as an extension of themselves and the company reflects their fundamental values (Chrisman *et al.*, 2007 [49]). Cennamo *et al.* [23] (following Westhead *et al.*, 2001 [50]) suggest that the firm is a mirror that reflects the self-esteem of family members. Similarly, Brickson

(2005) [51] argues that firms whose identity consists of reciprocal commitments and personal relationships are oriented towards increasing the well-being and maximizing the wealth of a group that is larger than the firm itself. Baron (2008) [52] notes that altruism can dominate the family firm, and guide decision-making. Under these conditions, actions towards stakeholders are motivated by a broad concept of welfare. Finally, family members who are deeply rooted in their community are more concerned about environmental degradation and social problems [23].

Instrumental arguments relate to the hope of businesses that gains in social legitimacy and reputation will promote efficiency and consequently sustainability; in this case, societal performance increases the company's competitiveness (Jiao, 2010 [53]). McGuire *et al.*, (2012) [54] underline that interactions between the family and the business make the issue of reputation particularly sensitive. Firms' investments in their reputational capital create value with their key stakeholders (Fombrun, 1996 [55]). Cennamo *et al.* [23] note that these "goodwill" reserves act as an insurance to protect trust in the company, which is all the more important when families concentrate their capital in a single organization. Moreover, Cennamo *et al.* [23] and Berrone *et al.* [45] highlight the desire of the family to transmit the business to future generations, while for others the firm symbolizes tradition (Tagiuri and Davis, 1992 [56]). Therefore, the preservation of SEW implies a long-term investment in order to ensure that this tradition is passed on to future generations.

The PSE of family businesses is at least partially explained by the homogeneity of their value system, which emphasizes affective relationships, solidarity, loyalty, trust in the environment, and in their own abilities ([40]; Chami, 2001 [57]). An analysis in terms of social capital helps to understand the importance of the social dimension. Bourdieu (1986) [58] emphasizes that social capital consists of actual or potential resources that are linked to a durable network of institutionalized relationships of mutual recognition and respect. The family invests not only its financial wealth in the company, but also its human capital and its honor, even more so when the company bears the family name [23]. Consequently, the network of relationships is an asset that may be turned into organizational capital, and a source of value creation (Nahapiet and Ghoshal, 1998 [59]). This explains why family businesses have a good reputation ([56]; Lyman, 1991 [60]; Ward and Aronoff, 1991 [61]) and are keen to maintain it. Whetten and Mackey (2005) [62] explain the CSR of the family business by its need to forge an identity and project a positive image. The concern is to preserve the firms legacy, and has a qualitative dimension. Family businesses owners therefore regard unrest in the company or customer complaints as elements that may damage their business.

From this point of view, it is interesting to look at the concept of identification. This addresses the psychological factors at work, through the overlap between organizational and individual identity (Hogg, 2003 [63]; Hogg and Terry, 2001 [64]). The authors of [13] use the theory of organizational identity (Albert and Whetten, 1985 [65]) to explain the CSR of family businesses: such businesses orient their identity towards their stakeholders. Non-family firms make fewer engagements to socially responsible activities and only to the extent that they match individual identities. They consider stakeholders from a transactional perspective—in terms of the objective of creating value. In contrast, the identity of family firms is collective and relational; they create close links with stakeholders that are in line with their individual characteristics [13].

2.3. Socioemotional Wealth and the FIBER Model

The FIBER model was developed by [22] and provides an integrated framework for the analysis of the SEW of family businesses. It emphasizes five key dimensions: (i) Family control and influence; (ii) Identification of family members with the firm; (iii) Binding social ties; (iv) Emotional attachment of family members; and (v) Renewal of family bonds to the firm through dynastic succession. Based on this model, [23] argue that family firms engage proactively with both internal and external stakeholders. They engage with internal stakeholders in order to reinforce trust. This is all the more apparent as the family seeks to maintain control and influence the management of the firm, has a sense of the dynasty (which led it to adopt a long-term perspective), and values the company's reputation. It promotes engagements with external stakeholders (including those who have a more distant relationship with the firm) as the SEW of the family lies in its fundamental values, the strength of its internal social ties, and/or the emotional attachment of the firms owner.

2.4. Hypotheses

The literature review underlines the importance given by family businesses to their stakeholders and brings us to our hypotheses. Family shareholdings, which represent social capital, make it possible to structure and strengthen both internal and external links and relationships with principal stakeholders (Sirmon and Hitt, 2003 [66]). The commitment of managers to stakeholders appears to be a condition for sustainable development (Sloan, 2009 [67]).

The stakeholder approach [34–37] Jamali [68,69], led to the identification of the following six stakeholder categories: "human resources", "shareholders", "community", "environment", "suppliers", and "consumers", based on the model developed by [39]. These categories are similar to those identified by [34] (employees, suppliers, customers, community) and [37] (employees, consumers, community, investors, suppliers, environment).

Finally, [23] explain the PSE of family businesses by distinguishing between internal and external stakeholders. Their work is based on that of [22], and we retain the distinction between internal and external stakeholders in the formulation of our hypotheses, which are as follows:

H1: Family businesses are more engaged in social responsibility with respect to internal stakeholders than non-family businesses. This hypothesis can be decomposed into two sub-hypotheses:

H1.1: Family Businesses are More Engaged with Human Resources

Family businesses are thought to have better management practices. They focus on personal and family values rather than business values, and are known for their integrity and commitment to human relations (Lyman, 1991 [60]; Koiranen, 2002 [70]; Aronoff, 2004 [71]), which leads to greater job stability during periods of crisis [2]. They are characterized by trust, motivation, increased loyalty (Tagiuri and Davis [72]; Allouche and Amann [73]; Steier, 2001 [74]), and flexible working practices (Goffee and Scase, 1985 [75]; Poza *et al.*, 1997 [76]).

H1.2: Family Businesses are More Engaged with Shareholders

Family businesses are oriented towards the long term and aim to manage and increase the wealth of the family for the benefit of future generations (James, 1999 [77]; Hirigoyen, 2009 [78]). This long-term vision has a positive impact on the relationships between family businesses and their shareholders. Moreover, family businesses are characterized by better management of capital and resource allocation ([48]; Monsen, 1969 [79]; Astrachan, 1988 [80]).

H2: Family businesses are more engaged in social responsibility with respect to external stakeholders than non-family businesses. This hypothesis can also be decomposed as follows:

H2.1: Family Businesses are More Engaged with the Community

The idea of a virtuous circle between the engagement of family businesses to the community and value creation has been highlighted by [80]. They have a different relationship to risk and a better understanding of the resources available in their immediate environment; consequently they are better able to seize opportunities for growth and invest in sectors neglected by non-family firms. They not only contribute to increased employment, but also a dynamic economy and ultimately the well-being of the population. As a result, both economic and social developments are improved [15]. Vallejo Martos and Grand Torraleja (2007) [81] suggest a systemic approach in order to better understand the social responsibility of family businesses. They propose supplementing the three-circle model of Churchill and Hatten (1987) [82] (which describes the family, property, and the company) with community.

H2.2: Family Businesses are More Engaged with the Environment

The long-term vision of family businesses leads to a focus on sustainable development, which manifests itself as environmental, economic and social responsibility. Consistent with their values and the attention given to all their stakeholders, family businesses are likely to engage in sustainable and environmentally-friendly practices. At the firm level, the nonfinancial goals of family businesses include environmental actions [25,44].

H2.3: Family Businesses are More Engaged with Suppliers and Customers

The authors of [69] support the idea that family businesses are more attentive to the needs, expectations and reactions of their customers, and produce better-quality goods and services. This study found that the service provided to customers by these companies was marked by greater flexibility and adaptability; employees had greater autonomy in dealing with customer inquiries, which helped to strengthen the company's competitiveness. Similar arguments apply to suppliers [25,44].

Our model examines the diverse expectations of stakeholders that family businesses attempt to satisfy, in terms of international instruments related to six domains, namely: human resources, human rights, corporate governance, community involvement, environment and business behavior. Other explanatory and control variables (financial performance, company size, business sector, and geographic zone) are integrated in order to take into account other factors that may influence CSR. These factors are outlined in the methodology.

3. Methodology

The methodology consists of measuring the influence of the family business on CSR. The analysis is based on a longitudinal analysis, carried out on explanatory data covering a period of ten years (2001–2010), to explain CSR observed in 2010, on a dataset of 363 listed companies, spread over three geographic zones (Europe, North America, and the Asia-Pacific region). The data was assessed using bivariate and multivariate analyses. The following sections describe the dataset, operationalization of variables and the statistical methodology.

3.1. The Dataset

The dataset was taken from Vigeos database. Vigeo is a social responsibility rating agency. It assesses the social, environmental and governance performance of businesses against the institutional and international standards of the United Nations (UN), the International Labour Organization (ILO), the Organisation for Economic Co-operation and Development (OECD), the World Trade Organization (WTO), and the European Union (EU). The agency provides analyses to investors and asset managers in European, Asian, and North American companies to assist them in choosing their portfolios. It also conducts social responsibility audits that provide decision-making assistance to the managers of companies or local authorities. Vigeos methodology fully integrates the recommendations of the ISO 26000 Guidelines for Social Responsibility [2], which adopts a definition of social responsibility based upon the idea of respect for international standards of behavior. Its ratings therefore help companies to achieve ISO 26000 objectives and respond to stakeholders expectations (Crilly *et al.*, 2012 [83]). The Vigeo model assesses performance against a set of social responsibility objectives that are clear, enforceable and weighted; the evaluation consists of complementary analyses and ratings are divided into four hierarchical levels using a formalized scoring system.

Overall, Vigeos database contains a total of 1800 listed companies, spread over three geographical areas (Europe, North America, and the Asia-Pacific region), which have all received at least one rating by the agency since 1999. However, the following restrictions were applied:

- Only companies that had a rating for 2010 were retained. This was to eliminate bias due to irregular ratings and ensure consistency;

---

[2] This standard, published by the International Standards Organization, integrates the following dimensions of social responsibility applicable to companies, namely: stable employment, pay, health and safety, training, collective and individual social relations, the fight against discrimination, social actions, relationships with suppliers, the impact on local development and respect for the environment.

- Banks, credit institutions, finance companies, insurance companies, holding companies and real-estate companies were not included because of their financial characteristics;
- Companies that had not been listed throughout the ten year period (2001–2010) were not included (e.g., newly listed companies, delisted companies, companies that became insolvent or were placed into receivership);
- Other companies, where missing data prevented the satisfactory execution of the analysis, were also removed;

These restrictions resulted in a final sample of 363 companies, of which 58 were identified as family businesses using the criteria described below.

3.2. Variables

3.2.1. The Dependent Variable: Social Responsibility

The overall dependent variable was global corporate social responsibility (CSRG). However, one of the major contributions of the current study is to assess the various dimensions of social responsibility; this approach is in contrast to other studies that favor a comprehensive approach or only focus on one particular dimension. The selected domains were based on the approach taken by Vigeo.

The Vigeo analysis concerns six dimensions of activity (human resources, human rights, corporate governance, community involvement, environment and business behavior) that are created from a total of 38 generic criteria. These criteria are evaluated according to 200 action principles that enable an assessment of managerial systems. Each criterion is weighted according to its sectorial relevance. For each of the 35 sectors analyzed, the challenges are contextualized and weighted according to the degree of exposure of stakeholders and the risks or the competitive advantage they offer the company.

Moreover, for each of the 38 generic criteria, Vigeo examines in detail:

- Policies: business strategy, management processes, and the relevance of commitments based on a review of the content of stated policies and the extent to which they are adopted within the company;
- Deployment: the efficiency of policy implementation based on an examination of the resources made available, budgets and scope of application;
- Results: the performance achieved based on an analysis of quantitative performance indicators together with any complaints or disputes with stakeholders.

With these aims in mind, Vigeo uses multiple, traceable sources of information. Analysts first consult all publicly available documents (annual reports, sustainability reports, press releases, *etc.*), and contact the company for additional information. They then collect data from stakeholders (actors and observers on the ground, such as trade unions, NGOs and international organizations) to cross-check with information obtained from companies. They evaluate more than 250 indicators for each business, which make it possible to provide information and alerts on corporate commitments, performance, and risks on an ongoing basis.

The 38 generic criteria are consolidated into six domains.

(1) Human resources (HR): this dimension assesses industrial relations, employment relations, and working conditions;
(2) Human rights (HRTS): this dimension concerns respect for freedom of association, the promotion of collective bargaining, non-discrimination, the promotion of equality, the elimination of proscribed forms of work (child labor, forced labor), the prevention of inhuman or degrading treatment (such as sexual harassment), and the protection of privacy and personal data;
(3) Corporate Governance (CG): this dimension relates to the efficiency and integrity of governance. It not only concerns the independence and effectiveness of the Board of Directors (CG1), but also

the effectiveness and efficiency of audit and control mechanisms (CG2). This notably applies to the risks of social responsibility, respect for the rights of (particularly minority) shareholders (CG3), and the transparency and rationality of executive compensation (CG4);

(4) Community Involvement (CIN): this dimension evaluates the effectiveness and integration of managerial engagement, the company's contribution to the economic and social development of its host country and human communities, specific engagements to manage the social impact of products and services and, finally, contributions to good causes in general;

(5) Environment (ENV): this dimension focuses on the protection, safeguarding, and prevention of environmental damage, and the implementation of an appropriate management strategy. It applies to eco-design, biodiversity protection and the intelligent management of environmental impacts throughout the life-cycle of products or services;

(6) Business Behavior (BB): this dimension takes into account the rights and interests of customers, the integration of social and environmental standards in the selection of suppliers throughout the supply chain, respect for competition rules, and the implementation of effective anti-corruption measures.

Each dimension is rated on a scale of 0–100. A score of 0 indicates little commitment to social responsibility, and poor, to very poor risk management. A score of 100 demonstrates a mature commitment to CSR.

3.2.2. Explanatory and Control Variables

Explanatory variables include family and financial variables. Control variables include company size, industrial sector and geographic zone. They are described in detail in the following sections.

3.2.2.1. Explanatory Variables: The Family Business (FAM)

How the family business is defined has a strong bearing on empirical results (Westhead and Cowling, 1998 [84]). Since the founding definition of Donnelley (1964) [85], researchers have generally taken one of two approaches. On the one hand, some studies base the definition on quantitative criteria, such as family control and ownership of capital (Barry, 1975 [86]). On the other hand, researchers have used qualitative criteria, measured in terms of the involvement and influence that the family has on management (Beckhard and Dyer, 1983 [87]), corporate culture, how the family interacts with the business (Boswell, 1972 [88]), or the transfer of the business to subsequent generations [82].

A family business can be considered as a business in which a shareholder group, united by family ties, holds a significant portion of the capital and voting rights, and exerts an effective influence on managerial decisions. Following the work of Chrisman and Patel (2012) [89], we used a binary variable to distinguish family and non-family firms. Therefore, a family business was considered to be any business in which at least 5% of the capital was held by the family and in which at least one family member has served as a member of the top management team [89].

The qualification of a business involved a detailed analysis of the shareholder structure, the composition of the Board of Directors and executive bodies. This information was taken from financial databases provided by Osiris (BvDEP) and Infinancials. [3]

3.2.2.2. Explanatory Variables: Rate of Return on Assets (ROA)

This performance measure is commonly used in studies on the relationship between CSR and financial performance (McGuire *et al.*, 1988 [90]; Seifert *et al.*, 2003 [91]). It has already been used in

---

[3] It would have been desirable to take into account the potential impact of the presence of the founder of the company on the way it is managed or the number of successive generations that had run the company. Unfortunately, the database that was used did not provide this, more qualitative, information.

studies of family firms ([19]; Sraer and Thesmar, 2007 [92]; Villalonga and Amit, 2006 [93]). It was assessed as the ratio of net profit/total assets.

3.2.2.3. Control Variables: Company Size (SIZE)

The size of the company indicated the extent to which the company was humanized. It measured the influence of the hierarchical distance created by growth on the attention paid by management to staff problems. This variable was operationalized by the logarithm of the total number of full-time employees.

3.2.2.4. Control Variables: Industrial Sector (SECT)

Business performance must be assessed relatively, as it depends on the health of the sector and the financial flexibility it provides. Firms in the primary (extraction of natural resources, agriculture, fisheries, forestry and mining) and secondary sector (processing of raw materials) were combined into a single category. Those in the tertiary sector (service activities that do not fall into the first two categories) constituted a second category.

3.2.2.5. Control Variables: Geographic Zone

The impact of belonging to one of the three geographic zones (Europe, North America, the Asia-Pacific region) was tested. It is generally assumed that there are differences between the Anglo-Saxon and European (Rhenish) governance models, and the Japanese model is usually considered to be closest to the European model. The legal and political characteristics of national systems (La Porta *et al.*, 1997 [94]), together with cultural and managerial factors (Aoki, 1984 [95]), are thought to influence governance systems and, more broadly, the operation of companies, which is likely to impact the level of engagement with stakeholders. Therefore, the following three dichotomous control variables, corresponding to the three geographic zones were included: EUR (1 if the company is in Europe, 0 if not); AME (1 if the company is in North America, 0 if not); ASIA (1 if the company is in the Asia-Pacific region, 0 if not).

To reduce the impact of economic fluctuations, the average value of each of the explanatory and control variables over a ten year period (2001–2010) was calculated.

3.3. Statistical Analysis

Students *t*-test for the comparison of means was performed on the variables described above.

Logit regressions measured the impact of the family nature of the business and the various explanatory variables on CSR. This method is an example of a probabilistic choice model, where the objective is to determine the probability of occurrence of an event, and the variables that influence it. Logit regressions are useful for many reasons. In particular, the method does not attempt to highlight the impact of each explanatory variable in isolation, but rather to reveal the interaction between variables. This is probably their greatest strength, compared to a discriminant analysis or a least squares regression, which are additive.

The aim was to determine the probability that family businesses constituted a group of firms with a high level of CSR. This was made possible by the transformation of continuous variables (CSR scores) into dichotomous variables (CSR supported or not). Consequently, the sample was grouped into two categories: companies with a low level of CSR (scores between 0 and 49), and those with a high or very high level (CSR scores between 50 and 100).

The predictive variables are both continuous and binary, as required by logistical regression models. Moreover, the maximum likelihood estimation led to the use of the "descending" option in order to remove non-significant variables based on variation of the likelihood.

The (generic) model was tested as follows:

$$CSR = b_0 + b_1FAMI + b_2ROA + b_3SIZE + b_4SECTOR + b_5EUR + b_6AME + b_7ASLA$$

where:

CSR (binary variable) = CSRG (model 1), RH (model 2), HRTS (model 3), CG (model 4), CG1 (model 5), CG2 (model 6), CG3 (model 7), CG4 (model 8), CIN (model 9), ENV (model 10), BB (model 11).

Statistical tests were carried out using SPSS software.

4. Results

Of the 363 companies, 211 were European, 127 were in North America, and 25 were in the Asia-Pacific zone. A total of 259 were in the primary and secondary sectors, while 104 were in the tertiary sector. Finally, 58 were categorized as family businesses.

Table 1 presents the descriptive statistics, Table 2 presents social responsibility scores using Students t-test for means comparison between family and non-family businesses and Table 3 presents Logit regression analyses of the social responsibility of family businesses.

Bivariate tests showed no statistically significant differences between the CSR of family businesses and others. Although the means for family businesses are higher in the dimensions of human resources, community involvement, environment, and business behavior, Students *t*-test was not significant. Thus, family businesses are not characterized by a greater engagement towards their stakeholders, whether internal or external.

However, family businesses had statistically significantly lower scores for the overall corporate governance variable, and each of its sub-dimensions. Scores were significant at the 1% level for corporate governance (CG), balance of power and effectiveness of the Board (CG1) and executive compensation (CG4), while audit and control mechanisms (CG3) and engagement with shareholders (CG3) were significant at the 5% level. It is apparent therefore, that family businesses are characterized by a lower quality of governance, which gives rise to questions about power, and control of power exercised within them.

The principal result of the Logit analysis was that family businesses were less likely to operate a robust CSR policy (−0.936, significant at the 5% threshold). No statistically significant effect was observed for human resources, human rights, community involvement, environment and business behavior, which is entirely consistent with the bivariate tests. However, here again, it appears that family businesses are much less likely to have a high level of corporate governance (at the 1% threshold). This is particularly clear for the dimensions of balance of power and effectiveness of the Board (CG1) and executive compensation (CG4). Moreover, engagement with shareholders (CG3) and control and audit mechanisms (CG2) were negatively affected at the 5% and 10% thresholds, respectively.

Thus, not only are family businesses not characterized by higher levels of CSR, but their quality of governance appears to be lower.

Other explanatory variables, notably company size, also have an impact. This variable has a strong positive impact on CSR levels. It is significant at the 1% level for global social responsibility, human resources, human rights, balance of power and effectiveness of the Board, community involvement, environment, and business behavior.

Table 1. Descriptive statistics and Pearson correlations of continuous variables.

	Mean	SD	1	2	3	4	5	6	7	8	9	10	11	12	13
CSRG—Social responsibility—overall performance	39.51	10.608	1	0.813 **	0.740 **	0.388 **	0.403 **	0.339 **	0.138 **	0.243 **	0.657 **	0.857 **	0.741 **	−0.051	0.455 **
HR—Human resources	30.47	15.262	0.813 **	1	0.651 **	0.062	0.132 *	0.112 *	−0.024	−0.052	0.475 **	0.678 **	0.542 **	−0.174 **	0.357 **
HRTS—Human rights in the workplace	44.09	12.828	0.740 **	0.651 **	1	0.116 *	0.142 **	0.174 **	−0.018	0.051	0.460 **	0.552 **	0.601 **	−0.056	0.306 **
CG—Corporate Governance	50.83	13.466	0.388 **	0.062	0.116 *	1	0.813 **	0.690 **	0.597 **	0.831 **	0.228 **	0.136 **	0.193 **	0.130 *	0.057
CG1—Balance of power and effectiveness of the Board Directors	48.88	19.033	0.403 **	0.132 *	0.142 **	0.813 **	1	0.493 **	0.191 **	0.529 **	0.235 **	0.194 **	0.207 **	0.078	0.126 *
CG2—Audit and control mechanisms	60.25	13.786	0.339 **	0.112 *	0.174 **	0.690 **	0.493 **	1	0.175 **	0.547 **	0.252 **	0.135 *	0.236 **	0.101	0.110 *
CG3—Engagement with shareholders and shareholder structure	58.15	20.149	0.138 **	−0.024	−0.018	0.597 **	0.191 **	0.175 **	1	0.432 **	0.026	0.008	0.020	0.062	−0.079
CG4—Executive compensation	36.94	18.993	0.243 **	−0.052	0.051	0.831 **	0.529 **	0.547 **	0.432 **	1	0.169 **	0.036	0.113 *	0.157 **	0.000
CIN—Community involvement	42.67	17.003	0.657 **	0.475 **	0.460 **	0.228 **	0.235 **	0.252 **	0.026	0.169 **	1	0.581 **	0.423 **	0.05-9	0.314 **
ENV—Respect for the environment	33.40	17.062	0.857 **	0.678 **	0.552 **	0.136 **	0.194 **	0.135 *	0.008	0.036	0.581 **	1	0.555 **	−0.072	0.463 **
BB—Business behavior	43.34	11.988	0.741 **	0.542 **	0.601 **	0.193 **	0.207 **	0.236 **	0.020	0.113 *	0.423 **	0.555 **	1	−0.073	0.346 **
ROA—Rate of return on assets	6.147	5.4627	−0.051	−0.174 **	−0.056	0.130 *	0.078	0.101	0.062	0.157 **	0.059	−0.072	−0.073	1	−0.097
SIZE—Company size	4.2552	0.67870	0.455 **	0.357 **	0.306 **	0.057	0.126 *	0.110 *	−0.079	0.000	0.314 **	0.463 **	0.346 **	−0.097	1

***/**/* Significant at the 1%, 5% and 10% levels respectively.

Table 2. Social responsibility scores using Students t-test for means comparison between family and non-family businesses.

	Mean for Non-Family Business	Mean for Family Business	Student t-test
CSRG: Social responsibility—overall performance	39.45	39.81	−0.237
HR: Human resources	30.16	32.09	−0.880
HRTS: Human rights	44.32	42.86	0.795
CG: Corporate Governance	52.00	44.67	3.870 ***
CG1: Balance of power and effectiveness of the Board	50.07	42.60	2.763 ***
CG2: Audit and control mechanisms	60.91	56.76	2.115 **
CG3: Engagement with shareholders	59.21	52.59	2.307 **
CG4: Executive compensation	38.68	27.83	4.072 ***
CIN: Community involvement	42.43	43.93	−0.617
ENV: Environment	32.85	36.33	−1.425
BB: Business behavior	43.01	45.07	−1.198

***/**/* Significant at the 1%, 5% and 10% levels respectively.

Table 3. Logit Regression analyses of the social responsibility of family businesses.

Variables	Model 1 CSRG	Model 2 HR	Model 3 HRTS	Model 4 CG	Model 5 CG1	Model 6 CG2	Model 7 CG3	Model 8 CG4	Model 9 CIN	Model 10 ENV	Model 11 BB
CONSTANT	-11.372 *** 53.471	-12.262 *** 35.474	-4.909 *** 30.026	-2.221 *** 8.446	-2.329 *** 10.575	-0.080 0.040	0.0480 *** 6.729	-2.507 *** 55.296	-5.117 *** 34.110	-7.076 *** 36.114	-4.552 *** 29.038
FAMI	-0.936 ** 4.684			-1.465 *** 19.431	-0.940 *** 8.926	-0.662 * 3.741	-0.756 ** 6.056	-1.054 *** 6.701			
ROA		-0.095 ** 5.277		0.039 * 3.187				0.061 ** 5.508			
SIZE	1.831 *** 33.703	1.783 *** 22.252	1.067 *** 27.595	0.413 ** 6.045	0.453 *** 7.574				1.057 *** 29.063	1.339 *** 27.297	0.797 *** 17.934
SECT	-0.910 ** 5.614	-1.643 *** 10.569	-1.012 *** 12.042				0.670 ** 6.121	0.722 *** 6.784			
EUR	2.866 *** 32.320	3.868 *** 14.056		0.777 *** 11.477	0.754 *** 11.124	1.413 *** 10.198	0.404 * 2.920	1.339 *** 20.690			0.555 ** 5.215
AME			-0.641 ** 5.983			2.734 *** 26.414			-0.442 * 3.056	-1.219 *** 11.187	
ASIA											
Chi-2	103.076 ***	94.796 ***	46.217 ***	34.816 ***	24.633 ***	34.513 ***	13.018 ***	35.861 ***	38.089 ***	47.666 ***	26.432 ***
-2 Log Lik.	252.890	188.785	408.649	468.406	477.597	327.109	441.848	363.946	425.394	302.502	426.910

*** / ** / * Significant at the 1%, 5% and 10% levels respectively.

The influence of other variables is more nuanced. Industrial sector (SECT) has a mixed effect. Belonging to the tertiary sector has a negative impact on global social responsibility (at the 5% level) and on human resources and human rights (at the 1% level). However, the same conditions appear to have a positive effect on engagement with shareholders (at the 5% level) and executive compensation (at the 1% level). Rate of return on assets (ROA) has a negative influence (at the 5% threshold) on the probability of developing socially responsible policies in the domain of human resources, but a positive influence in the domain of executive compensation (also at the 5% threshold).

Geographic variables merit particular attention. European companies (EUR) have a statistically significant probability of developing an active and robust CSR policy. The impact is significant at the 1% threshold for the global CSR indicator (CSRG), human resources (HR), and corporate governance (CG) and at the 5% threshold for the business behavior dimension (BB). American companies (AME) are more likely to have a higher level of governance in the audit and control mechanisms dimension, which is statistically significant at the 1% level. Conversely, there is a negative impact on the likelihood of developing socially responsible policies related to the environment (at the 1% threshold), and human rights (at the 5% threshold).

Consequently, all hypotheses are rejected.

5. Discussion and Conclusions

5.1. Contributions

This study of a sample of listed companies, showed that family businesses are not characterized by higher levels of CSR, based on the selected measures. There are no statistically significant differences between family and non-family firms in ratings of human resources, human rights, community involvement, environment and business behavior. Moreover, this is the first time, to our knowledge, that a study has highlighted a negative relationship between family companies and corporate governance, both as a constituent dimension of social responsibility and its various sub-dimensions (balance of power and effectiveness of the Board, audit and control mechanisms, engagement with shareholders and shareholder structure, and executive compensation). These results were obtained from a broad sample of companies spread over three geographic zones and are based on a business classification that distinguishes family businesses based on both their ownership structure and management mode.

The finding that family firms do not show a greater engagement towards their stakeholders contradicts theoretical predictions that their presumed closer relationship with stakeholders is at the origin of their economic success and superior performance [80]. It also qualifies the results of other empirical studies, notably those of Uhlaner *et al.* (2012) [96], who, based on a sample of small- and medium-sized Dutch businesses, showed a conditional influence of family businesses on their commitments, which favored environmentally-friendly practices. Similarly, while the study by [13], on a sample of large, publicly-traded S&P 500 companies, partially confirms our hypotheses, it also suggests that in North America there is a positive relationship between family businesses and some dimensions of CSR—in particular those related to community initiatives and employee relations. Their results suggested that the effect increases with the level of family involvement in the business. For their part, Block and Wagner (2011) [97] argue that the effect of family ownership can differ across various CSR dimensions. Family firms can be responsible and irresponsible regarding CSR at the same time. Their results show that family ownership is negatively associated with community related CSR performance and positively associated with diversity-, employee-, environment-, and product-related aspects of CSR. They note the largest positive effect of family ownership on CSR performance exists with regard to product-related aspects of CSR.

Our results are more in line with the work of [11], who carried out a study on a sample of 612 small- and medium-sized Spanish companies, or that of [12], who have looked at a sample of large publicly-traded SandP 500 companies. Based on a sample of North American companies, [12] found no difference between family and non-family firms in terms of social initiatives for the period 1991–2000. Nevertheless, any differences or similarities in results must be treated with caution given the various contextual, geographical and temporal fields of investigation, and variations in measures of social responsibility.

Our observation that scores related to human resources and human rights are not higher in family firms is surprising, given the generally accepted view that they are more engaged in human relations [69–71]. Moreover, our results show that family businesses do not demonstrate greater engagement with employment relations, labor relations, working conditions, or respect for social rights.

Another surprising result is the similarity in scores relating to community involvement in family and non-family businesses. This does not support the idea that family businesses have a closer relationship with either host countries or their local communities, nor are they more engaged in managing the social impact of their products and services. It challenges the view that, due to their position at the heart of the community, they enjoy a special relationship with their environment (Uhlaner *et al.*, 2012 [96]; Sharma and Sharma, 2011 [98]), and a sense of shared belonging with stakeholders, employees, customers and suppliers [11]. The observation that scores related to environment and business behavior are very similar is entirely consistent with previous work, although family businesses could be expected to be more responsive both to the environmental consequences of their production activities, and also to the needs, expectations and reactions of their customers [69].

Several factors may explain our results. First, there are some general factors. The dataset was composed of large, listed companies whose requirements, in terms of competitiveness and corporate governance, are very similar regardless of their shareholder structure or type of management. The life-cycle of family firms means that their managerial characteristics come to resemble those of non-family businesses. Such firms change significantly over time, from the first generation founding father, via sibling partnerships to the confederation of cousins (Ward, 1991 [99]). The influence of the family weakens with the appointment of external directors (either to head the company or as members of the executive committee) and as their share of capital decreases. These factors mean that both family and non-family listed firms (who evolve in the same economic, legal and regulatory environment) develop similar organizational structures and management styles. Being quoted on the stock exchange homogenizes behavior. In both cases, short-term concerns tend to dominate over long-term objectives. In these conditions, and consistent with traditional financial theory, the objective of shareholder value creation prevails. In this sense, our results confirm the convergence of corporate governance systems in listed companies. It may therefore be the case that differences in behavior are seen at the level of unlisted family firms; something that remains to be confirmed by further works.

Secondly, there may be factors specific to family businesses. Such businesses are characterized by the family's engagement with them and the benefits they bring to the family, which risks becoming self-centered and inward-looking. The key objective of the family-run business is the preservation, development and transfer of their legacy. The family identifies with the company, shares and forms its values, and is committed to its growth for the benefit of future generations—a factor that sometimes leads to decisions that favor family members at the expense of other stakeholders.

On a theoretical level, it is interesting to analyze these results in the light of socioemotional theory [25,45], which is based upon the behavioral agency model [26]. On the one hand, our results seem to contradict those of [22], who investigated the conditions that encourage family companies to demonstrate PSE. On the other hand, they tend to confirm the conceptual analysis of Kellermanns *et al.* (2012) [100], according to which the five dimensions of SEW (family control and influence, identification of the family with the firm, binding social ties, emotional attachment of family members and transgenerational intentions) are associated with a lack of PSE. The authors of [100] draw upon affect infusion theory (Forgas, 1995 [101]; Loewenstein and Adler, 1995 [102]) to argue that SEW can be perceived as negatively or positively valenced, and high levels of SEW can be associated with poor levels of stakeholder care. They point out although family firms do not have an aversion to risk, they do have an aversion to the loss of SEW, which can lead to decisions that are unfavorable for stakeholders.

The utility function of the family shareholding is complex, as it leads to a trade-off between private consumption, the value of business assets (Mahérault, 1999 [103]), cash income over its lifetime, and the wellbeing of the next generation (Bhattacharya and Ravikumar, 1999 [104]). Basco and Perez Rodriguez (2011) [105] underlined the diversity of family businesses and established a typology of firms based on their orientation: "family oriented" businesses (which place greatest emphasis on the principles and values of the family in their decision-making, and give priority to its needs and objectives); "business oriented" companies (in which strategic decisions principally respond to the companys goals and its needs); and "family-business oriented" companies (which set priorities by finding a balance between the needs of the family and those of the company). This interpretation may explain why the interests of the family and the business impact the interests of various non-family stakeholders. This is all the more true, given that family shareholders run a significant personal risk resulting from both managerial decisions and the consequences of these decisions on their personal wealth and that of the family. Xiao *et al.* (2001) [106] showed that although family shareholders are exposed to individual risk, it is less relevant at the level of global business risk since there is little capacity to diversify their personal asset portfolio.

Moreover, it could be claimed that the birth of a family business brings with it agency costs associated with behavioral biases ([57]; Schulze *et al.* 2003 [107]). Following Habbershon *et al.* (2003) [108], Hirigoyen (2008) [109] highlighted the need to update the three-circle model of Gersick *et al.* (1997), which assumes that the behavior of actors involved in the family business is homogeneous and monolithic. The author of [109] suggests adding a fourth individual circle, to explicitly take into account the evolving preferences of individuals, which may give rise to behavioral biases. These biases are as much cognitive and emotional, as individual and collective. Differences in expectations between external stakeholders and the family can create cognitive agency costs. Altruism, in particular, is likely to alter managerial perceptions and limit their ability to monitor and effectively discipline family members, at the expense of other internal and external stakeholders. O'Boyle *et al.* (2012) [110] therefore argue that it is necessary to analyze the symbolic capital of the family shareholding and how it creates a particular competitive advantage; in particular they recommend refining the concept of the role of the family shareholding to take into account altruism, growth strategy, and leadership styles.

5.2. Managerial Implications

Various factors may so explain the weaknesses of family businesses according to our definition of governance. In our study this manifests as weaknesses in the balance of power and the effectiveness of the Board, audit and control mechanisms, engagement with (particularly minority) shareholders and the determination of executive compensation. Clearly, the emotional and cognitive biases highlighted by previous literature may have an impact on the remuneration of managers, which, like the recruitment of other family members, the evaluation of their performance, and their career progression is not necessarily guided by economically rational considerations. In family firms, the satisfaction of family interests seems to prevail over those of other stakeholders, in the matter of remuneration and other areas. Similarly, the rights of majority shareholders belonging to the family prevail over those of minority shareholders. These considerations may explain our finding that the Board of Directors is less efficient, and audit and control mechanisms are weaker in family firms. The Board of Directors is a key facet of corporate governance and its disciplinary role becomes more important as capital is controlled by the family (Charreaux and Pitol-Belin, 1990 [111]). The issue is significant: a study in the United States of over 80 family businesses run by at least the third generation, showed that the existence of an active board that was not controlled by the family was the most important element in the sustainability these companies [99]. Other empirical studies have shown that the performance and value of family firms are lower, relative to non-family businesses when the Board has relatively few independent directors (Anderson and Reeb, 2004 [112]). Other studies have shown a positive relationship between the proportion of independent directors and the existence of an audit committee, which is considered to be one of the factors for improving governance in family businesses (Chau and Leung, 2006 [113]). In family businesses the audit committee is composed of directors who are family members, and (depending on how capital and ownership is structured) by directors representing other shareholders (for example other businesses, banks, financial institutions, investment funds and pension funds) who hold a share of the capital and have objectives that are more financial than strategic. The more decisions are influenced by directors who are family members (and who attempt to preserve or enhance family control of the company's capital and management), the more the balancing power(s) of non-family directors is weakened. This is particularly true in companies where those who own the company's capital simultaneously exercise managerial and administrative functions.

However, in order to bring real added-value to the governance of this type of business, the Board of Directors must play an active role in monitoring managerial actions, checking the quality of internal control procedures, and succession planning. It must also act as a strategic think tank that assesses confidential information and helps in decision-making, while at the same time operating as the interface between the business and the family. It is clear that the Board cannot properly carry out these functions when there is confusion between the roles of shareholders, directors and managers who are family members. Nevertheless, this does not negate the role of family or non-independent directors, who, according to the resource-based view (Wernerfelt, 1984 [114]), facilitate relationships with the environment and access to certain resources (skills, finance, *etc.*). This underlines the importance of different conceptual frameworks in the analysis (Bammens *et al.*, 2011 [115]).

Another important factor is the extension of the family, which further complicates the question of corporate governance. As the business evolves, subsequent generations take up the reins. Over time, the family loses its unity and homogeneity [99]. Divergent interests and disagreements appear. Conflicts surface when strategic and financial decisions have to be taken. Dividend policy is a typical example, where differences of opinion arise between family shareholders who prefer to reinvest profits in the business, and non-managerial, minority family shareholders who want a distribution of profits that provides them with an annuity. Such conflicts have a negative impact on the operation and efficiency of the Board. One of the challenges for family businesses is to find advisors who have the expertise and independence to act in the best interests of the company. These individuals should be able to define strategy and lay out general guidelines for the company; they should exercise genuine control over both the management and controlling shareholders (through appropriate mechanisms such as the audit) and ensure that the interests of minority shareholders are protected.

5.3. Limitations and Future Research

It is important to note that the results obtained are only valid in the context of the explanatory capacity of the selected variables and their operationalization. The research assesses the social responsibility of the organizations studied, and not the socially responsible behavior of the family members who control the capital of the business or have shareholdings. These people can, either in an individual or collective capacity, engage in responsible action at the societal level using their own financial resources and not those of the business. Family members can, of course, mobilize private funds to support causes they believe in: the environment, health, the protection of human rights, poverty reduction, the struggle against injustice, the development of local communities or support for local associations.

Our findings suggest two future avenues of research. On the one hand, it would be appropriate to broaden the scope of the analysis by identifying (in addition to the impact of the structure of ownership) other explanatory factors that may have a positive or negative impact on social responsibility. These may include the institutional, legal and regulatory environment, the cultural background, religious beliefs of management, and the history and traditions of the company. A comparison of listed and unlisted firms would enrich the analysis, as becoming listed naturally favors decisions oriented towards the interests of shareholders. The hypothesis that unlisted family firms have a greater social engagement with their stakeholders merits attention. The corporate governance model would be different in listed and unlisted companies, in particular familiness, "the unique set of resources of a family business which arise from the interactions between the family system as a whole, the individual family members, and the business itself" (Habbershon and Williams, 1999 [116]), would more be developed. It would be interesting to use different theoretical perspectives to inquire the diffusion of CSR among family SMEs, for example stewardship theory or social capital perspective, that seem to be more effective to understand the why and the how of CSR diffusion and/or relative obstacles in family firms. Similarly, it would be interesting to analyze the potential relationship between stakeholder engagement with the company (both familial and not) and the engagement of these same companies to their stakeholders. Qualitative methodologies, based on case studies and interviews with business leaders would be useful here. On the other hand, it would be relevant to examine the impact of social responsibility on the economic, financial, and stock performance of the company, and to identify, where appropriate, recursive causal links between social and financial performance. In the wake of research devoted to family businesses, the avenues opened up by CSR offer promising prospects.

Acknowledgments: The authors thank the VIGEO social responsibility rating agency for its support.

Author Contributions: The authors contributed equally in all aspects of the paper.

Conflicts of Interest: The authors declare no conflict of interest.

References

1. Friedman, M. The Social Responsibility of Business is to Increase its Profits. *New York Times Magazine.* 13 September 1970.
2. Lee, M.P.D. A review of the theories of corporate social responsibility: Its evolutionary path and the road ahead. *Int. J. Manag. Rev.* **2008**, *10*, 53–73. [CrossRef]
3. Bowen, H.R. *Social Responsibilities of the Businessman*; Harper: New York, NY, USA, 1953.
4. Jones, T.M. Corporate social responsibility revisited, redefined. *Calif. Manag. Rev.* **1980**, *22*, 59–67. [CrossRef]
5. Wartick, S.L.; Cochran, P.L. The evolution of the corporate social performance model. *Acad. Manag. Rev.* **1985**, *10*, 758–769.
6. Wood, D.J. Corporate Social Performance Revisited. *Acad. Manag. J.* **1991**, *16*, 691–718.
7. Blair, M. *Ownership and Control: Rethinking Corporate Governance for the Twenty First Century*; The Bookings Institution: Washington, DC, USA, 1996.
8. McWilliams, A.; Siegel, D. Corporate social responsibility: A theory of the firm perspective. *Acad. Manag. Rev.* **2001**, *26*, 117–127.
9. Margolis, J.D.; Walsh, J.P. Misery loves companies: Rethinking social initiatives by business. *Adm. Sci. Q.* **2003**, *48*, 268–305. [CrossRef]
10. Makni, G.R.; Francoeur, C.; Bellavance, F. Causality between Corporate Social Performance and Financial Performance: Evidence from Canadian firms. *J. Bus. Ethics* **2009**, *89*, 409–422. [CrossRef]
11. De la Cruz Déniz Déniz, M.; Cabrera Suarez, K. Corporate Social Responsibility and Family Business in Spain. *J. Bus. Ethics* **2005**, *56*, 27–41. [CrossRef]
12. Dyer, W.G.; Whetten, D.A. Family Firms and Social Responsibility. *Entrep. Theory Pract.* **2006**, *30*, 785–802. [CrossRef]
13. Bingham, J.B.; Dyer, G.D.; Smith, I.; Adams, G.L. A Stakeholder Identity Orientation Approach to Corporate Social Performance in Family Firms. *J. Bus. Ethics* **2011**, *99*, 565–585. [CrossRef]
14. Sharma, P.; Chrisman, J.J.; Chua, J.H. *A Review and Annotated Bibliography of Family Business Studies*; Kluwer Academic Publishers: Assinippi Park, MA, USA, 1996.
15. Neubauer, F.; Lank, A. *The Family Business*; McMillan Business: London, UK, 1998.
16. La Porta, R.; Lopez-de-Silanes, F.; Shleifer, A. Corporate ownership around the world. *J. Financ.* **1999**, *54*, 471–518. [CrossRef]
17. Faccio, M.; Lang, L. The ultimate ownership of Western European Corporations. *J. Financ. Econ.* **2002**, *65*, 365–395. [CrossRef]
18. Morck, R.; Yeung, B. Family control and the rent-seeking society. *Entrep. Theory Pract.* **2004**, *28*, 391–409. [CrossRef]

19. Anderson, R.C.; Reeb, D.M. Founding Family Ownership and Firm Performance: Evidence from the SandP 500. *J. Financ.* **2003**, *58*, 1301–1328.
20. PricewaterhouseCoopers. L'entreprise Familiale, un Modèle Durable. Family Business Survey—France. Available online: http://www.pwc.com/gx/en/pwc-family-business-survey/assets/FBS_2010_11_FR.pdf (accessed on 15 June 2014).
21. Gomez-Mejia, L.R.; Cruz, C.; Berrone, P.; DeCastro, J. The bind that ties: Socioemotional wealth preservation in family firms. *Acad. Manag. Ann.* **2012**, *5*, 1–79.
22. Berrone, P.; Cruz, C.C.; Gómez-Mejía, L.R. Socioemotional wealth in family firms: A review and agenda for future research. *Fam. Bus. Rev.* **2012**, *25*, 258–279. [CrossRef]
23. Cennamo, C.; Berrone, P.; Cruz, C.; Gomez-Mejia, L.R. Socioemotional Wealth and Proactive Stakeholder Engagement: Why Family-Controlled Firms Care More About Their Stakeholders. *Entrep. Theory Pract.* **2012**, 1153–1173.
24. Miller, D.; le Breton-Miller, I.; Lester, R.H. Family firm governance, strategic conformity and performance: Institutional *versus* strategic perspectives. *Organ. Sci.* **2012**, *24*, 189–209. [CrossRef]
25. Gomez-Mejía, L.R.; Haynes, K.T.; Núñez-Nickel, M.; Jacobson, K.J.L.; Moyano-Fuentes, H. Socioemotional wealth and business risk in family-controlled firms: Evidence from Spanish olive oil mills. *Adm. Sci. Q.* **2007**, *52*, 106–137.
26. Wiseman, R.M.; Gomez-Mejia, L.R. A Behavioral Agency Model of Managerial Risk Taking. *Acad. Manag. Rev.* **1998**, *23*, 133–153.
27. Lee, L. Social Responsibility and Economic Performance: An Empirical Examination of Corporate Profiles. Ph.D. Dissertation, US Alliant International University, San Diego, CA, USA, 1987.
28. Preston, L.; Post, J. *Private Management and Public Policy*; Prentice Hall: Upper Saddle River, NJ, USA, 1975.
29. Aguilera, R.V.; Rupp, D.E.; Williams, C.A.; Ganapathi, J. Putting the S back in corporate social responsibility: A multilevel theory of social change in organizations. *Acad. Manag. Rev.* **2007**, *32*, 836–863. [CrossRef]
30. Waddock, S.A. Parallel universes: Companies, academics, and the progress of corporate citizenship. *Bus. Soc. Rev.* **2004**, *109*, 5–42. [CrossRef]
31. Post, J. *Corporate Behavior and Change*; Reston Publishing Company: Reston, VA, USA, 1978.
32. DeFillipi, R.J. Conceptual Framework and Strategies for Corporate Social Involvement Research. In *Research in Corporate Social Performance and Policy*; JAI Press: Greenwich, CT, USA, 1982.
33. Freeman, R.E. *Strategic Management: A Stakeholder Approach*; Cambridge University Press: Cambridge, UK, 1984.
34. Longo, M.; Mura, M.; Bonoli, A. Corporate Social Responsibility and Corporate Performance: The Case of Italian SMEs. *Corp. Gov.* **2005**, *5*, 28–42. [CrossRef]
35. Abreu, R.; David, F.; Crowther, D. Corporate Social Responsibility in Portugal Empirical Evidence of Corporate Behavior. *Corp. Gov.* **2005**, *5*, 3–18. [CrossRef]
36. Uhlaner, L.M.; van Goor-Balk, A.; Masurel, E. Family Business and Corporate Social Responsibility in a Sample of Dutch Firms. *J. Small Bus. Enterp. Dev.* **2004**, *11*, 186–194. [CrossRef]
37. Papasolomou-Doukakis, I.; Krambia-Kapardis, M.; Katsioloudes, M. Corporate Social Responsibility: The Way Forward? Maybe Not! *Eur. Bus. Rev.* **2005**, *17*, 263–279. [CrossRef]
38. Sharma, S. Managerial interpretations and organizational context as predictors of corporate choice of environmental strategy. *Acad. Manag. Rev.* **2000**, *43*, 681–697. [CrossRef]
39. Mitchell, R.K.; Agle, B.R.; Wood, D.J. Toward a Theory of Stakeholder Identification and Salience: Defining the Principle of Who and What really Counts. *Acad. Manag. Rev.* **1997**, *22*, 853–886.
40. Mitchell, R.K.; Agle, B.R.; Chrisman, J.J.; Spence, L.J. Toward a Theory of Stakeholder Salience in Family Firms. *Bus. Ethics Q.* **2011**, *21*, 235–255. [CrossRef]
41. Chrisman, J.J.; Chua, J.H.; Steier, L. Sources and Consequences of Distinctive Familiness: An introduction. *Entrep. Theory Pract.* **2005**, *29*, 237–247. [CrossRef]
42. Pearson, A.W.; Carr, J.C.; Shaw, J.C. Toward a Theory of Familiness: A Social Capital Perspective. *Entrep. Theory Pract.* **2008**, *32*, 949–969. [CrossRef]
43. Gomez-Mejia, L.; Makri, M.; Larraza Kintana, M. Diversification decisions in Family-Controlled Firms. *J. Manag. Stud.* **2010**, *47*, 223–252. [CrossRef]
44. Zellweger, T.M.; Nason, R.S. A Stakeholder Perspective on Family Firm Performance. *Fam. Bus. Rev.* **2008**, *21*, 203–216. [CrossRef]

45. Berrone, P.; Cruz, C.C.; Gómez-Mejía, L.R.; Larraza Kintana, M. Socioemotional wealth and corporate responses to institutional pressures: Do family-controlled firms pollute less. *Adm. Sci. Q.* **2010**, *55*, 82–113. [CrossRef]
46. Kets De Vries, M.F.R. The Entrepreneurial Personality: A Person at the Cross Roads. *J. Manag. Stud.* **1977**, *14*, 34–57. [CrossRef]
47. Schein, E.H. The role of the founder in creating organizational culture. *Organ. Dyn.* **1983**, *12*, 13–28. [CrossRef]
48. Dyer, W.G., Jr. *Cultural Change in Family Firms: Anticipating and Managing Business and Family Transitions*; Jossey-Bass: San Francisco, CA, USA, 1986.
49. Chrisman, J.J.; Sharma, P.; Taggar, S. Family influences on family businesses: An introduction. *J. Bus. Res.* **2007**, *60*, 1005–1011. [CrossRef]
50. Westhead, P.; Cowling, M.; Howarth, C. The development of family companies: Management and ownership imperatives. *Fam. Bus. Rev.* **2001**, *14*, 369–382.
51. Brickson, S.L. Organizational identity orientation: Forging a link between organizational identity and organizations relations with stakeholders. *Adm. Sci. Q.* **2005**, *50*, 576–609.
52. Baron, R.A. The role of affect in the entrepreneurial process. *Acad. Manag. Rev.* **2008**, *33*, 328–340. [CrossRef]
53. Jiao, Y. Stakeholder Welfare and Firm Value. *J. Bank. Fin.* **2010**, *34*, 2549–2561. [CrossRef]
54. McGuire, J.; Dow, S.; Dow, S. All in the Family? Social Performance and Corporate Governance in the Family Firm. *J. Bus. Res.* **2012**, *65*, 1643–1650. [CrossRef]
55. Fombrun, C.J. *Reputation: Realizing Value from the Corporate Image*; Harvard University Press: Cambridge, UK, 1996.
56. Tagiuri, R.; Davis, J.A. Bivalent Attributes of the Family Firm. *Fam. Bus. Rev.* **1996**, *9*, 199–208.
57. Chami, R. *Whats Different About Family Businesses?* IMF Working Paper IMF WP 01/70. Available online: http://www.imf.org/external/pubs/ft/wp/2001/wp0170.pdf (accessed on 2 January 2014).
58. Bourdieu, P. The Forms of Capital. In *Handbook of Theory and Research for the Sociology of Education*; Richardson, J.G., Ed.; Greenwood: New York, NY, USA, 1986; pp. 241–258.
59. Nahapiet, J.; Ghoshal, S. Social Capital, Intellectual Capital, and the Organizational Advantage. *Acad. Manag. Rev.* **1998**, *23*, 242–266.
60. Lyman, A.R. Customer service: Does family ownership make a difference? *Fam. Bus. Rev.* **1991**, *4*, 303–324.
61. Ward, J.L.; Aronoff, C.E. Trust gives you the advantage. *Nations Bus.* **1991**, *79*, 42–45.
62. Whetten, D.A.; Mackey, A. *An Identity-Congruence Explanation of Why firms Would Consistently Engage in Corporate Social Performance*; Working Paper; Brigham Young University: Provo, UT, USA, 2005.
63. Hogg, M.A. Social Identity. In *Handbook of Self and Identity*; Leary, M.R., Tangney, J.P., Eds.; Guilford Press: New York, NY, USA, 2003; pp. 462–479.
64. Hogg, M.A.; Terry, D.J. *Social Identity Processes in Organizational Contexts*; Psychology Press: Philadelphia, PA, USA, 2001.
65. Albert, S.; Whetten, D.A. *Organizational Identity*; Cummings, L.L., Staw, B.I.M., Eds.; Research in Organizational Behavior; JAI Press: Greenwich, CT, USA, 1985; Volume 7; pp. 263–295.
66. Sirmon, D.G.; Hitt, M.A. Managing Resources: Linking Unique Resources, Management, and Wealth Creation in Family Firms. *Entrep. Theory Pract.* **2003**, *27*, 339–358. [CrossRef]
67. Sloan, P. Engagement des dirigeants envers les parties prenantes: Condition de succès du développement durable. *Gest* **2009**, *1*, 79–88.
68. Jamali, D. A Fresh Perspective into Theory and Practice. *J. Bus. Ethics* **2008**, *82*, 213–231.
69. Jamali, D.; Safieddine, A.M.; Rabbath, M. Corporate Governance and Corporate Social Responsibility Synergies and Interrelationships. *Corp. Gov.* **2008**, *16*, 443–459.
70. Koiranen, M. Over 100 years of Age but Still Entrepreneurially Active in Business: Exploring the Values and Family Characteristics of Old Finnish Family Firms. *Fam. Bus. Rev.* **2002**, 175–188.
71. Aronoff, C. Self-Perpetuation Family Organization Built on Values: Necessary Condition for Long-Term Family Business Survival. *Fam. Bus. Rev.* **2004**, *17*, 55–59.
72. Tagiuri, R.; Davis, J. On the goals of successful family businesses. *Fam. Bus. Rev.* **1992**, *5*, 43–62.
73. Allouche, J.; Amann, B. La confiance, une explication aux performances des entreprises familiales. *Econ. Soc.* **1998**, *25*, 129–154.
74. Steier, L.; Family firms. Plural forms of governance, and the evolving role of trust. *Fam. Bus. Rev.* **2001**, *14*, 353–367.
75. Goffee, R.; Scase, R. Proprietorial Control in Family Firms: Some Functions of Quasi-organic Management Systems. *J. Manag. Stud.* **1985**, *22*, 53–68. [CrossRef]
76. Poza, E.J.; Alfred, T.; Maheshwari, A. Stakeholder Perceptions of Culture and Management Practices in Family and Family Firms—A Preliminary Report. *Fam. Bus. Rev.* **1997**, *10*, 135–155.

77. James, H. Owner as Manager, Extended Horizons and the Family Firm. *Int. J. Econ. Bus.* **1999**, *6*, 41–55. [CrossRef]
78. Hirigoyen, G. Concilier finance et management dans les entreprises familiales. *Revue Française de Gestion* **2009**, *35*, 393–411. (in French). [CrossRef]
79. Monsen, J.R. Ownership and Management: The Effect of Separation on Performance. *Bus. Horiz.* **1969**, *12*, 46–52. [CrossRef]
80. Astrachan, J.H. Family Firm and Community Culture. *Fam. Bus. Rev.* **1988**, *1*, 165–189.
81. Vallejo Martos, M.C.; Grande Torraleja, F.A. Is Family Business More Socially Responsible? The Case of GRUPO CIM. *Bus. Soc. Rev.* **2007**, *112*, 121–136. [CrossRef]
82. Churchill, N.; Hatten, K. Nonmarket-based transfers of wealth and power: A research framework for family business. *Am. J. Small Bus. Manag.* **1987**, *11*, 51–64.
83. Crilly, D.; Zollo, M.; Hansen, M.T. Faking it or Muddling Through? Understanding Decoupling in Response to Stakeholder Pressures. *Acad. Manag. J.* **2012**, *55*, 1429–1448. [CrossRef]
84. Westhead, P.; Cowling, M. Family firm research: The need for a methodological rethink. *Entrep. Theory Pract.* **1998**, *23*, 31–56.
85. Donnelley, R.G. The Family Business. *Harv. Bus. Rev.* **1964**, *42*, 93–105.
86. Barry, B. The Development of Organisation Structure in the Family Firm. *J. Gen. Manag.* **1975**, *3*, 42–60.
87. Beckhard, R.; Dyer, W.G. Managing Change in the Family Firm—Issues and Strategies. *Sloan Manag. Rev.* **1983**, *24*, 59–65.
88. Boswell, J. *The Rise and Decline of Small Firms*; George Allen and Unwin Ltd.: London, UK, 1972.
89. Chrisman, J.J.; Patel, P.C. Variations in R&D Investments of Family and Nonfamily Firms: Behavioral Agency and Myopic Loss Aversion Perspectives. *Acad. Manag. J.* **2012**, *55*, 976–997. [CrossRef]
90. McGuire, J.B.; Sundgren, A.; Schneeweis, T. Corporate social responsibility and firm financial performance. *Acad. Manag. J.* **1988**, *31*, 854–872.
91. Seifert, B.; Morris, S.A.; Bartkus, B.R. Comparing big givers and small givers: Financial correlates of corporate philanthropy. *J. Bus. Ethics* **2003**, *45*, 195–211. [CrossRef]
92. Sraer, D.; Thesmar, D. Performance and behaviour of family firms: Evidence from the French stock market. *J. Europ. Econ. Assoc.* **2007**, *5*, 709–751. [CrossRef]
93. Villalonga, B.; Amit, R. How do family ownership, control and management affect firm value? *J. Financ. Econ.* **2006**, *80*, 385–417. [CrossRef]
94. La Porta, R.; Lopez-de-Silanes, F.; Shleifer, A.; Vishny, A. Legal determinants of external finance. *J. Financ.* **1997**, *52*, 1131–1150. [CrossRef]
95. Aoki, M. *The Cooperative Game Theory of the Firm*; Oxford University Press: Oxford, UK, 1984.
96. Uhlaner, L.M.; Berent-Braun, M.M.; Jeurissen, R.J.M.; de Wit, G. Beyond Size: Predicting Engagement in Environmental Management Practices for Dutch SMEs. *J. Bus. Ethics* **2012**, *109*, 411–429. [CrossRef]
97. Block, J.H.; Wagner, M. The Effect of Family Ownership on Different Dimensions of Corporate Social Responsibility: Evidence from Large US Firms. *Bus. Strategy Environ.* **2013**. [CrossRef]
98. Sharma, P.; Sharma, S. Drivers of Proactive Environmental Strategy in Family Firms. *Bus. Ethics Q.* **2011**, *21*, 309–334.
99. Ward, J.L. *Creating Effective Boards for Private Enterprise*; Jossey-Bass Publishers: San Francisco, CA, USA, 1991.
100. Kellermanns, F.W.; Eddleston, K.A.; Zellweger, T.M. Extending the Socioemotional Wealth Perspective: A Look at the Dark Side. *Entrep. Theory Pract.* **2012**, *36*, 347–367. [CrossRef]
101. Forgas, J.P. Mood and judgment: The affect infusion model. *Psychol. Bull.* **1995**, *117*, 39–66. [CrossRef]
102. Loewenstein, G.; Adler, D. A bias in the prediction of tastes. *Econ. J.* **1995**, *105*, 929–937. [CrossRef]
103. Mahérault, L. Comportement financier des entreprises familiales: Approche empirique. *Economies et Sociétés* **1999**, *33*, 247–272. (in French).
104. Bhattacharya, U.; Ravikumar, B. *Capital Markets and Evolution of Family Businesses*; Working Paper Series; Indiana University, Kelley School of Business: Indianapolis, IN, USA, 1999.
105. Basco, R.; Perez Rodriguez, M.J. Ideal Types of Family Business Management: Horizontal Fit between Family and Business Decisions and the Relationship with Family Business Performance. *J. Fam. Bus. Strategy* **2011**, *2*, 151–165. [CrossRef]
106. Xiao, J.; Alhabeeb, M.; Hong, G.; Haynes, G. Attitude Toward Risk and Risk-Taking Behavior of Business-Owning Families. *J. Consum. Aff.* **2001**, *35*, 307–325. [CrossRef]

107. Schulze, W.S.; Lubatkin, M.H.; Dino, R.N. Toward a Theory of Agency and Altruism in Family Firms. *J. Bus. Ventur.* **2003**, *18*, 473–490. [CrossRef]

108. Habbershon, T.G.; Williams, M.; MacMillan, I.C. A unified systems perspective of family firm performance. *J. Bus. Ventur.* **2003**, *18*, 451–465. [CrossRef]

109. Hirigoyen, G. Biais comportementaux dans l'entreprise familiale: Antécédents et impacts. *Economies et Sociétés* **2008**, *19*, 1901–1930. (in French).

110. O'Boyle, E.; Pollack, J.M.; Rutherford, M. Exploring the Relation between Family Involvment and Firms Performance: A Meta-Analysis of Main and Moderator Effects. *J. Bus. Ventur.* **2012**, *27*, 1–18. [CrossRef]

111. Charreaux, G.; Pitol-Belin, J.P. *Le Conseil D'administration*; Vuibert: Paris, France, 1990. (in French)

112. Anderson, R.C.; Reeb, D.M. Board Composition: Balancing Family Influence in S&P 500 Firms. *Adm. Sci. Q.* **2004**, *49*, 209–237.

113. Chau, G.; Leung, P. The Impact of Board Composition and Family Ownership on Audit Committee Formation: Evidence from Hong Kong. *J. Int. Account. Audit. Tax.* **2006**, *15*, 1–15. [CrossRef]

114. Wernerfelt, B. A Resource-Based View of the Firm. *Strat. Manag. J.* **1984**, *5*, 171–180.

115. Bammens, Y.; Voordeckers, W.; van Gils, A. Boards of Directors in Family Businesses: A Literature Review and Research Agenda. *Int. J. Manag. Rev.* **2011**, *13*, 134–152. [CrossRef]

116. Habbershon, T.G.; Williams, M.L. A resource-based framework for assessing the strategic advantages of family firms. *Fam. Bus. Rev.* **1999**, *12*, 1–26.

International Journal of
Financial Studies

MDPI

Article

Socio Emotional Wealth Preservation in the REIT Industry: An Exploratory Study

Magdy Noguera [1,*] **and Erick Paulo Cesar Chang** [2]

1   College of Business and Economics, University of Idaho, P.O Box 3161, Moscow, ID 83843-3161, USA
2   Department of Management and Marketing, College of Business, Arkansas State University, PO Box 59, State University, AR 72467, USA; echang@astate.edu
*   Author to whom correspondence should be addressed; mnoguera@uidaho.edu; Tel.: +1-(208)-885-6204.

Received: 4 May 2014; in revised form: 20 June 2014; Accepted: 23 June 2014; Published: 2 July 2014

Abstract: Our study uses the Socio Emotional Wealth Perspective (SEW) to test our contention that Real Estate Investment Trust (REIT) founders are more inclined to satisfy first their non-economic goals rather than satisfying the economic goals of REIT shareholders. We test our hypotheses with an unbalanced panel dataset that includes an average of 66 publicly-traded equity REITs from 1999–2012 that produced 921 REIT-year observations. Our exploratory results provide evidence of SEW preservation as REITs led by founders' successors tend to underperform; however, the family identification with the REIT affects performance positively. This is one of the first studies that merge the REIT and the family business streams of research. Future directions are suggested.

Keywords: REIT; socio emotional wealth; succession; family identification

JEL Classification: G29; G38

1. Introduction

The Socio Emotional Wealth perspective (SEW) (Gomez-Mejia *et al.* [1]) represents an emerging stream of family business literature that aims to explain why family controlled firms engage in behavioral activities that place emphasis on the attainment of non-economic goals over the economic ones. Studies that have explored theoretical explanations (e.g., Berrone *et al.* [2]) and provided empirical results (e.g., Berrone *et al.* [3]; Gomez-Mejia *et al.* [4]; Naldi *et al.* [5]) argue that the preservation of socio emotional endowments separate the governance of family controlled firms from those who are run by professional managers or have their ownership dispersed without a dominant coalition aligned with particular kinship ties. Although the incidence of family controlled firms tends to dominate different industries worldwide (Morck and Young [6]; La Porta *et al.* [7]), the economic implications of preserving socio emotional endowments to satisfy non-economic aspirations may affect stakeholders who are just looking to satisfy their own economic goals by acting as passive investors while seeking to attain their non-economic goals in other domains (Chrisman *et al.* [8]; Kellermanns *et al.* [9]; Berrone *et al.* [10]). Put differently, SEW preservation may drive a family to pursue a "self-serving behavior" [9] (p. 1179) that may even create liabilities when family members are in charge of running the firm (Naldi *et al.* [5]).

In the case of the Real Estate Investment Trusts (REITs), recent findings tend to call to attention that founder CEOs exert particular control over their boards, compromising their independence and effectiveness and in turn, REITs' performance (Noguera [11]). Even though REITs represent a particular investment vehicle that must pay significant dividends out to their shareholders and are believed to have strong corporate governance practices, many are still under the control of their founders or their founders' families (Ghosh *et al.* [12]; Noguera [11]). Particularly, a typical REIT is created from a family owning some valuable real estate properties. Subsequently, the REIT status is acquired as a growth strategy by the family who will later decide to list it in a stock exchange as a potential exit strategy for the family or as an investment vehicle that becomes available to other investors. Furthermore, the founding family not only reaps the benefit of making hard assets become liquid but also retains managerial control over the properties. As a result, it is reasonable to expect performance variances when founders and their family are capable of controlling and governing the REIT even with the presence of outsiders in the board of directors to comply with current regulations (Coates [13]; Duchin *et al.* [14]; Valenti [15]).

Our purpose in this paper is to engage in exploratory analysis of the most recent results in the REIT industry and provide some explanations that are rooted in the SEW perspective. We consider that the family plays an important role in the REIT industry in at least two aspects. First, we argue that REITs founders will focus more on preserving their socio emotional endowment on behalf of the family than on satisfying the performance demands of their primary stakeholders (in this case, their own REIT investors). Second, the founder's preference for choosing direct descendants to become the next REIT CEO and even chair of the board of directors implies the attainment of non-economic goals that may affect the REIT performance. In that regard, our arguments imply that the corporate governance mechanisms that pertain to REITs do not diverge significantly from those found in other industries where family-controlled firms provide a particular and unique approach to other types of organizational forms (Carney [16]; La Porta *et al.* [7]; Morck and Young [6]). To test our contentions, we engage in a series of exploratory analysis with an average sample of 66 publicly-traded equity REITs for the 1999–2012 period that resulted in 921 REIT-year observations.

Our results offer support to our theoretical developments and provide an initial understanding for why certain REITs led by direct descendants of the founders underperform other REITs led by either professional managers after succeeding the REIT founder or REITs led by their founders. Moreover, our results show evidence about the positive impact on performance when the founder uses the family name to identify the REIT. In addition, we encountered that family name and the presence of a successor moderate the relationship between ownership and control of the dominant family and performance. As a result, our empirical evidence supports our contention about the prevalence of non-economic goals in an industry that is heavily regulated (e.g., Internal Revenue Services [17]) and expected to perform above the average market returns for its investors. In that manner, our study provides a useful contribution that goes beyond the domain of the family business literature but also as an initial explanation to enhance the investigation of the dynamics surrounding REIT governance, management, and performance.

In the remainder of the paper, we proceed as follows. First, we develop our theoretical framework to set our hypotheses. Second, we provide our methodology and data analysis. Third, we present and discuss our empirical results. Fourth, we conclude with future directions for research and managerial implications.

2. Theory and Hypotheses

In their seminal piece about Spanish olive oil mills, Gomez-Mejia *et al.* [4] started to study the utilities that family owners attain from non-economic aspects to develop SEW or affective endowments that preserve the long run operation of the firms. These authors built behavioral agency models (Wiseman and Gomez-Mejia [18]) to argue that family owners will set a frame of reference in the management of the firm regardless of potential economic gains or losses. In their view, the attainment of non-economic goals such as the preservation and/or enhancement of the family's dominance in the firm sets them apart from other types of organizations where the lack of kinship ties becomes less relevant. In this situation, socio-emotional wealth can be considered as a unique feature for a family-controlled business because the dominant family-owner will exert a direct influence on everything that the firm does (Gomez-Mejia *et al.* [1]). In contrast, these authors argued, firms that lack certain levels of family influence will establish a clear separation in the relationship between the different stakeholders (e.g., owners, managers, employees) that can be considered transitory, economically-driven, or even individualistic. Put differently, the SEW enhances the interpretation of principal–principal or principal–agent conflicts emanating from the agency theory perspective (e.g., Gedajlovic *et al.* [19]; Gomez-Mejia *et al.* [1]; Wiseman and Gomez-Mejia [18]) because family owners will sacrifice the economic performance of the firm to satisfy their own agenda. This represents a particular phenomenon that drives family firms to rely on stocks of family influence where a self-serving behavior may evolve for focusing on particularistic aspects that will make them reach managerial decisions that do not occur in professional-managed entities so the needs of the controlling family are placed above those of other stakeholders (Kellermanns *et al.* [9]).

In an extended review, Berrone *et al.* [2] argue that SEW captures the owner's desires for exerting the family influence, appointing family members, retaining a strong family identity, or even renewing the intentions for transgenerational succession. As a result, the SEW construct can be considered as a multi-dimensional one where Berrone *et al.* [2] (pp. 262–264) identified it using the acronym FIBER: Family influence and control, Identification of the family members with the firm, Binding social ties, Emotional attachment, and Renewal of family bonds to the firm through dynastic succession. According to Chrisman *et al.* [8], the concept of SEW is also linked to the attainment of non-economic goals by owners and managers because families can accumulate wealth (monetary and non-monetary) in the long run as their long-term orientation may allow them to navigate under short-term periods of uncertainty and environmental turbulence.

2.1. REITs and Family

REITs can be considered as new entrants in the financial services industry where funds are collected from investors (institutional and general public) to invest in real estate properties ("equity REITs") and real estate mortgages or mortgage related securities ("mortgage REITs"). U.S. REITs were created by law in 1960 but really started to grow in the 1990s after the creation of UPREITs (a structure that provides tax deferral benefits and investment diversification to commercial property owners, who exchange ownership of appreciated property for operating partnerships units without immediate tax consequences) and a relaxation of the original rule by the IRS. This rule allowed equity REITs to select investment properties and manage their own assets, basically paving the way for more REITs to become internally rather than externally advised. In the US, REITs are highly regulated by the Securities and Exchange Commission (SEC) [20] and in order to be tax exempted at the federal level, they are required to distribute as dividends at least 90% of their taxable income. In addition, REITs must have a board of directors (trustees), have a dispersed ownership structure where five or fewer individuals can own no more than 50% of the shares, invest at least 75% of its total assets in real estate, and derive 95% of its income from dividends, interests, and property income (US Securities and Exchange Commission [20]; Internal Revenue Services [17]). In that regard, one can assume that the separation of ownership and control provides a balanced situation as REIT shareholders will seek to reap economic benefits and deposit their trust in the REIT managers and directors in their exchanges.

However, outside of the market returns that these investment vehicles will bring to shareholders, the REIT control from founders may resemble the similar scenarios depicted by Carney [16] who argued that family firms tend to be governed by personalism, particularism, and parsimony. Specifically, recent findings by Noguera [11] showed evidence of entrenchment from founder CEOs who use their influence on the structure of REIT boards as they are less independent and those situations result in lower performance when compared against the performance of REITs managed by non-founders. This situation may even sound contradictory as the SEC has exerted market controls since 2002 through the Sarbanes-Oxley Act that requires independent board members to exert control mechanisms on behalf of shareholders (Coates [13]). Consequently, it becomes an empirical question for determining the family effect on the performance of the REIT, and our key premise is that founders are seeking to preserve their socio-emotional endowments. Particularly, our central arguments are aligned with the intentionality of the founder to view the REIT as an extension of themselves and provide a sense of legacy to their family by way of non-economic goals before they can turn their attention to performance (e.g., Gedalojvic *et al.* [19]; Gomez-Mejia *et al.* [1]). In the next subsections, we use the SEW perspective to develop a set of our testable hypotheses. Particularly, we rely on three dimensions of the FIBER framework developed by Berrone *et al.* [2]: family influence and control; family identification; and renewal of family bonds to the firm through dynastic succession.

2.1.1. SEW Preservation and Performance

For preserving SEW, REIT founders may incur in different behaviors that ultimately affects REIT performance. The first one is related to the use of their own family name to identify the REIT. This is very critical for some REITs as they are new entrants in the industry, particularly, the ones trading in the stock exchanges, and need to position themselves in the minds of the general public. Dyer and Whettten [21] argue that carrying the name of the family provides a close link between the family and the firm with the desire of the owner to retain family control inside the firm (Astrachan *et al.* [22]). In their FIBER acronym, Berrone *et al.* [2] explain that the family identity placed on the company name signals to internal and external stakeholders that the family is viewing the firm as an extension of the family domain. Deephouse and Jaskiewicz [23] argue that family members are more invested in the family firm when the family name is part of the business. Particularly, there is a perception held by the family members toward enhancing the reputation of the business and giving a positive image to external stakeholders. In that manner, when REIT founders chose to use their names to identify the REIT, they are selling the notion to the general public of the good reputation of the family, its image, or even the notion of transcending over the long term (Gomez-Mejia *et al.* [1]).

However, using the family name for identifying the REIT cannot only be signaled towards SEW preservation as it creates a hurdle for founders and their directors to perform. For achieving long term stability and survival, the family will also require achieving financial performance thresholds; otherwise, the survival of the REIT will be at stake and the welfare of the family may also be compromised (Gedajlovic *et al.* [19]; Chrisman *et al.* [8]). In that regard, it is expected that attaching the founder's last name as part of enhancing SEW to the REIT will positively affect performance. Consequently:

Hypothesis 1: REIT founders preserve their SEW by using their own family name to positively influence REIT performance.

The second behavior is related to the willingness of the REIT founder to designate a family descendant as successor. From the FIBER acronym, this event represents a renewal by the family to continue its dominance in the firm (Berrone *et al.* [2]). As succession is a central element for characterizing a family firm (Chrisman *et al.* [24]; De Massis *et al.* [25]), designating a family member to become CEO and even Chairman of the REIT implies a commitment to retaining family influence or even meeting particular non-economic goals that satisfy the founder and the family's wishes. Gomez-Mejia *et al.* [1] argue intra-family succession is a fundamental driver for enhancing and preserving SEW as control remains within the family. Especially in the long run, the transfer of the baton to the next generation ensures the family influence and maintains the family identity and reputation (Zellwegger *et al.* [26]). Furthermore, family succession is highly desirable even though the incoming family member may not be the most qualified individual for the position (Cruz *et al.* [27]; De Massis *et al.* [25]). Henceforth, REIT founders count as part of their SEW endowment the future benefits of control by appointing a family successor.

However, SEW preservation in terms of intergenerational succession may imply that appointing family members to lead the REIT will be negatively related to performance. Given the founder's intentions toward preserving SEW; Gomez-Mejia *et al.* [1] argue that such event seeks to create a dynastic succession in the firm where the controlling family is willing to incur an economic cost by pursuing a family candidate. Even though, Jaskiewics and Luchak [28] considered the notion that appointing a non-family CEO is not going to seriously affect the SEW preservation of the family coalition, there is an image and a family commitment toward the CEO position (Berrone *et al.* [2]) that can be consistent with the identification of the family with the business in the long run. In general terms, empirical findings have shown that there is a negative market reaction to family-CEO appointments (Bennedsen *et al.* [29]; Villalonga and Amit [30]). Particularly, one can argue that these results are potential outcomes of principal–principal or principal–agent conflicts that are framed under the agency theory perspective (e.g., Gedajlovic *et al.* [18]) or that owners may exert a stewardship behavior to benefit their offspring as they may consider them to be aligned with the family regardless of their qualifications (e.g., Chrisman *et al.* [31]). [1] Even more, Naldi *et al.* [5] argue that a family CEO is a liability in terms of stock market situations because of the greater difficulty in balancing stakeholders' demands and implementing firm strategies. It can be also understood that a founder CEO will transfer the power to a descendant to perpetuate the family control and influence over the REIT even if this is not in the best economic interest of the firm (Miller *et al.* [32]).

Furthermore, passing the baton to the next generation rather than designating an incoming CEO in terms of professional experience or even competence and knowledge may also result in performance variations (e.g., Chrisman *et al.* [8]). For example, incoming CEOs with no kinship ties to the founders will behave as agents to work on behalf of the REIT shareholders as their level of compensation may be tied to the REIT performance. In contrast, successors taking the CEO position may tie their level of compensation outside of the economic performance as founders seek to maintain first the family influence and expect a sense of stewardship and altruism emanating from such a succession process (e.g., Gedajlovic *et al.* [19]; Hall and Nordqvist [33]). Furthermore, the CEO–Chairman duality tends to be used as a proxy for determining a stewardship characteristic in a family firm although the SEW perspective may also consider this situation as a direct effect of preserving SEW (e.g., Gomez-Mejia *et al.* [1]. In fact, Memili *et al.* [34] provided evidence that family owners are less reluctant to award compensation packages to non-family managers vis-à-vis family managers so a professional CEO (e.g., non-family) will seek to maximize shareholders' value to enhance the prospects of keeping his/her position in the REIT. Consequently, the presence of successors in CEO positions may negatively affect REIT performance and their designation may result in lower performance when compared to REITs that are professionally managed or that are still led by the founder. Thus, our next hypotheses imply that:

Hypothesis 2a: REIT founders preserve their SEW by designating a family member as the REIT CEO and this succession decision is negatively related to REIT performance.

Hypotheses 2b: REITs whose CEOs are descendants of the founder will underperform *versus* (1) those REITs whose CEOs have no family ties to the founder or (2) those that are still run by the REIT founder.

2.1.2. Moderating Effects in Ownership and Control

Our first set of hypotheses implies the contrasting relationships between SEW preservation and performance in terms of two FIBER dimensions: identification and succession (e.g., Berrone *et al.* [2]). We consider that these effects are not isolated from family power dynamics if we incorporate a third FIBER dimension: family influence and control. In that regard, we move a step forward from Berrone *et al.* [2] SEW conceptualization by stating that identification and succession will moderate the relationship between (a) family influence and control and (b) performance. Naldi *et al.* [5] argue that family ownership in a firm represents one way for preserving SEW because the family may also hold a significant proportion of voting power toward strategic decisions. Sometimes, such strategic decisions like engaging in transferring power to family successors may come at the expense of non-family

---

[1] It is important to note that agency theory or even the stewardship perspective may also present a competing theoretical framework to build these hypotheses. Please see Chrisman *et al.* [31] for a comparison and empirical tests of the agency versus stewardship theories in family firms. However, recent reviews of the family business literature (e.g., Gedajlovi *et al.* [19]) and SEW (e.g., Berrone *et al.* [2]; Gomez-Mejia *et al.* [1]) offered a more updated information to frame these relationships. However, it is out of the scope of this paper to provide theoretical and/or empirical developments to compare the SEW against agency and/or stewardship situations. We invite researchers to extend on this consideration, not only on the REIT literature but also on the mainstream family business literature.

shareholders (Morck and Young [6]). Even the potential controls exerted by independent directors may be diminished because the ownership concentration by the founder or his/her descendants may give the family unrestricted power (Jones *et al.* [35]). Even in general terms, outsiders are a minority in family firms' boards (Gersick *et al.* [36]) and oftentimes the CEO is also the chairperson of the board (Voordeckers *et al.* [37]). Especially, before the Sarbanex-Oxley Act, about one-third of the largest publicly traded companies in the U.S. where founding families exerted control of about 20% of board seats (Shleiffer and Vishny [38]). Noguera [39] found that after the Sarbanes-Oxley Act, a higher number of outside directors are sitting on REIT boards and fewer CEOs chair their boards, the latter because of SOX. However, her 2014 study [11] still found a significant prevalence of REITs founders who are not only the CEO but also the Chair of the board. Similar situations have been reported in other large companies that may question the effectiveness of independent directors (e.g., Duchin *et al.* [14]; Valenti [15]) due to the passing of the act. Furthermore, as the family controlling the REIT via the founder's successor, it is possible that the existence of outside directors may also be used to comply with regulations. However, as the board is chaired by a family member or even the ownership lies also in the family, there is an explicit indication about the influence from the family over the main strategic directions that the REIT may take.

As a result, we foresee that founders' SEW preservation moderates the relationship between ownership and control and REIT performance. Particularly, the REIT founder exerted a direct influence by naming the REIT after the family and designating a family member to become the next CEO. Hence, we formalize our hypotheses in this manner:

Hypotheses 3a: The relationship between ownership and REIT performance is negatively moderated by the presence of a founder's successor as CEO.
Hypotheses 3b: The relationship between control and REIT performance is negatively moderated by the presence of a founder's successor as CEO.
Hypotheses 4a: The relationship between ownership and REIT performance is positively moderated by the founder's use of the family name.
Hypotheses 4b: The relationship between control and REIT performance is positively moderated by the founder's use of the family name.

3. Methodology

3.1. Sample and Data

We collected equity REITs' financial data from Bloomberg, board data from proxy statements, and family and company information from secondary sources such as funding universe.com, Businessweek.com, Forbes.com, or the respective REITs' websites. The initial sample consisted of 1469 equity REIT-years (an average of 105 unique equity REITs per year, which represented 75% of the average number of equity REITs for the 1999–2012 period, in accordance with the NAREIT website, as last accessed on March 25, 2014. From the initial sample, 435 REIT-years were dropped due to missing either founder data or board data; 113 REIT-years were dropped because Bloomberg did not have the required financial variables for the analysis. The final unbalanced panel dataset includes 921 REIT-year observations, an average of 66 unique equity REITs per year. Table 1 shows a frequency distribution of the REITs identified as having a level of family influence from 1999–2012. The level of influence was determined if the REIT CEO is either the founder or the successor. The table is showing a decline in the frequency of these REITs starting in 2002 and reaching its minimum by 2008. Two particular explanations can be given to this decline: (a) the increase in mergers and acquisitions that has led to some level of consolidation in the REIT industry from 2006–2008; and (b) the number of founder CEOs who reached the retirement age and chose a non-kin descendant (e.g., professional manager) as the new CEO.

Table 1. Time series distribution of family sponsored Real Estate Investment Trusts (REITs).

Year	Family Influenced REITs *	All REITs in the Sample	Frequency (%)
1999	43	71	60.6
2000	46	75	61.3
2001	47	78	60.3
2002	41	70	58.6
2003	38	71	53.5
2004	34	68	50.0
2005	34	69	49.3
2006	28	56	50.0
2007	21	53	39.6
2008	18	46	39.1
2009	24	60	40.0
2010	27	68	39.7
2011	27	70	38.6
2012	28	69	40.6

* Led by founders or descendants of the founders.

3.2. Variables Description

For our dependent variable, performance, we use the return on assets calculated as the ratio of funds from operations to total assets, from Bloomberg data. Our set of independent variables includes three dummy variables to indicate if the last name of the founder is used to name the REIT (Family Name), if the CEO is a family successor of the founder (Family Successor as CEO), and if the CEO is also the chairman of the board (CEO Chairman). Ownership was measured in terms of the percentage of shares owned by the CEO (CEO Ownership). Our underlying assumption is that the CEO ownership will also be highly correlated with the family ownership as the founder will be transferring the shares to avoid potential sibling rivalry. In that regard, we only consider succession events (from founder-CEO to a family descendant) that occur during 1999–2012; thus, we are unable to identify those CEOs who may be part of a second or third generation of a particular family. In terms of unique REITs, 11 use the founder's last name (16.67%) and 13 family successors are acting as CEOs (19.70%). In terms of year-observations, the proportions are 12.8% and 10.64%, respectively. To identify the REIT family successors as CEOs, we relied on proxy statements or websites such as funding universe.com, Businessweek.com, Forbes.com, or the respective REITs website. Still, our sample shows evidence that a significant number of REITs, relative to non-REITs, are led by their founders during the sample period: 48 founders are still acting as CEOs (41.7%), and they represent almost 39% of the firm-year observations.

We controlled by using the natural log of firm age (Firm Age (Ln)) and firm size (Firm Size (Ln)); the proportion of debt to assets (Debt to Asset Ratio); and the proportion of outsiders on the board of directors (Outside Directors). Table 2 summarizes the variables description and its data source.

Table 2. Variable Descriptions.

Variable	Description	Source
Return on Assets	The ratio of funds from operations to total assets	Bloomberg
Firm Age (Ln)	The natural log of the number of years since the REIT initial public offering date (or the incorporation date if IPO date could not be found) purposes	Ambrose and Linneman [40], or Proxy Statement, or funding universe, yahoo finance or other website
Firm Size (Ln)	The natural log of REITs' total assets	Bloomberg
Debt to Asset Ratio	The ratio of debt to total assets	Bloomberg
Outside Directors	The proportion of outsides in the board of directors	Proxy Statement
CEO Ownership	Percentage of shares owned by the CEO	Proxy Statement
CEO Chairman	Dummy variable that equals one if the CEO chairs the board and zero otherwise	Proxy Statement
Family Successor as CEO	Dummy variable that equals one if the CEO of the firm is a descendant of the founder and zero otherwise	Proxy Statement or web sources (REIT website, funding universe, Business Week, Forbes)
Family Name	Dummy variable that equals one if the last name of the founder is used to name the REIT	Proxy Statement or web sources (REIT website, funding universe, Business Week, Forbes)

3.3. Data Analysis

We use SAS to run moderated ordinary least squares (OLS) regressions following Baron and Kenny [41]. Particularly, we followed McGrath's [42] suggestion to test moderation effects in separate models. Because of the nature of the data and the presence of interaction effects, we centered the independent variables to reduce potential concerns of multi-collinearity (Cohen and Cohen [43]; Tabachnick *et al.* [44]). However, we consider our regression results to be exploratory in nature as we were unable to attain statistical consistency in our results (signs were consistent though) when we performed panel data analyses with all our variables (independent, controls, and interactions). Results for the panel data analyses are omitted as we used them for robustness tests only.

4. Results

Tables 3 and 4 present the descriptive statistics and correlations of the variables that we used in our regression analysis before the independent variables were centered to create the interactions. The average REIT in the sample has a market capitalization of $6.5 billion, has been around for 14 years, has 71% of outsiders in the board of directors, a 43.81% leverage ratio, and 4.61% return on assets. In addition, CEOs own on average 5.66% of the REIT and 51% are also the chairman of the board. The highest bi-variate correlations ($p < 0.001$) occurred between Firm Size (Ln) and Firm Age (Ln) (-0.37); CEO Ownership and Family Name (0.33).

Table 5 provides means and medians of 10 variables from a panel of two CEO groups: (a) Family successor as CEO and (b) Non-family CEO. The table provides evidence that REITs led by successor CEOs are newer but bigger, and with higher leverage as in the case of founder CEOs (Ghosh *et al.* [12]). The successor CEO himself is younger, but with longer tenure and higher share ownership in newer REITs, compared to his counterparts. Unlike the case for founder CEOs (e.g., Noguera [11]),

CEO–chairman duality is not prevalent for the case of successors as the difference in means is not statistically significant. However, there is still evidence of successors' power over their boards as the successors coexist with a bigger board but are not as independent (as measured by a lower percentage of outsiders sitting on those boards) as in the case of REITs whose CEO has no ties with a family coalition.

Table 3. Descriptive Statistics.

Descriptive Statistics	Number	Mean	SD	Min	Max
Firm Age (Ln)	921	2.62	0.66	0.00	3.99
Firm Size (Ln)	921	22.60	1.42	18.57	26.28
Debt to Asset Ratio %	921	43.81	21.07	0.00	1.04
Outside Directors %	921	71.00	11.49	37.50	93.33
CEO Ownership %	921	5.66	10.03	0.00	79.13
CEO Chairman	921	0.51	0.50	0.00	1.00
Family Successor as CEO	921	0.11	0.31	0.00	1.00
Family Name	921	0.13	0.33	0.00	1.00
Return on Assets	921	4.61	5.00	−58.11	45.83

$+ p < 0.10$; $* p < 0.05$; $** p < 0.01$; $*** p < 0.001$.

Table 4. Correlations Matrix.

	1	2	3	4	5	6	7	8
1. Firm Age (Ln)	1.00							
2. Firm Size (Ln)	−0.37 ***	1.00						
3. Debt to Asset Ratio	−0.23 ***	0.17 ***	1.00					
4. Outside Directors	0.14 ***	0.05	−0.19 ***	1.00				
5. CEO Ownership	0.01	−0.10 **	0.24 ***	−0.19 ***	1.00			
6. CEO Chairman	−0.02	−0.01	0.09 **	−0.03	0.32 ***	1.00		
7. Family Successors as CEO	−0.08 **	0.03	0.01	−0.04	−0.06	−0.09 **	1.00	
8. Family Name	−0.06 +	−0.11 ***	0.16 ***	−0.04	0.33 ***	0.14 ***	0.19 ***	1.00
9. Return on Assets	0.13 ***	−0.16 ***	−0.21 ***	−0.02	−0.05	−0.04	−0.07 *	0.12 ***

$N = 921$; $+ p < 0.10$; $* p < 0.05$; $** p < 0.01$; $*** p < 0.001$.

Table 5. Descriptive Statistics Given CEO Profile.

Variable	Family Successor as CEO		Non-family CEO		
	N = 98		N = 465		
	Mean	Median	Mean	Median	p-value
Firm Size (Ln)	22.74	22.37	22.59	22.63	
Debt to Asset Ratio %	44.15	48.77	40.48	45.11	+
Firm Age (Ln)	2.47	2.48	2.79	2.83	***
CEO Age	50.05	50.00	53.19	53.00	***
CEO tenure	8.26	8.00	6.98	6.00	*
CEO Ownership %	4.20	2.61	2.97	0.92	*
Board Size	9.00	9.00	8.55	8.00	*
Outside Directors %	69.78	70.71	72.72	75.00	**
CEO chair	0.38	0.00	0.31	0.00	
Return on Assets %	3.63	3.74	4.96	4.64	*

$+ p < 0.10$; $* p < 0.05$; $** p < 0.01$; $*** p < 0.001$.

Table 6 presents the results of the regression models used to test the hypotheses. Model 1 entered the set of control and independent variables. Models 2–5 included one interaction effect. Model 6 includes all the variables and the interactions. The adjusted R^2 of the models ranged from 0.07 in Model 1 to 0.10 in Model 6. The set of control variables has significant influence on performance at the

0.05 level or better. Firm Age (Ln) was positively related while Firm Size (Ln), Debt to Asset Ratio, and Outside Directors were negatively related to performance.

Model 1 provides evidence to support H1 and H2a as both the Family Name and the Family Successor as CEO are significant at the 0.05 level and in the hypothesized directions. In that manner, the model provides evidence of SEW preservation by the founder that influences REIT performance.

To test H2b, we ran a t-test for comparing the return on assets of REITs led by family successors and (1) non-family CEOs and (2) founders. The difference was significant ($p < 0.05$) as the average performance was 3.63 for REITs with successors as CEOs and 4.73 for REITs with other types of CEOs. This analysis complements what has been presented in Table 2 where the average performance for REITs with non-family CEOs is 4.96. Thus, we provide evidence that professionally managed REITs will attain a relatively higher performance than those with family control.

Table 6. Regression Results using Return on Assets as Dependent Variable.

	Model 1	Model 2	Model 3	Model 4	Model 5	Model 6
Intercept	15.01 *** (3.15)	15.02 *** (3.15)	13.80 *** (3.14)	14.85 *** (3.14)	14.30 *** (3.17)	12.39 *** (3.16)
Firm Age (Ln)	0.61 * (0.27)	0.63 * (0.27)	0.64 * (0.26)	0.57 * (0.26)	0.60 * (0.27)	0.61 * (0.26)
Firm Size (Ln)	−0.30 * (0.12)	−0.30 * (0.12)	−0.27 * (0.12)	−0.29 * (0.12)	−0.27 * (0.12)	−0.22 + (0.12)
Debt to Asset Ratio	−4.72 *** (0.82)	−4.72 *** (0.82)	−4.69 *** (0.81)	−4.65 *** (0.81)	−4.81 *** (0.82)	−4.76 *** (0.81)
Outside Directors	−4.50 ** (1.44)	−4.51 ** (1.44)	−3.75 ** (1.45)	−4.70 ** (1.44)	−4.38 ** (1.44)	−3.59 * (1.45)
CEO Ownership (Own)	−0.11 (0.18)	−0.05 (0.22)	−0.12 (0.18)	−0.25 + (0.19)	−0.12 (0.18)	−0.19 (0.22)
CEO Chairman (Chair)	−0.18 (0.17)	−0.18 (0.17)	0.17 (0.17)	−0.16 (0.17)	−0.15 (0.17)	−0.10 (0.17)
Family Successor as CEO (Successor)	−0.40 * (0.16)	−0.37 * (0.17)	−0.52 ** (0.17)	−0.31 + (0.17)	−0.31 + (0.17)	−0.30 + (0.18)
Family Name (Family)	0.38 * (0.18)	0.39 * (0.18)	0.28 (0.18)	0.15 (0.20)	0.27 (0.19)	−0.08 (0.20)
Successor x Own		0.20 (0.42)				0.29 (0.41)
Successor x Chair			−0.62 *** (0.17)			−0.78 *** (0.17)
Family x Own				0.35 ** (0.13)		0.29 * (0.14)
Family x Chair					0.33 + (0.18)	0.45 * (0.14)
F-Value	10.21 ***	9.09 ***	10.71 ***	9.93 ***	9.46 ***	9.36 ***
R^2	0.08	0.08	0.10	0.09	0.09	0.11
Adjusted R^2	0.07	0.07	0.09	0.08	0.08	0.10
Change in Adjusted R^2			0.013 ***	0.006 **	0.002 +	0.02 ***

N = 921; $+ p < 0.10$; $* p < 0.05$; $** p < 0.01$; $*** p < 0.001$; Standard errors in parenthesis.

Model 2 was used to test H3a and the hypothesis is not supported as the interaction of Family Successor as CEO and CEO Own is not significant. Model 3 was used to test H3b and the hypothesis is supported as the interaction of Family Successor as CEO and CEO Chair is negative and significant ($p < 0.001$). In addition, the adjusted R^2 increased to 0.09 with a change of 0.013. Model 4 was used to test H4a and the hypothesis is supported as the interaction of Family Name and CEO Own is positive and significant ($p < 0.01$). In addition, the adjusted R^2 increased to 0.08 with a change of 0.006. Model 5 was used to test H4b and the hypothesis is partially supported as the interaction of Family Name and CEO Chair is positive and marginally significant ($p < 0.10$). In addition, the adjusted R^2 increased to 0.08 with a change of 0.002.

Model 6 is presented for completeness as the four interactions are entered with the set of controls and independent variables. The adjusted R^2 increased to 0.10 with a change of 0.021. It provides support for H4b as the interaction of Family Name and CEO Chair is positive and significant ($p < 0.05$). The model also provides further support to H3b and H4a as the interactions effects were significant at the 0.05 level or better.

For further explanation of our results, we plotted the three significant moderations effects. We followed the procedure explained by Cohen and Cohen [10] for plotting the interaction effects by

Int. J. Financial Stud. **2014**, *2*, 220–239

setting high and low levels at +/−1 standard deviation. Figure 1 plots the Family Successor as CEO and CEO Chair. It can be noted the negative slope in the high proportion of duality (CEO and Chair). Figures 2 and 3 plot the Family Name and CEO Own and CEO Chair, respectively, where it can be noted the positive slopes in the high proportion of both moderators. Overall, our exploratory analysis provides empirical support for all of the hypotheses except H3a.

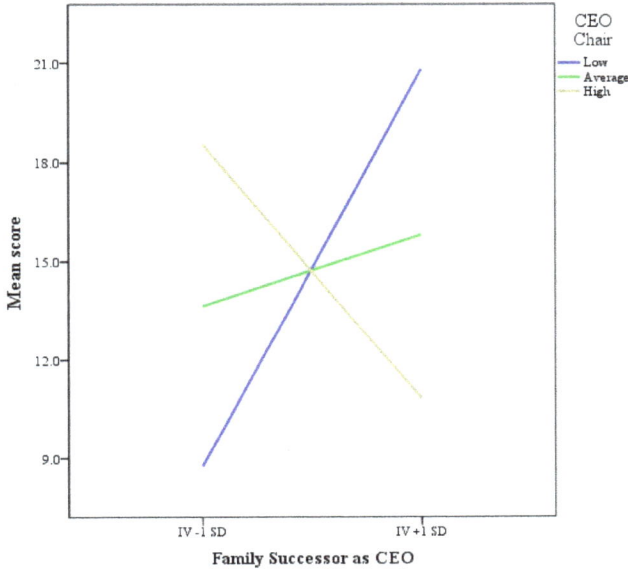

Figure 1. Interaction Plot: Family Successor and CEO Chair.

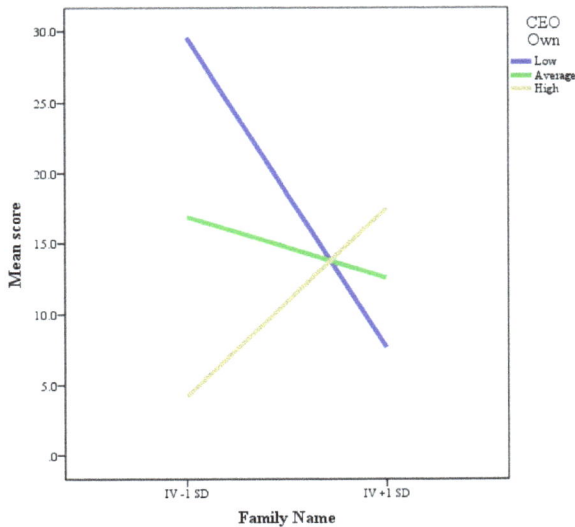

Figure 2. Interaction Plot: Family Name and CEO Own.

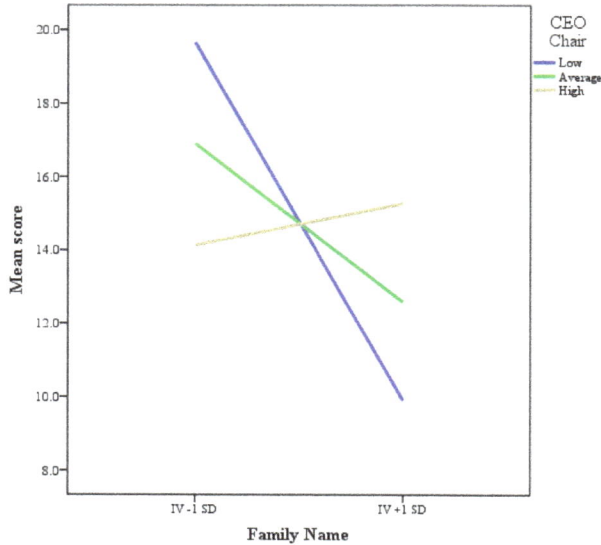

Figure 3. Interaction Plot: Family Name and CEO Chair.

4.1. Robustness Tests

We engaged in a series of robustness tests to provide further support to our hypotheses. First, we used Tobin's Q as a dependent variable. Tobin's Q represents a typical measure of performance for REITs, available at Bloomberg. We re-ran the models discussed above and the overall results were consistent in terms of significant levels and hypothesized relationships. However, the main difference is the adjusted R^2 of the models that ranged from 0.02–0.045 so we opted for not including the results in subsequent tables. Second, we created a new variable that included the family successors and the founder-CEO to re-run the regression models to assess, and the results did not differ. Third, we ran panel data analysis using a random effect model (a fixed effect model controlling for year effects will render no results for the founder status variable, since it is time invariant) with both Return on Assets and Tobin's Q as dependent variables. We obtained mixed results in our hypothesized relationships. On one side, we attained a consistency in the signs of the coefficients as we described in our hypotheses. On the other side, we were unable to attain levels of significance ($p < 0.10$) for our hypotheses. The panel data results could only provide support for H1 as the family name was positively related to Tobin's Q ($p < 0.05$) and the R^2 of such model was 0.39.

5. Discussion and Conclusion

Our central argument developed in this paper considers that REIT founders aim to preserve SEW by using the family name to identify the REIT and designate family members to attain CEO or chair positions once they retire. Although their intentions create performance implications—positively for family name and negatively for intergenerational transfers of power—they are also exerting a moderation effect between ownership and control and REIT performance. Our theoretical developments relied on three of the five Berrone *et al.* [2] FIBER conceptualizations of SEW: family influence and control, family identification, and renewal of family bonds through succession. Particularly, we consider that these three dimensions may interact (e.g., family influence and control interacting with identification and renewal) rather than being treated as independent factors behind the main SEW construct. In fact, our empirical evidence provided support for such contention as family business researchers who have studied these dimensions outside of the SEW perspective have attained similar results (e.g., Gedalojvic *et al.* [19]).

Our empirical results from an average sample of 66 REITs that produced 921 year-observations confirm our hypothesized relationships. These are very interesting findings because of two reasons. On one hand, our results support the desires of the founder to use the family name as an intangible resource that can bring further recognition to external stakeholders (e.g., Berrone *et al.* [10] Deephouse and Jaskiewicz [23]). On the other hand, the lower performance of REITs where the successor is the CEO implies that the founder may be benevolent and opt to pass the baton without paying attention to professionalizing the REIT (e.g., De Massis *et al.* [25]; Gedalojvic *et al.* [19]; Gomez-Mejia *et al.* [1]). In that manner, the family influence towards achieving non-economic goals (e.g., Chrisman *et al.* [8]) exerts a critical role in a commodity-like industry where the attainment of economic performance is critical for being competitive or even surviving in the long run. In addition, it is important to note the significant and negative relationship between outside directors and performance. Besides potential evidence of CEO entrenchment that may occur in rent-seeking family-controlled firms (Morck and Young [6]), it is evident that CEOs exert higher levels of controls over the management of the REIT.

From our knowledge, this is the first integration of the family business domain within the REIT research stream. We consider this to be our first contribution to the literature as the SEW perspective is also present in this industry and family influence toward the management of a publicly-traded investment vehicle is exposed to identify performance variances. In that regard, we validate the claims made by Gomez-Mejia *et al.* [1] about the uniqueness of SEW to explain the phenomena towards seeking non-economic goals beyond the normal economic ones (e.g., Chrisman *et al.* [8]) that can be even extended to particular tax advantages attained by families whose asset diversification strategy may also be tied to the REIT market performance. Particularly, our measures tend to agree with three dimensions of the FIBER proposal suggested by Berrone *et al.* [2], not only in regards to the direct effects of identification and renewal but also the interaction effects of these two dimensions with family influence and control. Our second contribution is related to the ambivalence that SEW preservation may bring to REITs. Especially, the desires of REIT founders to pass the baton to the next generation diminish performance, which may affect the competitive position of the REIT among its direct rivals. Such a scenario provides empirical evidence to the arguments developed by Kellermanns *et al.* [9] about the dark side of SEW because the enhancement of the endowments of the family controlling the REIT may end up being considered as a liability in having a successor running the operations (e.g., Naldi *et al.* [5]) or discouraging non-family stakeholders to benefit from either the economic performance of the REIT (as investors) or having governance and management conflicts (as independent directors or managers). Even though Jaskiewicz and Luchak [28] stated that non-family leaders may not be at conflict with the demands of the controlling family, we noticed that REIT performance is lower when successors of the founder become the next CEO. Particularly, this is a critical aspect if we consider the fact that publicly-traded REITs are subjected to competitive pressures or even analysts' opinions. Even though the SEW preservation will keep the family control in the hands of the successor, having a continuous record of lower performance against non-family CEOs may call the attention of non-family shareholders who may even question the successor's tenure. Furthermore, the reputation of the firm (or even the controlling family's reputation) may be at stake if non-family shareholders become dissatisfied with the founder's selection of the next CEO (e.g., Deephouse and Jaskiewicz [23]). As a result, the potential benefits toward SEW preservation may end up endangering the market survival of the REIT in the long run.

We also need to address our limitations in this study. First, we consider our results to be exploratory in nature as we did not obtain full support of our contentions by using panel data analysis. Our regression results were very consistent and our data did not present evidence of multicollinearity among the variables; however, multicollinearity becomes a problem when one starts to run interactions. Although we relied on McGrath [42] for testing one interaction at a time, once we introduced the four interactions, the levels of significance in the independent variables were altered.

However, our robustness tests discussed earlier demonstrated a consistency in the results. Second, our data collection efforts focused on short-term performance so it can be argued that the family successors may require some tenure to really prove their qualifications for the position. Third, we encountered data collection problems that restricted our sample size so we considered situations where the founder is still controlling the REIT or just transferred the baton to either a descendant or to a professional manager. Fourth, we relied on naming the REIT after the founder as an objective proxy for identification without considering subjective elements within the REIT. For example, there is the possibility that a REIT founder may have used a symbol or another family-related event that could have led to an increase in the number of REITs identified as family.

Our methodological limitations provide opportunities for future investigation to enhance our understanding of family influence in the REIT sector. In addition, future investigation is needed to explore the effectiveness of having independent directors to govern the direction of the REIT. Particularly, outsiders can also enable a sense to respond to the economic demands of non-family shareholders or even comply with the Sarbanes-Oxley Act (Coates [13]). A second extension for further investigation is to explore the other two components of the FIBER framework proposed by Berrone *et al.* [2]—emotional intelligence and binding social ties—as these may be used to enhance understanding of the strategic behavior of REIT founders and their intentions toward SEW preservation. Third, it is encouraged to investigate situations where older REITs may be facing a succession transfer to the third generation and analyze if SEW preservation was enough to maintain family dominance or market forces will require the REIT to involve outsiders (e.g., Gersick *et al.* [36]). Fourth, future investigations may want to use other performance measures such as CAPM adjusted or multi-factor adjusted one-year excess returns as a potential measure of risk and return. [2] This measure can be considered as an alternate explanation for determining the exposure of the family toward SEW preservation. These considerations may not only apply to the REIT industry but also to family firms operating in different industries and/or countries. Fifth, future investigations may also need to establish the potential implications of naming family successors in balancing the reputation of the firm in the long run. As suggested by Deephouse and Jaskiewicz [23], stakeholders may have limits in accepting the non-economic goals of the family firm to support their SEW preservation; however, financial performance may remain a key element to determine the level of satisfaction with the family successor. Otherwise, the survival of the business will be at stake if the successor is unable to meet the market and stakeholder thresholds.

In terms of practical implications, our study can also be used for developing strict guidelines and policies toward succession. Especially, family descendants will need adequate training and rely on professionals and outsiders, not only for the family benefit in terms of economic and non-economic wealth preservation but also for the rest of the stakeholders. Furthermore, it is important that family firms that opt to become publicly traded recognize that attaining particular non-economic goals (e.g., reaping benefits from tax minimization due to lower market returns) may not satisfy the wealth maximization of non-family investors. In the case of REITs, our results implied that not only do successors underperform non-family ones, but also that independent board members are not exerting a positive influence on governing the REIT. Even though the family may be reaping benefits for keeping control in the family, the long-term image of the family may be at stake if there are not proper guidelines or incentives to have outsiders (e.g., non-kin related managers and directors) that may demotivate non-family shareholders to maximize their investment. Put differently, families may need to establish their limits before being subjected to shareholder activism and/or other market controls.

In conclusion, it is our hope that researchers can build on our conceptual and empirical developments as both family business and REIT literature are emerging streams that deserve attention in the future.

---

[2] We thank this suggestion from a reviewer.

Int. J. Financial Stud. **2014**, *2*, 220–239

Acknowledgments: We would like to thank Jim Chrisman for his valuable suggestions on a prior version of this article.

Author Contributions: Both authors contributed equally to this paper.

Conflicts of Interest: The authors declare no conflict of interest in the results provided in this manuscript.

References

1. Gomez-Mejia, L.R.; Cruz, C.; Berrone, P.; De Castro, J. The bind that ties: Socioemotional wealth preservation in family firms. *Acad. Manag. Ann.* **2011**, *5*, 653–707. [CrossRef]
2. Berrone, P.; Cruz, C.; Gomez-Mejia, L.R. Socioemotional wealth in family firms: Theoretical dimensions, assessment approaches and agenda for future research. *Fam. Bus. Rev.* **2012**, *25*, 258–279. [CrossRef]
3. Berrone, P.; Cruz, C.; Gomez-Mejia, L.R.; Larraza-Kintana, M. Socioemotional Wealth and Corporate Responses to Institutional Pressures: Do Family-Controlled Firms Pollute Less? *Adm. Sci. Q.* **2010**, *55*, 82–113. [CrossRef]
4. Gómez-Mejía, L.R.; Haynes, K.T.; Núñez-Nickel, M.; Jacobson, K.J.L.; Moyano-Fuentes, H. Socioemotional wealth and business risk in family-controlled firms: Evidence from Spanish olive oil mills. *Adm. Sci. Q.* **2007**, *52*, 106–137.
5. Naldi, L.; Cennamo, C.; Corbetta, G.; Gomez-Mejia, L. Preserving Socioemotional Wealth in Family Firms: Asset or Liability? The Moderating Role of Business Context. *Entrep. Theory Pract.* **2013**, *37*, 1341–1360. [CrossRef]
6. Morck, R.; Young, B. Family control and the rent seeking society. *Entrep. Theory Pract.* **2004**, *28*, 391–409. [CrossRef]
7. La Porta, R.; Lopez-de-Silanes, F.; Shleifer, A. Corporate ownership around the world. *J. Financ.* **1999**, *54*, 471–517. [CrossRef]
8. Chrisman, J.J.; Sharma, P.; Steier, L.P.; Chua, J.H. The Influence of Family Goals, Governance, and Resources on Firm Outcomes. *Entrep. Theory Pract.* **2013**, *37*, 1249–1261. [CrossRef]
9. Kellermanns, F.W.; Eddleston, K.A.; Zellweger, T.M. Extending the Socioemotional Wealth Perspective: A Look at the Dark Side. *Entrep. Theory Pract.* **2012**, *36*, 1175–1182. [CrossRef]
10. Berrone, P.; Cennamo, C.; Cruz, C.; Gómez-Mejía, L.R. Socioemotional wealth and proactive stakeholder engagement: Why family-controlled firms care more about their stakeholders. *Entrep. Theory Pract.* **2012**, *36*, 1153–1173. [CrossRef]
11. Noguera, M. The Effect of Founder CEOs on the Structure of REIT Board of Directors and REIT Performance. *R. Estate Finance* **2014**. forthcoming.
12. Ghosh, C.; Giambona, C.; Harding, J.; Sirmans, C.F. How entrenchment, incentives, and governance influence REIT capital structure. *J. Real Estate Econ.* **2011**, *43*, 39–72. [CrossRef]
13. Coates, J.C. The Goals and Promise of the Sarbanes-Oxley Act. *J. Econ. Perspect.* **2007**, *21*, 91–116. [CrossRef]
14. Duchin, R.; Matsusaka, J.G.; Ozbas, O. When are outside directors effective? *J. Financ. Econ.* **2010**, *96*, 195–214. [CrossRef]
15. Valenti, A. The Sarbanes-Oxley Act of 2002: Has It Brought About Changes in the Boards of Large U.S. Corporations? *J. Bus.* **2008**, *81*, 401–412.
16. Carney, M. Corporate governance and competitive advantage in family-controlled firms. *Entrep. Theory Pract.* **2005**, *29*, 249–265. [CrossRef]
17. Internal Revenue Services. Internal Revenue Code Section 856. Available online: http://www.irs.gov/pub/irs-drop/rr-98-60.pdf (accessed on 10 April 2014).
18. Wiseman, R.M.; Gomez-Mejia, L.R. A behavioral agency model of managerial risk taking. *Acad. Manag. Rev.* **1998**, *22*, 133–153.
19. Gedajlovic, E.; Carney, M.; Chrisman, J.J.; Kellermanns, F.W. The adolescence of family firm research: Taking stock and planning for the future. *J. Manag.* **2012**, *38*, 1010–1037.
20. U.S. Securities and Exchange Commission. Investor Bulletin: Real Estate Investment Trusts (REITs). Available online: http://www.sec.gov/investor/alerts/reits.pdf (accessed on 10 April 2014).
21. Dyer, G.W.; Whetten, D.A. Family firms and social responsibility. Preliminary evidence from the S&P500. *Entrep. Theory Pract.* **2006**, *30*, 785–802. [CrossRef]
22. Astrachan, J.H.; Klein, S.B.; Smyrnios, K.X. The F-PEC scale of family influence: A proposal for solving the family business definition problem. *Fam. Bus. Rev.* **2002**, *15*, 45–58.
23. Deephouse, D.L.; Jaskiewicz, P. Do Family Firms Have Better Reputations Than Non-Family Firms? An Integration of Socioemotional Wealth and Social Identity Theories. *J. Manag. Stud.* **2013**, *50*, 337–360. [CrossRef]

Int. J. Financial Stud. **2014**, *2*, 220–239

24. Chrisman, J.J.; Memili, E.; Misra, K. Non-family managers, family firms, and the winner's curse: The influence of non-economic goals and bounded rationality. *Entrep. Theory Pract.* **2014**. [CrossRef]

25. De Massis, A.; Chua, J.H.; Chrisman, J.J. Factors preventing intra-family succession. *Fam. Bus. Rev.* **2008**, *21*, 183–199. [CrossRef]

26. Zellweger, T.M.; Kellermanns, F.W.; Chrisman, J.J.; Chua, J.H. Family Control and Family Firm Valuation by Family CEOs: The Importance of Intentions for Transgenerational Control. *Organ. Sci.* **2012**, *23*, 851–868.

27. Cruz, C.; Justo, R.; De Castro, J. Does family employment enhance MSEs performance? Integrating socioemotional wealth and family embeddedness perspectives. *J. Bus. Ventur.* **2012**, *27*, 62–76. [CrossRef]

28. Jaskiewicz, P.; Luchak, A.A. Explaining Performance Differences Between Family Firms With Family and Nonfamily CEOs: It's the Nature of the Tie to the Family That Counts! *Entrep. Theory Pract.* **2013**, *37*, 1361–1367. [CrossRef]

29. Bennedsen, M.; Meisner, N.; Perez-Gonzalez, F.; Wolfenzon, D. Inside the family firm: The role of families in succession decisions and performance. *Q. J. Econ.* **2007**, *20*, 647–691.

30. Villalonga, B.; Amit, R. How do family ownership, control and management affect firm value? *J. Financ. Econ.* **2006**, *80*, 385–417. [CrossRef]

31. Chrisman, J.J.; Chua, J.H.; Kellermanns, F.W.; Chang, E.P.C. Are family managers agents or stewards? An exploratory study in privately held family firms. *J. Bus. Res.* **2007**, *60*, 1030–1038. [CrossRef]

32. Miller, D.; Steier, L.; Le Breton-Miller, I. Lost in time: Intergenerational succession, change and failure in family business. *J. Bus. Ventur.* **2003**, *18*, 513–531. [CrossRef]

33. Hall, A.; Nordqvist, M. Professional Management in Family Businesses: Toward an Extended Understanding. *Fam. Bus. Rev.* **2008**, *21*, 51–69. [CrossRef]

34. Memili, E.; Misra, K.; Chang, E.P.C.; Chrisman, J.J. The propensity to use non-family manager incentive compensation in SME family firms. *J. Fam. Bus. Manag.* **2013**, *3*, 62–80. [CrossRef]

35. Jones, C.D.; Makri, M.; Gomez-Mejia, L.R. Affiliate directors and perceived risk bearing in publicly traded, family-controlled firms: The case of diversification. *Entrep. Theory Pract.* **2008**, *32*, 1007–1026. [CrossRef]

36. Gersick, K.; Davis, J.; Hampton, M.; Lansberg, I. *Generation to Generation: Life Cycles of the Family Business*; Harvard Business School Press: Boston, MA, USA, 1997.

37. Voordeckers, W.; Van Gils, A.; Van den Heuvel, J. Board composition in small and medium-sized family firms. *J. Small Bus. Manag.* **2007**, *45*, 137–156. [CrossRef]

38. Shleifer, A.; Vishny, R. Liquidation values and debt capacities: A market equilibrium approach. *J. Financ.* **1992**, *47*, 1343–1365. [CrossRef]

39. Noguera, M. The Impact of the Sarbanes-Oxley Act on the Structure of REIT Board of Directors. *J. Real Estate Financ. Econ.* **2012**, *45*, 869–887. [CrossRef]

40. Ambrose, B.W.; Linneman, P. REIT organizational structure and operating characteristics. *J. Real Estate Res.* **2001**, *21*, 141–162.

41. Baron, R.M.; Kenny, D.A. The moderator-mediator variable distinction in social psychological research: Conceptual, strategic, and statistical considerations. *J. Personal. Soc. Psychol.* **1986**, *51*, 1173–1182. [CrossRef]

42. McGrath, R.G. Exploratory learning, innovative capacity, and managerial oversight. *Acad. Manag. J.* **2001**, *44*, 118–131. [CrossRef]

43. Cohen, J.; Cohen, P. *Applied Multiple Regression/Correlation Analysis for the Behavioral Sciences*, 2nd ed.; Erlbaum: Hillsdale, NJ, USA, 1983.

44. Tabachnick, B.G.; Fidell, L.S. *Using Multivariate Statistics*, 3rd ed.; HarperCollins College Publishers: New York, NY, USA, 1996.

International Journal of
Financial Studies

MDPI

Article

Family-Concentrated Ownership in Chinese PLCs: Does Ownership Concentration Always Enhance Corporate Value?

Jin-Hui Luo [1,*] and Heng Liu [2]

[1] Department of Accounting, School of Management, Xiamen University, No. 422 Siming South Road, Xiamen 361005, China

[2] Department of Business Administration, Lingnan College, SUN YAT-SEN University, Guangzhou 510275, China; liuheng8@mail.sysu.edu.cn

* Author to whom correspondence should be addressed; jinhuiluo@xmu.edu.cn; Tel.: +86-182-0592-9133; Fax: +86-0592-218-5870.

Received: 5 December 2013; in revised form: 11 February 2014; Accepted: 14 February 2014; Published: 28 February 2014

Abstract: In this paper we investigate the relationship between family ownership structure and corporate value across a sample of 1314 firm-year observations of China's family publicly listed companies (PLCs), from 2004 to 2008. We find a significant inverse-U-shaped relationship between the controlling family's ultimate cash-flow rights and corporate value; as measured by Tobin's Q. That is, as family-ownership concentration increases, corporate value first increases and then decreases. This finding refreshes our understanding of the relationship between family-ownership concentration and corporate value in emerging economies such as found in China. We corroborate prior findings that when controlling families hold excess control over cash-flow rights, corporate value is significantly lowered, while multiple large shareholders structure is significantly associated with higher corporate value. In addition; board independence is found to significantly improve corporate value in the context of family-concentrated ownership. We also test for potential endogeneity between family ownership and corporate value and find our results to be robust.

Keywords: China; corporate value; family concentrated ownership; family firms; ultimate ownership structure

1. Introduction

Since China's economic reform began in 1978, China has become the largest and fastest-growing emerging economy in the world (Allen *et al.* [1]). During the past three decades, China's economic reform has seen declining state ownership and rising private sector ownership (Ding *et al.* [2]). As the private sector has developed substantially, the Chinese stock market has been increasingly listing family-controlled firms. However, research has provided little understanding about family ownership in Chinese publicly listed companies (PLCs). In this study, we explore empirically the governance effect of family-concentrated ownership in China's unique institutional context. In particular, we describe and compare the ultimate ownership structures in Chinese state-owned and family PLCs, and then analyze the relationship between family ownership structure and corporate value in Chinese family-controlled PLCs.

Concentrated ownership is common throughout the world (Claessens *et al.* [3], Faccio and Lang [4], La Porta *et al.* [5]), especially in emerging economies, such as found in China. On one hand, minority shareholders may show free-ride behaviors, but large shareholders have the incentive and voting power to collect information, monitor the management, and, thus, improve corporate value (Grossman and

Hart [6], Jensen and Meckling [7]). On the other hand, large shareholders have a general interest and enough control to pursue their own benefits at the expense of minority shareholders (Alsan and Kumar [8], Shleifer and Vishny [9]), especially when large shareholders with relatively smaller shares, nevertheless, control the firms through control-enhancing mechanisms, such as a pyramid structure, cross-holding, and dual-class shares (Adams and Ferreira [10], Lin *et al.* [11,12], Johnson *et al.* [13], Friedman *et al.* [14]). As ownership concentration increases, large shareholder's interests may become more aligned with minority shareholder interests and, thus, reduce the likelihood and degree minority shareholders would be expropriated (Claessens *et al.* [3], Dyck and Zingales [15]). That is, ownership concentration and corporate value may have a positive linear relationship (La Porta *et al.* [5], Claessens *et al.* [3]).

However, in practice, many of China's controlling families use their high ownership to expropriate minority shareholders, ultimately reducing corporate value. Controlling families respond, not only to firm-level imperatives, but also to country/region level institutions. In particular, emerging economies, such as China's, are in the process of economic reform. Their formal institutions are in transition, and legal system for protecting investors and enforcing protections are still weak and uneven. In this special institutional context, controlling families have low cost and little risk of being captured for expropriating minority shareholders and are, thus, prone to pursue their own utility at the expense of minority shareholders, causing serious conflicts of interests. High ownership is accompanied by high voting rights. Without effective power balance from other large shareholders, high ownership does not always align controlling family interests with minority shareholder interests in emerging economies. Hence, family-ownership concentration and corporate value should have a non-monotonic relationship rather than a simple linear relationship (Bai *et al.* [16], De Miguel *et al.* [17], Morck *et al.* [18], Tian and Estrin [19], Yeh *et al.* [20]). However, thus far, we know little about relationships for ultimate family-ownership structure in China.

Accordingly, we use a panel data set of 1,314 firm-year observations from Chinese family-controlled PLCs from 2004 to 2008. Consistent with our argument and prediction, we find strong evidence of a significant nonlinear inverse-U-shaped relationship between ultimate family ownership and corporate value in China. As the level of ultimate family ownership increases, corporate value, as measured by Tobin's Q, first increases and then decreases. That is, family-concentrated ownership has two competing effects: interest-alignment and entrenchment. The level of family ownership determines which effect dominates.

Similar to prior findings (e.g., La Porta *et al.* [5], Yeh *et al.* [20], Yeh [21]), we find that diverging control and cash-flow rights significantly and negatively affect corporate value. Meanwhile, of several other governance mechanisms, we find that only multiple large shareholders structure and strong board independence conditions are significantly associated with higher corporate value. These findings suggest that in the context of concentrated ownership, multiple large shareholders and independent directors provide the power and balance to play an effective governance role in restricting the controlling family's expropriation activities. Nevertheless, other governance mechanisms, such as management ownership and CEO duality, play a limited role (Berglöf and Pajuste [22], Claessens and Fan [23], Morck *et al.* [24]). As a result, our findings have important implications for corporate governance practice in China and other emerging market economies.

We make three main contributions to the literature. First, we enrich the growing map of ultimate ownership structures around the world by describing and comparing in detail ultimate corporate ownership structures between China's family-owned and state-owned PLCs and between PLCs in China and in other East Asian Economies (Claessens *et al.* [25], Faccio and Lang [4], La Porta *et al.* [26]). Second, because evidence is mixed regarding the influence of family ownership on firm performance/value (e.g., Anderson and Reeb [27], Andres [28], Goergen [29], Morck *et al.* [30]), we argue that family ownership and corporate value have a non-monotonic relationship rather than a simple linear relationship, and then find strong and robust corroborating evidence from a sample of data from China's family-controlled PLCs. Thus, we contribute to the literature by suggesting that the level of family-ownership concentration changes the dominant interest-alignment and entrenchment effects of family-concentrated ownership. Third, we find that traditional governance mechanisms are inadequate in the context of concentrated ownership. Instead, different governance mechanisms, such as multiple large shareholders and independent directors, are required to resolve conflicts of interests between the controlling families and minority shareholders.

The rest of this paper is structured as follows. Section 2 briefly introduces the ultimate ownership structures of Chinese PLCs. Section 3 drives our testable hypotheses. Section 4 describes the data set and variables. Section 5 presents regression results. Section 6 concludes.

2. Ultimate Ownership Structures of Chinese PLCs

In 1978, China undertook economic reform to turn its central-command economic system into a market economy. Since then, China has become the world's largest and fastest-growing emerging economy (Allen *et al.* [1]). During the past three decades, China's economic reform has led to the decline of state ownership and the rise of private sectors (Ding *et al.* [2]).

In the early 1990s, the Chinese government launched SOEs reform to clarify former SOEs' property rights, improve their corporate governance, and promote their operating performance. To restructure and renovate former SOEs, especially to help SOEs raise funds, the Chinese government established the stock market. As a result, many former SOEs were restructured to form joint stock companies. However, central or local governments still control former-SOE joint stock companies (Ding *et al.* [2]). To decentralize control rights from the State to firm managers who specialize in managing state assets no longer diluted by state ownership in case of losses, the government usually owns the listed companies through a pyramidal structure consisting of one to several intermediate companies, generally non-listed, solely government-owned SOEs (Fan *et al.* [31], Watanabe [32]). That is, Chinese state-owned PLCs commonly feature pyramidal ownership structures with weak divergence between ultimate cash-flow and control rights (see column B in Table 1).

Table 1. Summary of ownership structures in family listed companies around East Asia.

Column A: Ultimate Ownership and Control Structure in East Asian Corporations (the Largest Shareholder)					
	Mean (Median)				
Country/Region	*Cash flow rights*	*Control rights*	*Ratio of cash flow rights to control rights*	No. of obs.	Sample Period
Japan	6.90 (4.00)	10.33 (9.71)	0.60 (0.60)	1117	1996
Korea	13.96 (10.10)	17.78 (20.00)	0.86 (1.00)	211	1996
Singapore	20.19 (20.00)	27.52 (29.35)	0.79 (0.800)	211	1996
Indonesia	25.61 (24.00)	33.68 (30.19)	0.78 (0.86)	178	1996
Malaysia	23.89 (19.68)	28.32 (29.72)	0.85 (1.00)	238	1996
Philippines	21.34 (19.22)	24.36 (21.00)	0.91 (1.00)	99	1996
Thailand	32.84 (30.00)	35.25 (39.52)	0.94 (1.00)	135	1996
Taiwan	15.98 (14.42)	18.96 (21.28)	0.83 (0.98)	92	1996
Hong Kong	24.30 (18.67)	28.08 (19.64)	0.88 (1.00)	330	1996

See Table 2 for the definitions of variables.

Table 1. *Cont.*

Country/Region	Column A: Ultimate Ownership and Control Structure in East Asian Corporations (the Largest Shareholder)				
	Mean (Median)				
	Cash flow rights	*Control rights*	*Ratio of cash flow rights to control rights*	No. of obs.	Sample Period
	Column B: Ultimate Ownership and Control Structure in Mainland China (the Largest Shareholder)				
Total	39.14 (37.84)	44.42 (44.46)	0.85 (1.00)	880	
State-owned firms	43.02 (42.70)	46.77 (47.49)	0.91 (1.00)	718	2004
Family firms	21.92 (21.18)	34.01 (29.52)	0.62 (0.60)	162	
Total	36.91 (35.05)	42.52 (41.76)	0.84 (1.00)	937	
State-owned firms	40.76 (39.65)	44.75 (45.11)	0.90 (1.00)	754	2005
Family firms	21.07 (20.29)	33.34 (29.49)	0.62 (0.60)	183	
Total	31.27 (29.41)	37.28 (36.10)	0.82 (1.00)	991	
State-owned firms	35.32 (33.70)	39.45 (39.62)	0.89 (1.00)	723	2006
Family firms	20.34 (18.58)	31.42 (27.85)	0.63 (0.65)	268	
Total	31.98 (29.72)	37.76 (36.77)	0.83 (1.00)	1043	
State-owned firms	35.22 (33.75)	39.33 (39.12)	0.89 (1.00)	729	2007
Family firms	24.44 (21.79)	34.10 (30.59)	0.70 (0.75)	314	
Total	32.68 (30.55)	38.74 (38.02)	0.83 (1.00)	1124	
State-owned firms	35.36 (33.80)	39.81 (39.62)	0.88 (1.00)	737	2008
Family firms	27.59 (24.75)	36.68 (33.77)	0.73 (0.80)	387	
Total	34.19 (32.02)	39.96 (38.91)	0.83 (1.00)	4975	
State-owned firms	37.94 (36.55)	42.03 (41.74)	0.89 (1.00)	3661	2004–2008
Family firms	23.75 (21.39)	34.20 (29.89)	0.67 (0.70)	1314	

See Table 2 for the definitions of variables.

As economic reform has deepened in China, many private firms have emerged to become increasingly important to the rapid economic development. In 1992, with the first private-owned company listed on the Chinese stock market, a small but increasing number of private-owned firms, especially family-controlled firms, have been listed on the Chinese stock market (Ding *et al.* [2], Fan *et al.* [31]). For example, by the end of 2008, the Chinese stock market had about 387 family-controlled PLCs, about 34.43% of the total number (1124) of non-financial listed companies (see column B in Table 1). To create internal capital markets and thus relieve financial constraints, entrepreneurs/families also control these PLCs through pyramids. However, entrepreneurs/families usually lack full ownership of the intermediate companies, along the pyramids, resulting in huge divergence between their ultimate control and cash-flow rights (Fan *et al.* [31]).

Although China's state-owned and family-owned PLCs commonly have pyramidal structures, ultimate ownership structures differ. As column B of Table 1 shows, state-owned PLCs have much higher ultimate-ownership concentration than do family-owned PLCs. In state-owned PLCs, the largest shareholder's ultimate control and cash-flow rights diverge much less than they do in family-owned PLCs, as indicated by the ratio of ultimate cash-flow rights to control rights. Column A of Table 1 also shows that in ten countries/regions of East Asia, the ratio of controlling families' ultimate cash-flow rights and control rights, a reverse estimator of the divergence between ownership and control, is the second lowest in mainland China (0.67) with the lowest in Japan (0.60). This indicates common and serious disproportional ownership in Chinese family-owned PLCs, and indicates serious possible conflicts of interests between controlling families and minority shareholders (Friedman *et al.* [14]).

Due to different ultimate ownership structures for state-owned and family-owned PLCs in the Chinese stock market, previous findings on ownership concentration and corporate value/performance relationships drawn from samples combining Chinese state-owned and family-owned firms would be problematic and unconvincing (e.g., Bai *et al.* [16], Tian and Estrin [19], Wei *et al.* [33]). As a result, we focus on Chinese family-owned PLCs to gain more knowledge about ultimate family ownership structures and draw convincing comparable results regarding relationships between family-concentrated ownership and corporate value in China.

3. Hypotheses Development

Unlike cases of diffuse ownership, universal large shareholders can help resolve traditional agency problems between shareholders and managers, but would also cause conflicts of interests between majority shareholders and minority investors (Grossman and Hart [6], Jensen and Meckling [7], Shleifer and Vishny [9,34]). In other words, family-ownership concentration has two competing effects: interest-alignment and entrenchment (Claessens *et al.* [3], Dyck and Zingales [15]).

Under low family-ownership concentration, entrenchment effect will be very weak so that conflicts of interests between controlling families and minority shareholders would generate relatively low costs. As controlling families would lack the voting rights to expropriate minority shareholders, interest-alignment effects may turn to be pronounced. As early as 1980, some degree of ownership concentration was suggested to help resolve problems of free-riders in monitoring managers (Grossman and Hart [6]). In contrast, small investors often "vote with their feet" when a firm is performing poorly, so block shareholders (*i.e.*, controlling families in this study) have enough voting power and incentives to collect information and monitor managerial opportunistic behaviors and then help resolve traditional agency problems between shareholders and managers (Andres [28], Grossman and Hart [6], Jensen and Meckling [7], Shleifer and Vishny [9,34]). In emerging economies, such as in China, this interest-alignment effect of family-concentrated ownership may be much more pronounced. Conflicts of interests between shareholders and managers is much more serious in emerging economies because of poor legal systems, uneven enforcement (North [35]), and developing corporate governance.

However, under highly concentrated family ownership, controlling families may expropriate firm resources for their own utility at the expense of minority shareholders. As high ownership concentration enables controlling families to manipulate and even appoint management, they can more easily pass privately beneficial decisions/proposals at the expense of overall corporate value. Meanwhile, high ownership concentration means that minority shareholders or coalitions of minority shareholder are weak in the power balance, and thus have no effective restrictions to counter self-beneficial behaviors. In other words, high family-ownership concentration may have a dominant entrenchment effect; controlling families and minority shareholders have serious interest conflicts with resulting poor corporate value. In emerging economies with weak institutions, the entrenchment effect will be more marked. For instance, in China, controlling families usually have outright firm control and management through pyramidal structures (Fan *et al.* [31]), making them much more powerful and able to use their super voting rights to appropriate the profits of companies lower on the tier.

Combining the interest-alignment and entrenchment effects of family-concentrated ownership, we suggest that as family ownership concentration gradually increases, corporate value first increases and then decreases, reflecting an inverse-U-shaped relationship between family ownership and corporate value. Those observations generated our first testable hypothesis:

Hypothesis 1: *An inverse-U-shaped relationship will occur between family-concentrated ownership and corporate value.*

Ultimate ownership structure also leads to the divergence of control and cash-flow rights. In Chinese state-owned PLCs, the government often directly/indirectly controls 100% of ownership (Watanabe [32]; also see the data in Table 1), however, in Chinese family-controlled PLCs, controlling families usually use pyramidal structures to control listed firms with relatively small ownership, so that control and ownership sharply diverge (Fan *et al.* [31]). Thus, ultimate ownership structures in Chinese family-controlled PLCs are distinct in the separation of control and ownership. Under this practical background, controlling families have much incentive to tunnel the lower-tier listed firm's profits and resources because other shareholders will bear the major tunneling costs, but expropriation provides exclusive benefits (Aslan and Kumar [8], Faccio *et al.* [36], Friedman *et al.* [14]). Thus, the major portion of the costs of tunneling will be born by controlling families and minority investors have worsened interest conflicts and increased agency costs (Claessens *et al.* [3], Lin *et al.* [11,12], Yeh *et al.* [20], Yeh [21]). As a result, aligned with prior studies (Claessens *et al.* [3], Dyck and Zingales [15], La Porta *et al.* [5]), the huge divergence between controlling families' ultimate control and cash-flow rights would reduce corporate value, leading to our second testable hypothesis:

Hypothesis 2: *The more divergence between controlling families' ultimate control rights and cash-flow rights, the lower will be corporate value.*

4. Research Design

4.1. Sample and Data

For our sample set, we gathered data regarding family-controlled PLCs in the 2004 to 2008 Chinese stock market. We defined companies as family-controlled PLCs if families or individuals were the largest PLC shareholders, with no less than 10% of ultimate control rights (Le Breton-Miller and Miller [37]). Second, the China Securities Regulatory Commission (CSRC) required Chinese PLCs to disclose details of control chains until 2003. Only a few PLCs disclosed this information in the first year, thus, we took 2004 as our initial sample year and selected firm-year observations from 2004 to 2008. Third, the government always treats the financial industry as a special domain and requires the industry to comply with very stringent legal requirements, thus, we eliminated all financial companies. Finally, to minimize outlier influences, we deleted firms also listed on other overseas markets, firms with issued debt more than asset value, firms that are under Special Treatment (ST), and firms with missing data. We finally obtained a five-year panel data set of 1314 firm-year observations. Firms in each sample year for 2004 to 2008 numbered 162, 183, 268, 314, and 387, respectively. In this study, we followed CSRC's *Guidelines for Classification of Listed Companies* (A through M) to classify our sample industry, including all but the financial industry.

We obtained financial data from the China Stock Market & Accounting Research (CSMAR) database designed and developed by GTA Information Technology, a major provider of China data. We hand-collected data about PLC control chains from PLC annual reports disclosed on the CRSC-appointed CNINFO website.

4.2. Variable Description

Since Tobin's Q is a widely used measure of valuation for listed companies, we followed this tradition and took Tobin's Q to measure the dependent variable: corporate value. Following previous researches (Wei *et al.* [33], Tian and Estrin [19]), we calculated *Tobinq* as the ratio of the market value of equity plus the book value of debt over the book value of total assets. However, Chinese PLC stock is classified as tradable and non-tradable. Illiquidity discounts of 70%–80% present a problem for pricing non-tradable stock (Chen and Xiong [38]). Referring to Bai *et al.* [16], we multiplied the tradable stock price by 30% and 20%, respectively, to use as the price of non-tradable stock and, thus, acquired another two measures for corporate value: *Tobin70* and *Tobin80*, respectively. As a whole, we used three alternative measurements for corporate value in this study: *Tobinq*, *Tobin70*, and *Tobin80*.

The independent variables are the controlling family's ultimate cash-flow rights and the divergence between the controlling family's ultimate control and cash-flow rights, denoted by *family ownership* and *wedge of control and ownership*, respectively. Pyramidal ownership structure is predominant in the Chinese stock market (Fan *et al.* [31]), so we cast back the firm's control chains and used La Porta *et al.*'s [5] method to calculate controlling families' ultimate cash-flow and control rights. Specifically, we computed controlled families' ultimate cash-flow rights as the sum of the product of the equity stakes along the control chains. The ultimate control rights were computed as the sum of the minimum voting stakes along the control chains. Then, *wedge of control and ownership* was measured as the ratio of the controlling family's ultimate control rights and cash-flow rights (Faccio and Lang [4]). Table 2 presents the definitions of other governance variables and control variables.

Table 2. Definition of variables.

Variable	Definition
Tobinq	A proxy of Tobin's Q as the adjusted market value of the firm. It is calculated as the ratio of the market value of common stock plus the book value of total debt over the book value of total assets.
Tobin70	A proxy of Tobin's Q adjusted for the illiquidity discount issue of non-tradable stock. It is calculated as the ratio of the market value of tradable and non-tradable stock plus the book value of total debt over the book value of total assets. The market price of non-tradable stock is proxied by 30 percent of the price of tradable stock.
Tobin80	A proxy of Tobin's Q adjusted for the illiquidity discount issue of non-tradable stock. It is calculated as the ratio of the market value of tradable and non-tradable stock plus the book value of total debt over the book value of total assets. The market price of non-tradable stock is proxied by 20 percent of the price of tradable stock.
Family ownership	The controlling family's ultimate cash-flow ownership. It is computed as the sum of the product of all the equity stakes along the control chains.
Family control	The controlling family's ultimate control rights. It is computed as the sum of the minimum voting stakes along the control chains.
Wedge of control and ownership	The divergence between control and cash-flow rights. It is measured as the ratio of controlling families' ultimate control and cash flow rights.
Multiple large shareholders	Multiple Large Shareholders. It is proxied by a dummy variable that takes the value one if the percentage of the second largest shareholder's ownership is no less than 5%.
Independent directors	The proportion of independent directors on the board of directors.
Management ownership	The sum of proportion of voting stakes by top managers and directors.
CEO duality	A dummy variable that takes the value one if the CEO is the chairman or a vice chairman of the board of directors.
Firm size	Firm Size. It is calculated as the log of total assets.
Firm age	Firm age. It is calculated as the log of years since focal firms listed on the stock market exchange.
Firm leverage	Firm Leverage. It is calculated as the sum of the book value of short term and long term debt deflated by the book value of total assets.
Tangible assets	Assets Tangibility. It is calculated as tangible assets over total assets.
ROA	Profitability. It is measured as the ratio of earnings before interest and tax (EBIT) and the book value of total assets.
Sales growth	Growth in Sales. It is calculated as percentage change in sales year-on-year.
Year indicators	Dummy variables that indicate the acquired companies' fiscal years. The year 2004 is the excluded category.
Industry indicators	Dummy variables that indicate the acquired companies' industrial types. The agriculture, forestry, animal husbandry, and fishing sector are the excluded categories.

4.3. Empirical Model Specification

To test our two hypotheses relative to the relationships between family ultimate ownership structure and corporate value, we used the following regression model:

$$y_{it} = \beta_0 + \beta_1(\text{family ultimate ownership structure}) + \beta_2(\text{other governance variables})$$
$$+ \beta_3(controlvariables) + \beta_4(industrydummies) + \beta_5(yeardummies) + \varepsilon_{it} \tag{1}$$

where y_{it} = corporate value was measured as *Tobinq*, *Tobin70*, and *Tobin80*. Family ultimate ownership structure refers to two variables: controlling families' ultimate cash-flow rights (*family ownership*) and the divergence of controlling families' ultimate control and cash-flow rights (*wedge of control and ownership*). Other governance variables include *multiple large shareholders*, *independent directors*, *management ownership*, and *CEO duality*. The control variables comprise *firm size*, *firm age*, *firm leverage*, *tangible assets*, *ROA*, and *sales growth*.

For our five-year panel data set, we used the fixed effects method to estimate our regression models. Ultimate family ownership structure changed substantially over the sample period, and by nature, the fixed effects model requires longitudinal variation in the data (Andres [28]). Therefore, this equation can identify fixed effects. In addition, we used fixed-effects IV regression models to address endogeneity issues between family-ownership structure and corporate value.

5. Empirical Results

5.1. Descriptive Results

Table 3 presents the descriptive statistics of the data and shows that the average corporate value, measured by *Tobinq*, was 2.22, much lower than 2.99 (in Bai *et al.* [16]), 2.92 (in Wei *et al.* [33]), and 2.68 (in Tian and Estrin [19]). The latter three studies included both family and state-owned PLCs in their samples, which suggests that family-owned PLCs have much lower corporate value than do state-owned PLCs in China. Meanwhile, controlling families' ultimate cash-flow rights averaged about 23.8%, and their ultimate control and cash-flow rights averaged 2.06, indicating that Chinese family-controlled PLCs have high ownership concentration and largely diverging ultimate control and cash-flow rights. Of the total sample firms, 70.7% had more than one large shareholder with no less than 5% ownership. On average, about 35.8% of directors were independent, much lower than that in developed Western countries. In the sample firms, top managers owned an average of only 2.1% of their companies' shares. Only 18.0% of the CEOs were also either chairmen or vice chairmen of the board of directors, much lower than 35% when both family and state-owned PLCs were included (in Bai *et al.* [16]). This result means that Chinese state-owned PLCs much more frequently have dual CEOs and (vice) chairmen on their boards of directors.

More specifically, to derive more insightful knowledge about ultimate family-ownership structure in Chinese PLCs, we summarized yearly statistics for family-ownership structure over the sample period of 2004 to 2008. Table 4 shows the results indicating that controlling families' ultimate cash-flow rights decreased yearly, from 2004 to 2006, but markedly increased from 2007 to 2008. However, controlling families' ultimate control and cash-flow rights diverged increasingly each year in the first three years, but substantially decreased in the last two years. For example, controlling families reaches their lowest average ultimate cash-flow rights of 20.3% in 2006 but the highest of 27.6% in 2008, while their ultimate control and cash-flow rights have their highest average ratio of 2.37 in 2006 but their lowest of 1.78 in 2008. Thus family ownership structure in Chinese PLCs changed substantially during the sample period of 2004 to 2008. This change predominantly tended toward the weakening divergence of control and cash-flow rights.

Table 3. Results of descriptive statistics.

Variable	Number	Mean	SD	Min	P25	Median	P75	Max
Tobinq	1314	2.222	1.503	0.311	1.293	1.737	2.534	12.400
Tobin70	1314	1.641	1.035	0.311	1.014	1.295	1.837	10.839
Tobin80	1314	1.558	0.979	0.311	0.970	1.231	1.719	10.620
Family ownership	1314	0.238	0.150	0.005	0.119	0.214	0.314	0.797
Wedge of control and ownership	1314	2.062	1.917	1.000	1.059	1.430	2.257	26.656
Multiple large shareholders	1314	0.707	0.455	0	0	1	1	1
Independent directors	1314	0.358	0.049	0.000	0.333	0.333	0.375	0.600
Management ownership	1314	0.021	0.076	0.000	0.000	0.000	0.000	0.692
CEO duality	1314	0.180	0.385	0	0	0	0	1
Firm size	1314	21.068	0.888	18.157	20.452	20.994	21.645	24.288
Firm age	1314	1.929	0.635	0.000	1.609	2.079	2.398	2.833
Firm Leverage	1314	0.493	0.183	0.009	0.371	0.500	0.625	0.994
Tangible assets	1314	0.292	0.173	0.001	0.164	0.274	0.403	0.916
ROA	1314	0.060	0.088	−0.778	0.032	0.059	0.094	0.950
Sale growth	1314	0.276	1.119	−0.945	−0.012	0.152	0.361	29.817

See Table 2 for the definitions of variables.

Table 4. Summary statistics for family ownership structure in Chinese publicly listed companies (PLCs).

Year	Variable	Number	Mean	SD	Min	P25	Median	P75	Max
	Family ownership	162	0.219	0.137	0.011	0.113	0.212	0.279	0.742
2004	*Family control*	162	0.340	0.129	0.104	0.261	0.295	0.444	0.742
	Wedge of control and ownership	162	2.245	1.901	1.000	1.183	1.660	2.439	13.491
	Family ownership	183	0.211	0.127	0.006	0.112	0.203	0.268	0.742
2005	*Family control*	183	0.333	0.130	0.104	0.249	0.295	0.416	0.742
	Wedge of control and ownership	183	2.287	2.412	1.000	1.181	1.678	2.439	26.656
	Family ownership	268	0.203	0.130	0.005	0.105	0.186	0.270	0.678
2006	*Family control*	268	0.314	0.127	0.100	0.225	0.279	0.392	0.802
	Wedge of control and ownership	268	2.373	2.527	1.000	1.125	1.538	2.500	22.413
	Family ownership	314	0.244	0.149	0.014	0.138	0.218	0.326	0.797
2007	*Family control*	314	0.341	0.143	0.103	0.229	0.306	0.427	0.797
	Wedge of control and ownership	314	1.919	1.508	1.000	1.014	1.327	2.032	10.026
	Family ownership	387	0.276	0.170	0.011	0.146	0.248	0.381	0.765
2008	*Family control*	387	0.367	0.160	0.104	0.238	0.338	0.468	0.959
	Wedge of control and ownership	387	1.779	1.334	1.000	1.000	1.250	1.943	10.870
	Family ownership	1314	0.238	0.150	0.005	0.119	0.214	0.314	0.797
Total	*Family control*	1314	0.342	0.143	0.100	0.233	0.299	0.434	0.959
	Wedge of control and ownership	1314	2.062	1.917	1.000	1.059	1.430	2.257	26.656

See Table 2 for the definitions of variables.

Table 5 shows the correlation coefficients between main variables included in regression models, illustrating that the absolute values of correlation coefficients are much smaller than 0.5 except for the coefficients among our three alternative corporate value measurements. Hence, multicollinearity does not appear to be a significant problem in this study.

Table 5. Pearson correlation coefficients (excluding industry and year indicators).

Variable	1	2	3	4	5	6	7
1 *Tobinq*	1.000	-	-	-	-	-	-
2 *Tobin70*	0.958 ***	1.000	-	-	-	-	-
3 *Tobin80*	0.939 ***	0.998 ***	1.000	-	-	-	-
4 *Family ownership*	0.114 ***	0.027	0.008	1.000	-	-	-
5 *Wedge of control and ownership*	−0.072 ***	−0.062 **	−0.059 **	−0.513 ***	1.000	-	-
6 *Multiple large shareholders*	0.094 ***	0.053 *	0.043	−0.101 ***	0.025	1.000	-
7 *Independent directors*	0.043	0.046 *	0.046 *	0.100 ***	−0.047 *	−0.091 ***	1.000
8 *Management ownership*	0.093 ***	0.050 *	0.040	0.252 ***	−0.135 ***	0.083 ***	0.018
9 *CEO duality*	0.046 *	0.034	0.032	0.053 *	0.014	−0.002	0.093 ***
10 *Firm size*	−0.257 ***	−0.199 ***	−0.184 ***	0.030	0.030	−0.183 ***	−0.033
11 *Firm age*	−0.060 **	0.040	0.062 **	−0.334 ***	0.134 ***	−0.150 ***	−0.007
12 *Firm Leverage*	−0.219 ***	−0.144 ***	−0.126 ***	−0.090 ***	0.061 **	−0.082 ***	−0.041
13 *Tangible assets*	−0.045	−0.034	−0.032	−0.135 ***	0.140 ***	−0.040	−0.072 ***
14 *ROA*	0.210 ***	0.183 ***	0.175 ***	0.200 ***	−0.059 **	0.013	−0.017
15 *Sale growth*	0.018	0.010	0.008	0.102 ***	−0.026	0.003	0.010

Variable	8	9	10	11	12	13	14
8 *Management ownership*	1.000	-	-	-	-	-	-
9 *CEO duality*	0.272 ***	1.000	-	-	-	-	-
10 *Firm size*	−0.111 ***	−0.062 **	1.000	-	-	-	-
11 *Firm age*	−0.428 ***	−0.117 ***	0.122 ***	1.000	-	-	-
12 *Firm Leverage*	−0.176 ***	−0.132 ***	0.302 ***	0.266 ***	1.000	-	-
13 *Tangible assets*	−0.017	0.022	−0.010	−0.064 **	−0.015	1.000	-
14 *ROA*	0.123 ***	0.010	0.173 ***	−0.149 ***	−0.192 ***	−0.070 **	1.000
15 *Sales growth*	−0.003	0.005	0.041	−0.024	0.036	−0.033	0.092 ***

***, **, * denote significance at the 0.01, 0.05, and 0.10 levels, (two tailed test).

5.2. Regression Results

Table 6 reports the results of fixed-effects (within) regressions of family ownership on our three corporate value measures of *Tobinq*, *Tobin70*, and *Tobin80*. In Models 1 and 2 we used *Tobinq* as the measure of corporate value, Models 3 and 4 used *Tobin70*, Models 5 and 6 used *Tobin80*. In all models, we included control variables (e.g., *Firm size*, *Firm age*, *Firm leverage*, *Tangible assets*, *ROA*, *Sale growth*) commonly used in studies of corporate value, as well as year dummy variables and industry dummy variables.

Table 6. Results of fixed-effects (within) regression.

Variable	*Tobinq*		*Tobin70*		*Tobin80*	
	Model 1	Model 2	Model 3	Model 4	Model 5	Model 6
Family ownership	0.620	1.942 ***	−0.223	0.918 *	−0.344	0.771
	(1.16)	(2.66)	(−0.58)	(1.76)	(−0.94)	(1.55)
Family ownership squared	-	−5.587 ***	-	−4.823 ***	-	−4.713 ***
	-	(−2.65)	-	(−3.20)	-	(−3.28)
Wedge of control and ownership	−0.041	−0.008	−0.044 *	−0.016	−0.044 **	−0.017
	(−1.28)	(−0.25)	(−1.94)	(−0.67)	(−2.05)	(−0.75)
Multiple large shareholders	0.252 **	0.268 **	0.103	0.117	0.081	0.095
	(1.97)	(2.10)	(1.12)	(1.28)	(1.28)	(1.09)
Independent directors	2.016 **	1.980 **	2.029 ***	1.999 ***	2.031 ***	2.002 ***
	(2.30)	(2.26)	(3.23)	(3.20)	(3.39)	(3.36)
Management ownership	1.012	1.067	0.402	0.449	0.314	0.361
	(0.81)	(0.86)	(0. 45)	(0.51)	(0.37)	(0.43)
CEO duality	0.057	0.053	0.034	0.031	0.031	0.028
	(0.44)	(0.41)	(0.37)	(0.33)	(0.35)	(0.31)

Table 6. *Cont.*

Variable	Tobinq		Tobin70		Tobin80	
	Model 1	Model 2	Model 3	Model 4	Model 5	Model 6
Firm size	−0.688 ***	−0.662 ***	−0.517 ***	−0.495 ***	−0.493 ***	−0.471 ***
	(−5.10)	(−4.91)	(−5.35)	(−5.14)	(−5.35)	(−5.13)
Firm age	0.065	0.005	0.466 **	0.415 *	0.524 **	0.473 **
	(0.21)	(0.02)	(2.14)	(1.91)	(2.52)	(2.29)
Firm leverage	−0.062	−0.219	0.366	0.231	0.427	0.295
	(−0.15)	(−0.54)	(1.27)	(0.80)	(1.56)	(1.07)
Tangible assets	−0.356	−0.378	−0.278	−0.297	−0.267	−0.285
	(−0.88)	(−0.94)	(−0.96)	(−0.103)	(−0.97)	(−1.04)
ROA	2.508 ***	2.390 ***	1.797 ***	1.696 ***	1.696 ***	1.596 ***
	(4.60)	(4.38)	(4.60)	(4.35)	(4.55)	(4.30)
Sales Growth	−0.026	−0.018	−0.033	−0.026	−0.034 *	−0.027
	(−0.93)	(−0.65)	(−1.61)	(−1.27)	(−1.74)	(−1.39)
Intercept	14.960 ***	14.379 ***	10.510 ***	10.010 ***	9.878 ***	9.387 ***
	(5.40)	(5.20)	(5.31)	(5.07)	(5.23)	(4.98)
No. of obs.	1314	1314	1314	1314	1314	1314
No. of firms	465	465	465	465	465	465
F value	43.91 ***	42.85 ***	44.83 ***	44.04 ***	44.42 ***	43.68 ***
R^2	0.581	0.585	0.586	0.591	0.584	0.589
Ajusted R^2	0.332	0.337	0.340	0.347	0.336	0.344

(i) ***, **, and * denote significance at the 0.01, 0.05, and 0.10 levels, (two tailed test); (ii) T-statistics are provided in parentheses; (iii) See Table 2 for the definitions of variables.

As Table 6 displays, when the regressions included only *Family ownership*, we found no significant relationship between family ownership and corporate value (see Models 1, 3, and 5 in Table 6). However, when we included *family ownership* and *family ownership squared* into the regressions at the same time, *family ownership* had positive and almost significant coefficients for our three corporate value measures, and *family ownership squared* had negative and significant coefficients at the 1% level (see Models 2, 4, and 6, in Table 6). These findings indicate that in China, a nonlinear inverse-U-shaped relationship, rather than a linear relationship, occurs between family-concentrated ownership and corporate value, consistent with hypothesis 1. Using the coefficients of *family ownership* and *family ownership squared* from Model 4 and taking *Tobin70* as the measure of corporate value, we got the turning point of the nonlinear inverse-U-shaped relationship. On the turning point, *family ownership* equals approximately 33.27%. This value implies that a positive relationship occurs between *family ownership* and *Tobin70* when controlling families' ultimate ownership is below 33.27%, the interest-alignment effect of family-concentrated ownership, but a negative relationship occurs between *family ownership* and *Tobin70* when the controlling family's ultimate ownership is no less than 33.27%, the entrenchment effect of family-concentrated ownership.

Our results are more or less consistent with previous research in Canada, family ownership was found to be negatively related financial performance (Morck *et al.* [30]). In another study, panel data on S&P 500 firms showed firm performance and family holdings to have a nonlinear but inverted-U-shape (Anderson and Reeb [27]). Panel data on 275 German listed companies showed family ownership to be significantly and positively related with accounting performance, but slightly significantly related with market valuation through a 10%-level nonlinear relationship (Andres [28]). Combining the evidence, we argue that low levels of family-concentrated ownership can help resolve agency problems between shareholders and managers, but high levels of family-concentrated ownership and thus outright control might allow owners to expropriate minority shareholders to maximize their own utility, especially in emerging economies, such as China's, where legal investor protections are poor. However, our findings sharply contrast with three studies on state shareholdings in China (Bai *et al.* [16], Wei *et al.* [33], Tian and Estrin [19]) that find a nonlinear-U-shaped relationship between state shareholdings and corporate value. Those differing results may occur mainly from different ownership state-owned and family-controlled structures in the Chinese stock market (see Table 1). Once again, to avoid drawing murky and inconsistent conclusions, future researchers focusing on the issues of Chinese corporate ownership structure should be aware that Chinese state-owned and family-controlled companies are vastly different.

In terms of the divergence of the controlling family's ultimate control and cash-flow rights, the *Wedge of control and ownership* coefficients were negative in all regression models, as Hypothesis 2 predicts. However, only some are statistically significant (see Models 3 and 5, in Table 6). As a whole, hypothesis 2 is weakly supported. That is, the divergence of controlling families' ultimate control and cash-flow rights may exacerbate the expropriation of minority shareholders and thus reduce corporate value in China, which coincides with prior studies (e.g., Claessens *et al.* [3], Lemmon and Lins [39], Lin *et al.* [11,12], Maury [40], Yeh [21]).

In the context of concentrated-ownership structure, do traditional governance mechanisms play an effective governance role and affect corporate value? To answer that question, we examined the effects of four most-frequently mentioned governance variables on corporate value. As Table 6 shows, the *Multiple large shareholders* variable was positively related to corporate value in all regression models, but only significantly related to corporate value, as measured by *Tobinq* (see Models 1 and 2). Overall, the results indicate that multiple large shareholders are associated with higher corporate value, consistent with previous empirical findings (Attig *et al.* [41], Maury and Pajuste [42]). The proportion of independent directors on the boards had positive coefficients in all regression models, which is significant at least at the level of 5%. Hence, our findings strongly indicate that board independence can play an effective governance role in preventing controlling families from expropriating minority shareholders, thus improving corporate value. More specifically, our findings suggest that although the independent director system has a short history in China, it is now mature enough to play an effective governance role as intended in Chinese PLCs. In addition, we found no significant effects of management ownership and CEO duality on corporate value, indicating that the two traditional governance factors do not affect corporate value. Taken as a whole, the role of traditional internal governance mechanisms is much limited in the context of concentrated ownership (Berglöf and Pajuste [22], Claessens and Fan [23], Morck *et al.* [24]).

Of the six control variables, the nature log of total assets (*Firm size*) was negatively associated with corporate value at the 1% level of significance in all regression models. This result corroborates previous findings (e.g., Bai *et al.* [16], Tian and Estrin [19], Wei *et al.* [33]) and indicates that smaller firms have higher corporate value in the Chinese stock market. Similar to prior evidences, *ROA* positively affects corporate value at the 1% level of significance in all regression models, suggesting that better accounting performance is associated with higher corporate market performance in Chinese family-controlled PLCs. However, our results show no signs of significant and consistent effects of *Firm age*, *Firm leverage*, *Tangible assets*, and *Sales growth* on corporate value in the Chinese stock market.

5.3. Analysis of Endogeneity of Family Ownership and Corporate Value

Our results potentially suffer from an endogeneity issue: our observed relationship between family ownership and corporate value might be the result of reversed causality. Ownership structures are firm-specific and affected by compensation plans, insider trading possibilities, and corporate takeovers (Demsetz and Lehn [43], Demsetz and Villalonga [44]), which indicates that firm performance/value affect the ownership structure. In our study, family ownership might be an endogenous variable. However, the argument for the endogeneity of family ownership is questionable. Many empirical findings (e.g., Andres [28], Gugler and Weigand [45], Holderness [46], La Porta *et al.* [26]) suggest that ownership structures, especially large shareholder ownerships, are relatively stable over time. Hence, it seems unlikely that large family shareholders will change their ownership quickly and frequently in light of the firm's temporary market valuation.

Despite the questionable argument of the endogeneity issue, we tested the robustness of our results by employing an IV-2SLS panel-data model; that is, fixed-effects (within) IV regressions. Specifically, the ultimate cash-flow rights of family-controlling shareholders (*family ownership*) are instrumented by lagged value in all regressions. Table 7 shows the regression results drawn by this method. After controlling for endogeneity, the inverse-U-shaped relationship between family ownership and corporate value was still significant for all three measures of corporate value: *Tobinq*, *Tobin70*, and *Tobin80*. The results indicate that serious reversed causality may not occur between family ownership and corporate value. In other words, endogeneity of family ownership does not drive the inverse-U-shaped relationship between family ownership and corporate value drawn in this study.

Table 7. Results of fixed-effects (within) IV regression.

Variable	*Tobinq*		*Tobin70*		*Tobin80*	
	Model 1	Model 2	Model 3	Model 4	Model 5	Model 6
(Instrumented) *Family ownership*	1.902	7.101 *	0.655	4.907	0.477	4.594
	(0.92)	(1.76)	(0.42)	(1.62)	(0.32)	(1.58)
(Instrumented) *Family ownership squared*	-	−17.160 *	-	−14.040 **	-	−13.590 **
	-	(−1.89)	-	(−2.06)	-	(−2.07)
Wedge of control and ownership	−0.069	0.202	−0.084	0.138	−0.086	0.128
	(−0.73)	(1.05)	(−1.20)	(0.95)	(−1.28)	(0.92)
Multiple large shareholders	0.393 **	0.466 **	0.221	0.280 *	0.196	0.253 *
	(2.11)	(2.32)	(1.58)	(1.86)	(1.46)	(1.75)
Independent directors	3.017 **	2.933 **	2.770 ***	2.701 ***	2.735 ***	2.668 ***
	(2.46)	(2.35)	(3.01)	(2.89)	(3.09)	(2.97)
Management ownership	−1.822	−1.464	−0.740	−0.447	−0.586	−0.302
	(−0.97)	(−0.76)	(−0.52)	(−0.31)	(−0.43)	(−0.22)
CEO duality	0.064	0.080	0.057	0.071	0.056	0.069
	(0.37)	(0.45)	(0.43)	(0.52)	(0.44)	(0.53)
Firm size	−0.866 ***	−0.812 ***	−0.624 ***	−0.579 ***	−0.589 ***	−0.546 ***
	(−3.68)	(−3.47)	(−3.53)	(−3.30)	(−3.46)	(−3.23)
Firm age	1.816 **	1.550 **	1.444 ***	1.227 **	1.391 ***	1.181 **
	(2.55)	(2.15)	(2.71)	(2.27)	(2.71)	(2.27)
Firm leverage	0.159	−0.340	0.478	0.071	0.524	0.129
	(0.30)	(−0.56)	(1.22)	(0.16)	(1.39)	(0.30)
Tangible assets	−0.907	−1.051 *	−0.744 *	−0.861 **	−0.720 *	−0.834 **
	(−1.62)	(−1.81)	(−1.77)	(−1.97)	(−1.78)	(−1.99)
ROA	2.446 ***	2.118 **	1.847 ***	1.579 **	1.761 ***	1.501 **
	(3.08)	(2.49)	(3.10)	(2.47)	(3.07)	(2.45)
Sales Growth	−0.002	−0.001	0.001	0.001	0.001	0.001
	(−0.05)	(−0.02)	(0.01)	(0.04)	(0.02)	(0.05)
Intercept	13.950 ***	12.180 ***	9.899 ***	8.601 ***	9.319 ***	8.090 **
	(3.23)	(2.75)	(3.05)	(2.59)	(2.99)	(2.53)
No. of obs.	821	820	821	820	821	820
No. of firms	333	332	333	332	333	332
Wald Chi2	6037.85 ***	5830.66 ***	6319.63 ***	6089.70 ***	6255.79 ***	6029.60 ***

(i) ***, **, and * denote significance at the 0.01, 0.05, and 0.10 levels, (two tailed test); (ii) Z-statistics are provided in parentheses; (iii) See Table 2 for the definitions of variables.

6. Conclusions

In this paper, we investigate the relationship between ultimate family-ownership structure and corporate value using a five-year panel data set of 1314 firm-year observations from China's family-controlled PLCs from 2004 to 2008. Unlike previous studies that propose a simple linear relationship between ownership concentration and corporate value, we argue and find a nonlinear inverse-U-shaped relationship between family ownership and corporate value in China's emerging economy where minority shareholders have poor legal protection. More specifically, we study the relationships between controlling families' ultimate cash-flow rights and corporate value, and between the divergence of controlling families' ultimate control and cash-flow rights and corporate value.

We find significant and consistent results. First, we find that the relationship between the controlling family's ultimate cash-flow rights and corporate value, as measured by Tobin's Q, exhibits a significant nonlinear inverse-U-shaped pattern, known as the interest-alignment and entrenchment effects of family-concentrated ownership. That is, the left half of the inverse-U-shaped curve reflects the interest-alignment effect of family-concentrated ownership, while the right half reflects the entrenchment effect. Second, we find evidence of a significant and negative relationship between the divergence of control and cash-flow rights and corporate value, which is consistent with prior studies. Third, we corroborate previous findings that both multiple large shareholders and high board independence are significantly associated with higher corporate value, but other governance mechanisms such as management ownership and CEO duality do not have significant and consistent effects on corporate value. These findings suggest that in the context of concentrated ownership, some traditional governance mechanisms would be ineffective for reducing agency costs and improving corporate value. Finally, our robustness tests of potential endogeneity between family ownership structure and corporate value future suggest that our results are robust.

Our findings add to our understanding of the relationship between family ownership structure and corporate value. Specifically, family-concentrated ownership has two competing effects: interest-alignment and entrenchment. The level of family-ownership concentration determines which effect dominates. In other words, increased family-ownership concentration does not always enhance corporate value. Controlling family-ownership concentration plays its best governance roles at moderate levels. Moreover, in the context of family-concentrated ownership, both multiple large shareholders and high board independence can play effective governance roles by restricting controlling families from expropriating minority shareholders, thus, enhancing corporate value. In practice, our findings suggest regulators (e.g., CSRC in China) should particularly supervise potential expropriation of minority shareholders in family-owned firms where controlling families hold high concentrated ownership, without multiple large shareholders structure, and/or having low board independence. For outside investors, they should avoid investing in family-owned firms with above features.

Despite these theoretical contributions and practical implications, future research should mainly address two limitations of this study. First, besides family ownership, family management is the other side of coin in family-controlled firms. How family management may interact with family ownership in driving firm performance would be an important research question in the future. Second, since firm performance is a complex function of many factors, it deserves research attention to go a step further to explore specific channels through which family-concentrated ownership affects firm performance.

Acknowledgments: Jin-Hui Luo acknowledge the financial support from the Chinese National Science Funds (Grant No. 71202061) and Fujian Provincial Social Science Planning Youth Project (Grant no. 2012C027), and Heng Liu acknowledge the financial support from the Chinese National Science Funds (Grant No. 71202093), the Postdoctoral Science Foundation of China (Grant no. 2011M500136 and 2013T60825), and the 985 Project (the innovation base for Chinese family business research) from Sun Yat-sen University. All remaining errors belong to us.

Author Contributions: Both authors contributed equally to this paper.

Conflicts of Interest: The authors declare no conflict of interest.

References

1. Allen, F.; Qian, J.; Qian, M. Law, finance, and economic growth in China. *J. Financ. Econ.* **2005**, *77*, 57–116. [CrossRef]
2. Ding, Y.; Zhang, H.; Zhang, J. Private *vs* state ownership and earnings management: Evidence from Chinese listed companies. *Corp. Gov.* **2007**, *15*, 223–238. [CrossRef]
3. Claessens, S.; Djankov, S.; Fan, J.; Lang, L. Disentangling the incentive and entrenchment effects of large shareholdings. *J. Financ.* **2002**, *57*, 2741–2771. [CrossRef]
4. Faccio, M.; Lang, L. The ultimate ownership of Western European corporations. *J. Financ. Econ.* **2002**, *65*, 365–395. [CrossRef]
5. La Porta, R.; Lopez-de-Silanes, F.; Shleifer, A.; Vishny, R. Investor protection and corporate valuation. *J. Financ.* **2002**, *57*, 1147–1170. [CrossRef]
6. Grossman, S.J.; Hart, O.D. Takeover bids, the free-rider problem, and the theory of the corporation. *Bell J. Econ.* **1980**, *11*, 42–64. [CrossRef]
7. Jensen, M.C.; Meckling, W.H. Theory of the firm: Managerial behavior, agency costs and ownership structure. *J. Financ. Econ.* **1976**, *3*, 305–360. [CrossRef]
8. Aslan, H.; Kumar, P. Strategic ownership structure and the cost of debt. *Rev. Financ. Stud.* **2012**, *25*, 2257–2299. [CrossRef]

9.   Shleifer, A.; Vishny, R. A survey of corporate governance. *J. Financ.* **1997**, *52*, 737–783. [CrossRef]
10.   Adams, R.; Ferreira, D. One share-one vote: The empirical evidence. *Rev. Financ.* **2008**, *12*, 51–91. [CrossRef]
11.   Lin, C.; Ma, Y.; Xuan, Y. Ownership structure and financial constraints: Evidence from a structural estimation. *J. Financ. Econ.* **2011**, *102*, 416–431. [CrossRef]
12.   Lin, C.; Ma, Y.; Malatesta, P.; Xuan, Y. Corporate ownership structure and bank loan syndicate structure. *J. Financ. Econ.* **2012**, *104*, 1–22. [CrossRef]
13.   Johnson, S.; La Porta, R.; Lopez-de-Silanes, F.; Shleifer, A. Tunneling. *Am. Econ. Re.* **2000**, *90*, 22–27. [CrossRef]
14.   Friedman, E.; Johnson, S.; Mitton, T. Propping and tunneling. *J. Comp. Econ.* **2003**, *31*, 732–750. [CrossRef]
15.   Dyck, A.; Zingales, L. Private benefits of control: An international comparison. *J. Financ.* **2004**, *59*, 537–600. [CrossRef]
16.   Bai, C.E.; Liu, Q.; Song, F.M.; Zhang, J. Corporate governance and market valuation in China. *J. Comp. Econ.* **2004**, *32*, 599–616. [CrossRef]
17.   De Miguel, A.; Pindado, J.; De la Torre, C. How do entrenchment and expropriation phenomena affect control mechanisms? *Corp. Gov.* **2005**, *13*, 505–516. [CrossRef]
18.   Morck, R.; Shleifer, A.; Vishny, R. Management ownership and market valuation: An empirical analysis. *J. Financ. Econ.* **1988**, *20*, 293–315. [CrossRef]
19.   Tian, L.; Estrin, S. Retain state shareholding in Chinese PLCs: Does government ownership always reduce corporate value? *J. Comp. Econ.* **2008**, *36*, 74–89. [CrossRef]
20.   Yeh, Y.; Lee, T.; Woidtke, T. Family control and corporate governance: Evidence from Taiwan. *Int. Rev. Financ.* **2001**, *2*, 21–48. [CrossRef]
21.   Yeh, Y. Do controlling shareholders enhance corporate value? *Corp. Gov.* **2005**, *13*, 313–325. [CrossRef]
22.   Berglöf, E.; Pajuste, A. Corporate Governance and Capital Flows in a Global Economy. In *Emerging Owners, Eclipsing Markets? Corporate Governance in Central and Eastern Europe*; Cornelius, P.K., Kogut, B., Eds.; Oxford University Press: Oxford, UK, 2003.
23.   Claessens, S.; Fan, J. Corporate governance in Asia: A survey. *Int. Rev. Financ.* **2002**, *3*, 71–103.
24.   Morck, R.; Wolfenzon, D.; Yeung, B. Corporate governance, economic entrenchment, and growth. *J. Econ. Lit.* **2005**, *43*, 655–720. [CrossRef]
25.   Claessens, S.; Djankov, S.; Lang, L.H.P. The separation of ownership and control in East Asian corporations. *J. Financ. Econ.* **2000**, *58*, 81–112. [CrossRef]
26.   La Porta, R.; Lopez-de-Silanes, F.; Shleifer, A. Corporate ownership around the world. *J. Financ.* **1999**, *54*, 471–517. [CrossRef]
27.   Anderson, R.C.; Reeb, D.M. Founding-family ownership and firm performance: Evidence from the S&P 500. *J. Financ.* **2003**, *58*, 1301–1328. [CrossRef]
28.   Andres, C. Large shareholders and firm performance—An empirical examination of founding-family ownership. *J. Corp. Financ.* **2008**, *14*, 431–445. [CrossRef]
29.   Goergen, M. *Corporate Governance and Financial Performance: A Study of German and U.K*; Edward Elgar Publishing Ltd.: Cheltenham, UK, 1999; Initial Public Offerings.
30.   Morck, R.; Strangeland, D.; Yeung, B. Inherited Wealth, Corporate Control and Economic Growth: The Canadian Disease. In *In Concentrated Corporate Ownership*; Morck, R., Ed.; University of Chicago Press: Chicago, IL, USA, 2000.
31.   Fan, J.; Wong, T.; Zhang, T. *The Emergence of Corporate Pyramids in China*; The Chinese University of Hong Kong: Hong Kong, China, 2005.
32.   Watanabe, M. Holding company risk in China: A final step of state-owned enterprises reform and an emerging problem of corporate governance. *China Econ. Rev.* **2002**, *13*, 373–381. [CrossRef]
33.   Wei, Z.; Xie, F.; Zhang, S. Ownership structure and corporate value in China's privatized firms: 1991–2001. *J. Financ. Quant. Anal.* **2005**, *40*, 87–108. [CrossRef]
34.   Shleifer, A.; Vishny, R. Large shareholders and corporate control. *J. Political Econ.* **1986**, *94*, 461–488.
35.   North, D.C. *Institutions, Institutional Change and Economic Performance*; Cambridge University Press: Cambridge, UK, 1990.
36.   Faccio, M.; Lang, L.H.P.; Young, L. Dividends and expropriation. *Am. Econ. Rev.* **2001**, *91*, 54–78. [CrossRef]
37.   Le Breton-Miller, I.; Miller, D. Agency *vs.* stewardship in public family firms: A social embeddedness reconciliation. *Entrep. Theory Pract.* **2009**, *33*, 1169–1191. [CrossRef]

38. Chen, Z.; Xiong, P. The Illiquidity Discount in China. Working Paper. International Center for Financial Research, Yale University: New Haven, CT, USA, 2002.

39. Lemmon, M.L.; Lin, K. Ownership structure, corporate governance, and corporate value: Evidence from the East Asian financial crisis. *J. Financ.* **2003**, *58*, 1445–1468. [CrossRef]

40. Maury, B. Family ownership and firm performance: Empirical evidence from Western European corporations. *J. Corp. Financ.* **2006**, *12*, 321–341. [CrossRef]

41. Attig, N.; Ghoul, S.E.; Guedhami, O. Do multiple large shareholders play a corporate governance role: Evidence from East Asia. *J. Financ. Res.* **2009**, *32*, 395–422. [CrossRef]

42. Maury, B.; Pajuste, A. Multiple large shareholders and corporate value. *J. Bank. Finance* **2005**, *29*, 1813–1834. [CrossRef]

43. Demsetz, H.; Lehn, K. The structure of corporate ownership: Causes and consequences. *J. Political Econ.* **1985**, *93*, 1155–1177.

44. Demsetz, H.; Villalonga, B. Ownership structure and corporate performance. *J. Corp. Finance* **2001**, *7*, 209–233. [CrossRef]

45. Gugler, K.; Weigand, J. Is ownership really endogenous? *Appl. Econo. Lett.* **2003**, *10*, 483–486. [CrossRef]

46. Holderness, C.G. A survey of blockholders and corporate control. *Econ. Policy Rev.* **2003**, *4*, 51–63.

International Journal of
Financial Studies

MDPI

Review

Review of Family Business Definitions: Cluster Approach and Implications of Heterogeneous Application for Family Business Research

Henrik Harms

Hamburg Institute of International Economics (HWWI), Heimhuder Straße 71, 20148 Hamburg, Germany;
harms@hwwi.org; Tel.: +49-40-340576-462; Fax: +49-40-340576-776

Received: 24 April 2014; in revised form: 12 July 2014; Accepted: 15 July 2014; Published: 23 July 2014

Abstract: This review article displays several attempts to define family businesses as well as a systematization approach to get new insights about the relationship between family business definitions and their application under different conditions such as legal framework, culture or regional understanding of family. Potential explanations for the ambiguity of what is meant by family firms are revealed by reviewing 267 journal articles. A consensus about the object of investigation would result in a deeper understanding of family firms' uniqueness, might lead to more reliable comparative studies as well as interdisciplinary work (e.g., finance and family firms) and enables a quicker consolidation of family business research, especially in contrast to research on small and medium-sized enterprises and entrepreneurship. Therefore, the present review contributes to the development of family business research by providing an initial attempt to comprehensively systematized existing family firm definitions which could be used by researchers in family business research.

Keywords: family business; systematic literature review; cluster approach to systemize family business definitions; reasons for heterogeneity in family business definitions; implications for business management

JEL Classification: D02; D20; D23; L25; L26

---

1. Introduction

While some studies identified only 15% of all enterprises as family businesses (Kayser and Wallau 2002 [1]), [1] others classified up to 79% of all companies as family firms (Chrisman *et al.* 2004 [2]). Therefore, family business studies do not build on a unified definition of the object of investigation so that the progress of the academic field might be hampered which could lead to a delayed consolidation of family business theory.

Admittedly, family business research gets more and more accepted as independent field of study in (business) economics, which can be observed by looking at the increasing number of newly published journals (e.g., Journal of Family Business Strategy), special issues (e.g., Entrepreneurship Theory and Practice, Volume 37, Issue 1, January 2013, Special Issue on Entrepreneurial and Family Business Teams) and conference tracks (e.g., Strategic Interest Group at European Academy of Management) on

---

[1]　The terms "family business" and "family firm" are used synonymously throughout this article since subdividing this group of companies does not contribute to the research objective. It should be analysed how the object of investigation is generally defined in refereed articles and not on which individual aspects of the heterogeneous group of family companies single articles focus. This is a common procedure in family business research but have to be separated from "family-owned businesses/firms" since these terms only focus on a specific aspect of family businesses, *i.e.*, ownership.

Int. J. Financial Stud. **2014**, *2*, 280–314

this specific group of companies. Moreover, many articles vividly discussing previous progress and future development potential have been published (e.g., Sharma *et al.* 2012 [3]) so that the importance of family business research is still accelerating.

However, one major deficit of family business research with regard to its consolidation and its ultimate establishment in economic sciences might be that there is still "no clarity what is meant by a family firm" (Chittoor and Das 2007 [4]). In spite of longstanding scientific research on family business issues and the considerable economic relevance of this group of companies, no jointly accepted definition exists within the research field. Results differ significantly depending on contextual issues such as the topic, the area under examination and the period of investigation. This in turn might impede comparative family business analyses as well as those pointed at the analysis of differences to small and medium-sized enterprises. Moreover, the understanding of the term "family" varies to a great extent in scientific analyses which again influences how researchers conceptualize "family firms". [2] Without a widely accepted broad understanding of the characteristics influencing family businesses' behavior and outcomes, a common starting point for a joint approach to define family firms which is also suitable for comparative analyses is missing. In the absence of an accurate definition, conclusions would be taken without sufficiently considering family businesses' strategic and personal orientation or its behavior which might lead to invalid findings. This lack of consensus on a unified family business definition not only limits the development of a theory of the family firm which might be suitable to distinguish this specific group of companies from other organizational structures but also hampers interdisciplinary work on issues such as financial management in family firms.

2. Objective and Research Questions

This article tries to conduct a comprehensive review about the application of family business definitions in studies published in highly ranked and family business specific journals. Expect from a study published by Chrisman *et al.* 2010 [5] identifying and reviewing the 25 most influential articles in family business research and an analysis conducted by Siebels and Knyphausen-Aufsess 2012 [6] about theoretical perspectives applied in family business research and its implications for corporate governance structures, hardly any comprehensive review on family businesses exists. Thus, the present study focuses on the specific aspect of defining family firms and integrates a broader range of articles into the review to contribute to come closer to a widely accepted definition of family businesses. Another important goal is to raise awareness of the possibility to systematically define family firms and the consequences of having multiple definitions for theory building and empirical studies, which might be particularly relevant for scholars from other disciplines who like to examine family businesses. Thereby, the review pursues a twofold research objective. First, the article groups existing studies about family businesses to afore developed definitional clusters. Thereby, this review does not aim at providing a new definition in addition to the numerous existing ones, but would like to provide a classification approach which enables researchers to get an overview about previously applied definitions.

Thus, the first central research question can be formulated as follows:

> Which existing definitions have family business researchers mainly applied in their studies to date and how can these definitional approaches be clustered?

Future researchers might benefit from getting a better comprehension of which family business definitions have been used in previous studies, especially concerning specific topics or within a

---

[2] Although an increasing amount of literature about the definition and understanding of the term "family" exists, this review does not intend to comprehensively discuss this aspect because previous research in the family business field has hardly addressed this issue. However, it should be referred to the literature from the field of family studies which is recommended to consider in future family business analyses.

certain timeframe, because they get the opportunity to locate their own (intended) study within the "family business theory jungle" (Rutherford *et al.* 2008 [7] (p. 1102)).

However, even if it might be helpful to review and cluster different family business definitions for the further improvement of a unified family business research, this study should be supplemented by a deeper look at the reasons for the current heterogeneity in defining the object of investigation. Therefore, the article's further purpose is to detect the underlying reasons for the continuous absence of a unified family business definition in spite of the long lasting scientific research on the topic and the considerable economic relevance of the object of investigation.

Hence, the second research question to be answered can be formulated as follows:

> Why have family business researchers not found a consensus on a single, commonly accepted definition which can be applied in family business studies?

Thus, the present review aims to refine attempts to systematically examine the numerous definitional approaches. By exclusively focusing on the status quo and the development of family business definitions and by integrating recently published articles, this study extends existing review articles. Instead of developing further family business definitions or a sub-classification schemes, this review-article aims to sensitize researchers to the issue and to give recommendations for dealing with the definitional ambiguity. Thus, it is intended to allow future researchers to classify their chosen definition before starting a specific analysis which might particularly facilitate to conduct issue-specific or comparative studies because research results cannot be compared if studies are not based on the same assumptions concerning the variable of interest. It should prevent that findings in family business research are based on samples not consistently defined. This might lead to skewed empirical evidence because especially "performance results are sensitive to family firm definitions" (Sacristan-Navarro *et al.* 2011 [8]) and "different definitions offer different findings" (Astrachan and Zellweger 2008 [9]).

Consequently, a literature review covering 267 family business articles has been conducted to find indications to respond to the central research questions and to contribute to a consolidation of the field of family business research. [3] By being part of the *International Journal of Financial Studies* Special Issue on family firms, this review will provide a foundation for finance scholars and academics in other disciplines to frame their work toward investigating family firms.

3. Literature Review

Only a few reviews on different aspects of family businesses' distinctiveness have been carried out in the last decade. However, these studies mostly focused on specific topics such as financial performance [9], familiness (Frank *et al.* 2010 [10]), corporate governance [6] or internationalization (Pukall and Calabrò 2013 [11]), but did not aim to analyze how researchers define their object of investigation, the family businesses. They often placed special emphasis on particular issues without discussing about the choice of a suitable definition in detail instead of explicitly trying to systematically analyze which definition should be applied under which conditions (e.g., Mazzi 2011 [12]). Academics should not be accused for this behavior since they intend to further elaborate existing research on specific topics. Nevertheless, research on family business definitions is also crucial to enhance findings in the entire field of family firms so that the definitional issue should be again set on the agenda because the necessary condition for the development of an independent theory of family businesses is an unambiguously defined population. Even if sufficient conditions for high-quality research, such as reliable assumptions concerning the empirical investigation, are fulfilled, scientific goals can hardly be reached in the absence of the necessary condition, an explicitly defined family business variable (Bhattacherjee 2012 [13]).

---

[3] All researchers interested in getting the entire list of journal articles considered for the review are welcome to contact the author.

First review studies, which refer to the ongoing debate about a consistent concept to uniformly define family businesses, predominantly discussed advantages and drawbacks of different definitional approaches and pointed to the need to undertake efforts so as to establish a basis for a unified definition. However, they have not found ways to solve the definitional ambiguity to date (e.g., Dekker *et al.* 2013 [14]). One of the latest comprehensive studies on definitional issues has been conducted by Sharma in 2004 [15]. This overview about the field of family business studies focused on reasoning why family firms should be analyzed separately by exclusively looking at the level of family involvement. Sharma stated that existing research succeeded in distinguishing family businesses from non-family firms since they differ in terms of control mechanisms, visions or the creation of resources. However, the study did not primarily concentrate on a systematic classification of family business definitions. Moreover, the assumption stated by Sharma in 2004 that general purpose classification systems to distinguish between family and nonfamily firms and between different types of family businesses will be developed soon did not come true until today—at least not in the sense that a commonly accepted definitional classification scheme exists.

In order to illustrate how the applied definitions can be clustered so that the systematization can serve as orientation for future research, this section should briefly outline principle developments and problematic areas that arose over time concerning the family business definition.

The development of family business research as an autonomous academic field began with Donnelley's article "The family business", published in Harvard Business Review in 1964 [16]. He pointed to specific features of family businesses such as family members' involvement in the business, consequences of their influence on key business success factors, the composition of the management board or succession decisions (Zachary 2011 [17]). Thus, Donnelley defined a family business as follows:

> "A company is considered a family business when it has been closely identified with at least two generations of a family and when this link has had a mutual influence on company policy and on the interests and objectives of the family." [17] (p. 94)

Donnelley points to multiple conditions being of importance for family business research instead of focusing on single dimensions such as ownership, family involvement in the business or generational transfer, as observed in most previous and subsequent studies (Handler 1989 [18]).

After years of advancements, research on family businesses apparently reached a breakthrough with the release of Family Business Review (1988), the first regularly published self-contained journal. In their editorial, Lansberg *et al.* 1988 [19] dealt with the question why it is of great importance to define what is meant by family businesses as distinctive organizational structures. The authors pointed to the need to systematically demarcate this type of business from others due to environmental developments such as the increasing number of upcoming succession decisions in the American economy or the changing interrelation between family and working issues. However, Lansberg *et al.* did not give an explicit definition of what they understand by family firms but rather critically considered that previous studies had neglected family firms as unique organizational structures. Notwithstanding, Lansberg *et al.* made a substantial contribution to the theoretical development because their editorial initiated a systematic discussion about the relevance of family business definitions.

In the following years, researchers increasingly devoted their knowledge to the field. They analyzed numerous different subjects ranging from general effects related to ownership, family involvement in management, generational transfer and governance to specific topics such as innovative behavior or the role of trust for firms' cooperative behavior (for an overview see Yu *et al.* 2012 [20]). To name just a few selected researchers, who have been most frequently cited in family business studies and therefore played a decisive part in developing an extensive theory in early family business research, it should be referred to Handler [18], Litz 1995 [21], Wortman 1995 [22], Shanker and Astrachan 1996 [23], Gersick *et al.* 1997 [24], Wall 1998 [25] or Westhead and Cowling 1998 [26]. All these studies investigated in finding angles to systematically define family firms in manifold ways, for instance by emphasizing companies' distinctiveness in contrast to their non-family counterparts or by classifying family firms along multiple dimensions such as family involvement in ownership and management. These studies include newly developed approaches, modifications of already established definitions as well as sub-classifications to define family businesses.

While Daily and Dollinger found in 1992 [27] that there seems to be no possibility to reliably define family firms a priori, researchers outlined in recent publications that disagreement about the definition of a family business persists, but stressed hope to come closer to a unified definition. A well-known conclusion regarding the way of dealing with the numerous definitions was offered by Chrisman *et al.* 2005 [28] stating that ideally all researchers should start with a common family business definition, but also emphasizing that:

> "[...] the definition of a family business must be based on what researchers understand to be the differences between the family and nonfamily businesses." [28] (p. 557)

Thus, the discussion about a unified definition of the object of investigation is evidently not a thing of the past, but continues to be of great importance. For instance, O'Boyle *et al.* 2012 [29] recently conducted a meta-analysis about the predictive explanatory power of studies analyzing the relationship between family involvement and firm performance. With regard to the definitional ambiguity they found that:

> "Our search confirmed this [a lack of consensus as to how to operationalize family involvement; author's note] as we identified over thirty definitions of family involvement across included studies. These articles used between one and eight criteria to determine the family involvement of a firm." [29] (p. 8)

Although numerous persuasive reasons to use a self-developed definition might exist (and will be discussed in Section 6), it could potentially lead to an increasing heterogeneity in the use of family business definitions to apply them without trying to build upon existing definitions. This in turn might foster the tendency to insufficiently define the object of investigation and to neglect the necessity to find a consensus concerning the definitional issue.

4. Methods

4.1. Selection of Journals and Articles

To respond to the major research questions, the author identified 267 journal articles through a tripartite selection process.

In a first step, the selection process was aimed at restricting the comprehensive amount of family business publications to a manageable number of studies with regard to relevance and time. Therefore, only studies published as journal articles were considered for the analysis. Monographs, dissertations and "grey literature" such as conference papers or unpublished articles were excluded due to the assumption that only peer-reviewed publications could guarantee an appropriate quality level. To limit the extent of reviewed journals and to ensure a reasonable degree of actuality, the first issue of Family Business Review [19] was chosen as starting point for the analysis. In place of trying to include as many family business related publications as possible to give an all-embracing historical overview on the development of family business research, this review focuses on the most influential (citied) articles since 1988 identified through corresponding lists provided by academic publishing companies such as Sage Publications or Elsevier. This not only represents a common procedure to give a summary of existing approaches to handle a specific research question (e.g., [15]; [5]; Kraus *et al.* 2011 [30]; [12]; or Sharma and Carney 2012 [31] for other review articles about family business related topics) but also enables researchers and other interested groups to easily understand the scientific discourse about family business research—especially considering the dynamics in the chronological development and in terms of contents.

Secondly, the selection of journals has been restricted to all refereed family business journals as well as those from related disciplines such as small business research to ensure that the journal's main issue is to address family business topics and to guarantee a sufficient degree of journal quality. Thus, the most important journals for the field have been taken into account; with particular attention to Family Business Review (88 articles), Entrepreneurship Theory and Practice (25 articles), Journal of Family Business Strategy (24 articles), Journal of Business Research (12 articles), Journal of Small Business Management (11 articles) and Journal of Business Venturing (10 articles). Additionally, the remaining 97 articles are composed of studies directly pointed at family business issues and published in highly ranked journals (A+ or A) according to the official journal classification of the German Academic Association for Business Research. The VHB-JOURQUAL2 rates international publications regarded as relevant for business research and identified 64 journals classified as A+ or A (Schrader and Hennig-Thurau 2009 [32]). The selection procedure should ensure that only family business related publications of high quality are considered for this review. [4]

Thirdly, all journal articles identified through the first steps were inspected using a keyword search. Apart from the terms "Family (Owned) Business", "Family Business Characteristics", "Family Firm" and "Definition/Define", each article's section outlining applied methods or the sample selection was checked for indications of a family business definition. Therefore, electronic full-text databases, such as ProQuest, EBSCO Host and Academic OneFile, have been utilized and an additional keyword search in each article (as Adobe PDF) has been manually conducted.

After having conducted these three selection steps, the general topic of each article has been considered as additional exclusion criteria to decide whether there is a particular need to define family business. Although researchers are advised to determine their object of investigation as precisely as possible in any case [13], it is even more important in analyses with a special focus on theory development, performance issues or strategic behavior. In these subject areas, a precise definition of what is meant by family business is crucial because reliable results with regard to these topics, which can be compared with those for other types of enterprises, could only be yielded by taking family firms' distinctiveness into account. Instead of integrating numerous articles which do not match some of the criteria discussed in the selection process (relevance, quality, topic, date of publication), only those articles should be considered which necessarily require an appropriate family business definition since articles' findings might be otherwise prone to biases or at least incomparable results.

In total, 267 journal articles have been reviewed in detail. Only (business) economic studies or those from closely related fields which have been passed through the described selection process have been included—independent of their theoretical or methodological orientation.

4.2. Development of Clusters for Analytical Approach

After having identified articles of importance from refereed and/or family business journals which played a major role for the theoretical progress of family business research, definitional clusters should be developed. First of all, the general target of this cluster approach is to focus on main trends concerning the definition identified in family business research in recent decades rather than to develop another extensive differentiation of family business subgroups. Thereby, it should be contributed to a better understanding of topics frequently discussed in family business research and one of its central challenges, *i.e.*, to find a widely accepted and measurable definition to theoretically and empirically test previously developed hypotheses.

These clusters have been established by firstly screening the most cited articles published in the afore-mentioned journals in a chronological order to detect frequently used family firm definitions. For that purpose, a manually conducted keyword search—analogous to the procedure to detect family business definitions within the considered journal articles—has been conducted. This not only yielded

---

[4]   A list covering all journals under review is provided in Table A2 in Appendix 7.4.

to which of the following six clusters the articles have to be assigned to but also allowed for inference about several additional criteria such as journal, region under study, theoretical grounding, topic or date of publication. The connections between the applied definitional approach and these examination criteria shed light on general trends in the application of family business definitions by researchers. Are there any relationships between the theoretical approach and the family firm definition applied by authors? Do some journals favor articles in which the analysis can be traced back to certain family business definition? These and other two-dimensional coherences can be scrutinized by integrating the afore-mentioned variables. Thereby, the definitional approach should be regarded as central unit of analysis because this review's overall target is to identify and to some extent explain which family business definitions have been predominantly applied to date, how they can be clustered and why no widely accepted family business definition still exist.

To identify which conceptualization complies with the requirements of a consistent family business definition scheme, studies published between the first issue of Family Business Review in 1988 and the end of 2012 have been worked through. Thereby, examinations focusing on definitional or conceptual issues of family business research should meet the following crucial criteria to be potentially selected as cluster for this review. All relevant elements identified to be of importance to differentiate between family firms and other businesses should be considered, for instance ownership structure, involvement of the family in management decisions and transgenerational issues (e.g., [28]). Moreover, the definition has to be widely accepted in the research area, which means it has been disproportionately often applied by other family business researchers. Thereby, modifications in the theoretical or methodological approach as well as alterations in terms of content can cause that definitions are selected for classification in this review. Knowing that multiple other options exist how to systemize family business definitions, e.g., in terms of theoretical orientation or empirical investigation, this review follows the described intention to trace its classification back to operationalization issues and contents which have been changes in the course of time. [5]

5. Clustering Approach

In this section, a description of the six identified clusters and its emergence will be followed by some references about the main contents of the respective approaches to define family businesses. Each of the identified 267 journal articles was assigned to one of the six categories for a detailed analysis.

5.1. Cluster 1: Components of Involvement Approach and Essence Approach

Since Chua *et al.* conducted a first well-known comprehensive review of family firm definitions in 1999 [33] in which they proposed an attempt to systematically define the object of investigation by differentiating between components- and essence-based approaches, this method provides the basis for cluster 1. Although the concepts could also be regarded as distinct means to define family firms since they differ in terms of theoretical and empirical orientation [33], components and essence jointly depict essential elements of family businesses which are subject of discussion since several years. In these debates, current research came to the agreement that both concepts should be integrated in a well-grounded family business definition. Chua *et al.* in 1999 [33] as well as Chrisman *et al.* in 2005 [28] state that the concepts are complementary rather than competing and every consistent definition should be traced back on elements from both approaches since otherwise crucial characteristics of family businesses might be ignored. This classification has been chosen since Chua *et al.* had been the first authors claiming that the components of involvement have been linked to essence factors. Subsequently, the authors provided a definition on which multiple following studies are grounded so

---

[5] The cluster approach tries to depict a wide range of definitions, but does not raise a claim to completeness. Although, other definitional clusters can—if sufficiently justified—be applied, the author advocates for the use of this systematization in further studies in the interests of comparability.

that the complementary approaches of components and essence should be treated as basis of cluster 1. Taking the fundamental propositions of both approaches into account means that studies consider all relevant elements identified by Chua *et al.* to precisely define family firms [28]. Chua *et al.* explicitly pointed to the need to complement the previously applied components of family involvement approach. They noticed that the involvement approach, which was typically used in operational definitions, did not reliably predict actions which could be traced back to family business specific intentions [33]. Therefore, they integrated additional elements to the family business definition and specified those companies as:

> " . . . a business governed and/or managed with the intention to shape and pursue the vision of the business held by a dominant coalition controlled by members of the same family or a small number of families in a manner that is potentially sustainable across generations of the family or families." [33] (p. 25)

Chua *et al.* criticized that previous research exclusively focused on components of involvement such as ownership, control, management and transgenerational succession because this may lead to the insufficient simplification that " . . . family business definitions should be based upon multiple dimensions of family involvement" (Fiegener 2010 [34] (p. 313)), as studies emphasized, especially those based on Handler [18]. Instead of solely considering combinations of these elements of family involvement, the authors recommended to integrate "soft" factors such as family members' visions and intentions. Otherwise, it is only possible to differentiate family firms from non-family businesses which "simply represent the extremes of a continuum" (Audretsch *et al.* 2010 [35] (p. 4)). However, the distinctive behavior of different groups of family businesses can be detected by taking essence factors into account (e.g., [33]). Thus, this modification of existing theoretical approaches to define family businesses extended the scope of theory. Thereby, two ways of proceeding were conceivable; researchers either strictly build on Chua *et al.* approach or further advanced the described definition.

Updates to Chua *et al.* definition were written by Chrisman *et al.* 2003 [36] and 2005 [28] who also focused on components of family involvement and the essence of family businesses. They explicitly followed Chua *et al.* approach which can be shown by the following statement:

> "We call these human processes the 'politics of value determination' in family firms. This concept is entirely consistent with the two concepts of transgenerational intentionality and the familial coalition's vision that was used by Chua *et al.* (1999) to develop a theoretical definition of family firms and the systems perspective proposed by Habbershon *et al.* 2003 [37]." [36] (p. 470)

Furthermore, they pointed to the different characteristics family businesses possess so that this definitional cluster served as trigger for further thoughts about the family business definition and as catalyst for the progress of the research area.

Ultimately, family businesses had no longer been solely considered as homogeneous entities different from other companies but rather as having specific features among themselves (e.g., Marchisio *et al.* 2010 [38]). Attention within family business research partly turned to an extended concept of what constitutes family firms' distinctiveness (e.g., Lumpkin *et al.* 2008 [39]). An exclusive focus on factors describing family's involvement in the day-to-day business might be the necessary condition to classify a firm as family business. However, researchers realized that a significant influence of family essence has to be given additionally to be defined as family business. Only this sufficient condition ensures that a family firm behaves in a fashion different from non-family businesses [28]. In this context, essence can be considered as mediator between family involvement and family business performance [10].

In sum, approaches refining Chua *et al.* definition contributed to an extended comprehension of the heterogeneity of family firms without overly deviating from the initial definition. In total, this review yielded that 25 out of 267 studied publications follow the fundamental work by

Chua *et al.* 1999 respectively updates to this article published by Chrisman *et al.* in 2003 and 2005. Even if the definitional concept introduced in cluster 1 has been used in numerous subsequent studies (e.g., Sirmon *et al.* 2008 [40]; Basco and Pérez Rodríguez 2011 [41]; Lumpkin and Brigham 2011 [42]), some researchers did not trace back their definitions on these established ones and focused on specific aspects of family firms. Based especially on Chua's and Chrisman's findings, some academics extended the basic classification by sub-classifications (e.g., Uhlaner 2005 [43]), own applications (e.g., Björnberg and Nicholson 2007 [44]) or the integration of other research disciplines' approaches (e.g., [39]) as alternative ways to refine family firm definitions and to further promote theory development in family business research. Selected results for the overall distribution with respect to particular aspects are displayed in the following Figures 1–4. [6]

On the one hand, this led to more detailed analyses on particular family business cases since researchers elaborated on additional factors shaping family firms. This review tries to capture this development by classifying articles which place special emphasis on the impact of essence elements on family businesses while others prioritize the components of involvement (*cf.* cluster 2 to 4). On the other hand, it should be pointed to the risk of a—potentially exaggerated and misleading—differentiation of the described classification. This might be due to the observation that some articles do not refer to existing family firm definitions (*cf.* cluster 5) or even do not explicitly explain how they demarcate family from non-family businesses (*cf.* cluster 6).

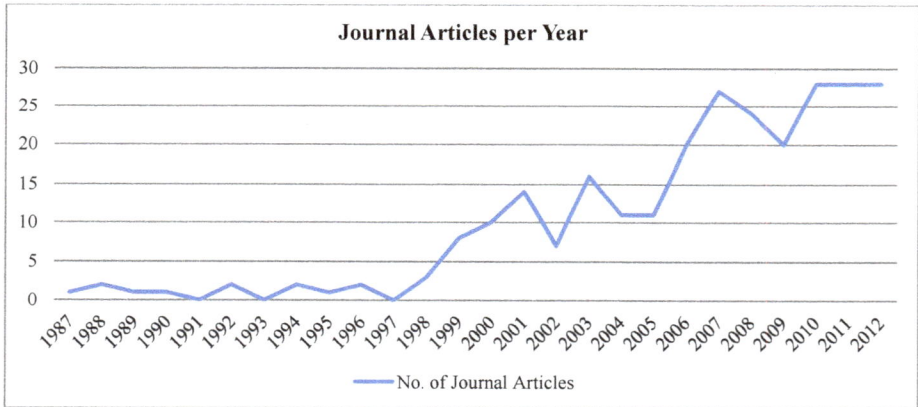

Source: own illustration.

Source: own illustration.

Figure 1. Journal Articles under Review per Year (all clusters).

---

[6] An overview about the distribution of articles among the individual clusters is given in Table A1 in Appendix A. Results for the overall distribution with respect to particular aspects are available on request. Interested academics are welcome to contact the author.

Region under Study

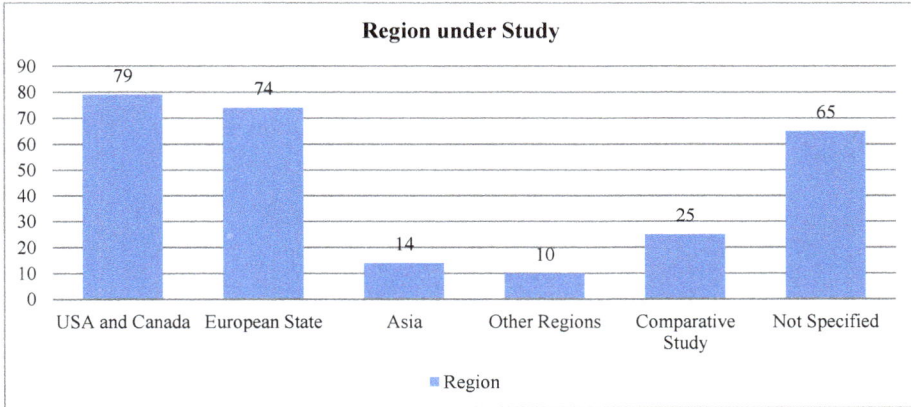

Figure 2. Journal Articles under Review, clustered by region (all clusters).

Theoretical Approach of Articles

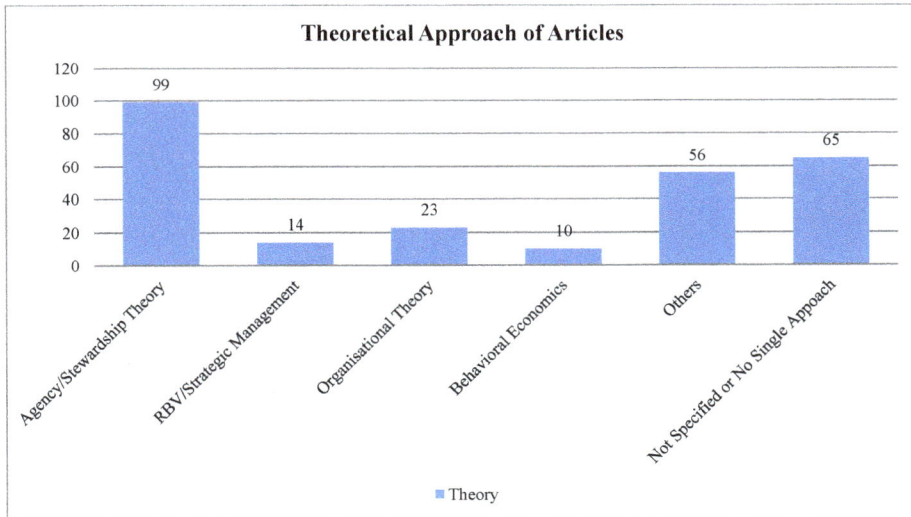

Figure 3. Journal Articles under Review, clustered by theory (all clusters).

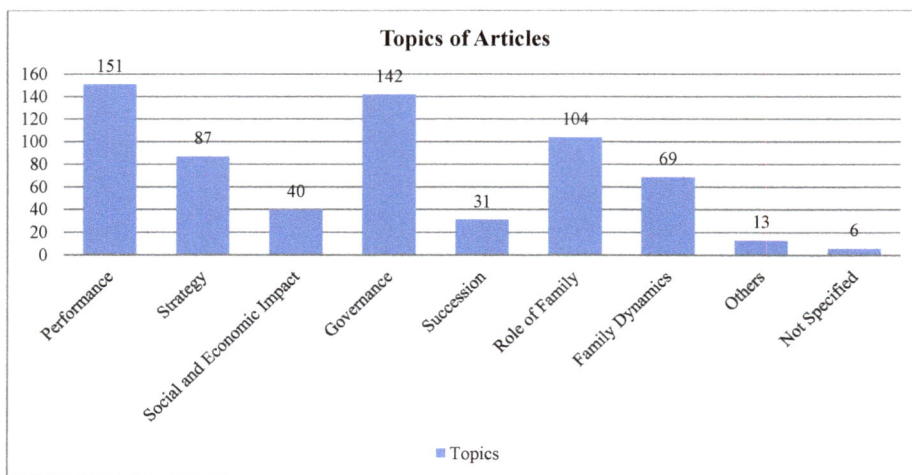

Topics of Articles

Source: own illustration.

Figure 4. Journal Articles under Review, clustered by topic (all clusters).

5.2. Cluster 2: F-PEC Scale/Familiness

Based on the discussion of elements assigned to the essence approach, "soft" factors of family businesses have been included in numerous studies. Astrachan *et al.* 2002 [45], for instance, developed the so called F-PEC (Family, Power, Experience, Culture) to differentiate family firms on a continuous rather than a dichotomous scale. Therefore, the authors conducted a literature review on family business studies and found that family firms are mainly defined depending on the categories content, purpose and form. This means that researchers either try to analyze the influence of components, such as ownership or management composition, or subdivide their sample to explain the specific behavior of family business subgroups [45]. Although many previous studies focused on aspects of content (e.g., [18]; [21]), Astrachan *et al.* emphasized that an increased attention should be attached to "soft" factors. While they subordinate components elements such as ownership, governance and management to their power subscale, the relevance of essence elements is displayed by the subscales experience and culture, in which they focus on family's values and commitment to the business [45]. Furthermore, the approach integrated multiple elements of the "familiness concept", which was firstly mentioned by Habbershon and Williams in 1999 [46] and which refers to a unique set of resources arising from interactions between the family system, family members and the business. Thereby, attention should be paid to the fact that F-PEC and familiness concept differ in terms of its fundamental intention as well as in its theoretical grounding. While the F-PEC aims at providing a method to operationally measure the influence a family could have on the business [45], the familiness approach refers to family firm-specific behavioral and social phenomena [46]. Furthermore, a major contribution of the F-PEC to family business research consists in the advantage to integrate different theoretical perspectives [45], whereas Habbershon and Williams [46] applied the resource-based view as single theoretical framework to investigate family firms' competitive advantages [5].

Core advantages of the F-PEC are the possibility to measure family's influence on the business on a continuous scale instead of in a dichotomous mode and the integration of both, the components and the essence approach [10]. In consequence, there is no further need to differentiate between family firms and non-family businesses since the differences can be displayed and measured without selecting a single family business definition (Danes *et al.* 2008 [47]). In addition, the integration of components and essence variables as well as elements of the familiness concept provided researchers with an enhanced understanding to what extent family's involvement and behavior can influence business decisions and results (Klein *et al.* 2005 [48]).

However, it should be pointed to the fact that the F-PEC is indeed able to depict family's potential involvement in a given company, but the scale does not capture the extent to what this involvement can be exploited in order to create the essence of a family business which in turn might influence company's performance. Therefore, some authors recommend not to exclusively working with this concept since it possesses a limited applicability in empirical studies (e.g., [7]).

Overall, both approaches, F-PEC scale [45,48] and familiness concept [37,46], represent theoretical conceptualizations whose underlying family firm definitions gather some elements from Chua *et al.* findings and thereby further enhanced the theoretical progress in the field of family business research. Studies assigned to cluster 2 differ from those in cluster 1 since they focus on "familiness elements" initially introduced by Habbershon and Williams in 1999 [46] which had not been integrated into Chua *et al.* approach. Thus, although it would be possible to split cluster 2 into two subsamples, the current systematization has been chosen to highlight the close consideration of "soft" factors as combining element in both approaches. Although F-PEC and familiness are grounded on different theoretical underpinnings and they are directed to slightly different targets, they share that they concentrate on "soft" factors which explain family firms' distinctiveness [45,46]. Thus, the concepts are jointly considered as cluster 2. This also contributes to avoid an over-clustering in the sense of having multiple categories with a small number of observations which in turn does not help other academics to get an overview about existing structures in family business research.

Studies following this classification scheme display important characteristics to comprehensively define family firms and contribute to a vivid and active discussion about how these elements can be captured in empirical analyses. In total, 24 articles of this review are based on this approach to define family businesses.

5.3. Cluster 3: Definitions with Empirical Orientation

The afore-mentioned fundamental approaches can be described as the most commonly used applications in family business research because lots of academics build upon the components of involvement and essence approach or the F-PEC respectively the familiness approach and other concepts highlighting the role of "soft" factors [12]. However, in addition to these classifications, a third category of articles has been identified for this review. All articles assigned to cluster 3 are aimed at applying and measuring family business variables in empirical studies trying to analyse performance aspects which does not hold true for the already described clusters. While the approaches presented in cluster 1 and 2 are to some extent also suitable to examine empirical relations, the subsequent approach, initially yielded by Anderson and Reeb 2003 [49], specifies operational criteria of family businesses. Therefore, this definition is explicitly applicable in empirical studies, mainly on financial performance. The authors concentrated on the question whether there is a significant difference in the relation of family ownership and firm performance for family and non-family businesses. While Anderson and Reeb [49] focused on publicly traded family firms and do not distinguish ownership from control, Villalonga and Amit provided a definition for all groups of family firms in which they integrate additional selection criteria (Villalonga and Amit 2006 [50]). Even if these definitions are not based on one of the already analysed clusters, they might create added value for a systematic review of family business definitions. Contrary to systematizations following cluster 2, these approaches are explicitly geared to empirical studies with a specific focus on performance issues. Furthermore, they are context-specific in the sense that definitions assigned to cluster 3 have often been applied to empirical studies based on datasets on publicly traded family firms. This means that theoretical definitions applied to empirical investigations should include a wide range of variables potentially differentiating family from non-family firms in order to discover and classify homogeneous groups of family businesses. Hence, already Chua *et al.* [33] stated that "in empirical research, an inclusive definition will lead to a more thorough understanding of the family business" [33] (p. 23).

Anderson and Reeb used the Standard & Poor's 500 as their initial sample, excluded banks and public utilities and collected additional data from corporate statements, for instance on board structure or CEO characteristics. In a second step, the authors tried to extract family firms by using fractional equity ownership of the founding family and the presence of family members on the board of directors. Villalonga and Amit based their analysis on Anderson and Reeb but conducted additional sensitivity analyses after having integrated different minimum thresholds for family ownership and control. Besides, they break down their sample, gathered from the Fortune 500 between 1994 and 2000, into different groups of family firms to illustrate the heterogeneity of family businesses.

Thus, Anderson and Reeb as well as Villalonga and Amit refrained from analysing definitional details a priori in favor of the possibility to easily operationalize family businesses. In sum, 21 of the 267 reviewed articles employ these definitions.

5.4. Cluster 4: Application of other Definitions

A fourth category has been opened due to the fact that some reviewed articles had been published before the definitions described in the first clusters were developed (e.g., Nam *et al.* 1999 [51]; McConaughy 2000 [52]; Davis and Harveston 2000 [53]). Moreover, some authors applied specific definitions to account for their study's special objective (e.g., Danes *et al.* 2007 [54]; [38]). For instance, the definition used in Danes *et al.* 2007 [54] applied selected criteria provided by Heck and Trent in 1999 [55] which is a well-considered study in family business research but did not influence other academics' understanding of family firms fundamentally. This cluster can be regarded as category containing all studies which are grounded on elaborated family business definitions but do not fit into one of the afore-mentioned clusters. Thereby, the conscious choice of specialized definitions must not influence study's reliability in a negative way. Nevertheless, by applying numerous varying family firm definitions, family business research might miss the opportunity to conduct comparative empirical studies which in turn might hamper the further theoretical development of the research field. For instance, Astrachan *et al.* [45] noticed that "definitions that differ only slightly make it difficult not only to compare across investigations but also to integrate theory" [45] (p. 46). This statement shows that it would be beneficial for the consolidation of family business research to agree on some widely accepted definitional classifications; especially since this would facilitate sample selection processes and the operationalization of family business characteristics. Overall, articles in this cluster applied definitions which have been published before 1999 which is the reference point for cluster 1 so that they cannot be influenced by definitions explained in the clusters 1 to 3. Ultimately, 42 articles of the review were assigned to cluster 4 due to the different described reasons.

5.5. Cluster 5: Self-Developed Definitional Approaches

Studies applying definitions assigned to cluster 5 should be distinguished from those assigned to cluster 4 (and all other already described clusters) since in the former category the authors neglected existing definitions and based their analyses on self-developed definitional approaches. These definitional approaches triggered a further diversification of family business research, which might have positive impacts due to additional insights concerning aspects not being able to examine without an explicit focus on certain family business characteristics (e.g., family effect on firm performance, analyzed in Dyer 2006 [56]). However, adverse effects may also occur since an increased heterogeneity of family business types could reinforce the problem of uniformly operationalizing family firms which again might impede comparative analyses. Therefore, Habbershon *et al.* [37] critically mentioned that:

> "[...] attempts to define a family firm or to delineate between the performance requirements of so-called family firms and nonfamily firms have left family business leaders confused at best." [37] (p. 452)

Int. J. Financial Stud. **2014**, *2*, 280–314

Even if significant progress has been achieved in recent years, this review reveals that some researchers still develop new sub-classifications (e.g., [43]) or own approaches (e.g., [44]) without regard to existing definitions and thereby accept the risk to contribute to definitional fuzziness.

While Westhead and Howorth 2007 [57] based their study on findings of Westhead and Cowling [26] and hereby respond to the increasing insight that family firms are not homogeneous entities, other researchers did not draw on previous definitions. Westhead and Howorth identified seven clusters and explained their uniqueness without tremendously deviating from existing approaches. [7] While the authors also detected that family firms cannot be considered as homogeneous entities as the majority of previous studies claimed, their analysis differs from the current study by focusing solely on agency and stewardship theory instead of integrating all theoretical and empirical approaches. Furthermore, Westhead and Howorth did not conduct a literature review on existing family firm definition but rather tried to elaborate on the links between private family firms' structure (ownership, management, objectives) and their financial and non-financial performance. However, for instance, May and Koeberle-Schmid 2011 [58] tried to delineate different types of family firms but did not apply an already broadly accepted definition or at least refer to one. In order to develop a model which depicts the specific intentions and challenges of different types of family firms, the authors analysed the ownership structure, the governance composition and investment decisions. Thereby, they identified 64 different types of family businesses which are supposed to possess distinctive features. Besides, some academics critically pointed to the ongoing development concerning the definitional vagueness but, nevertheless, recommended their colleagues to apply new concepts such as the "Family Business Definition Index" [12]. In this approach, Mazzi 2011 emphasizes the need to find another angle to distinguish family firms from companies without family influence. The author tries to capture different levels of the already established familiness approach but recommends extending this typology by including several additional factors [12].

In the light of this development, family business research arrived at a point on which academics started to review existing studies not only about family business definitions but also about family firm typologies (e.g., [14]) which indicates that the diversification still continues and a consensus on a unified family business definition has not been reached to date. Finally, the described behavior was utilized by authors of 68 reviewed articles.

5.6. Cluster 6: Without Explicit Definition

The difference between the clusters 5 and 6 consists in the underlying definitional approach applied in the analyses. While studies assigned to cluster 5 used self-generated definitions without referring to already established ones, authors assigned to cluster 6 did not even point to the source they utilised to define family firms. Some even solely described the data without quoting which selection criteria have been used to differentiate family firms from non-family businesses. Thus, the last cluster contains articles in which authors did not apply an explicit family business definition but only pointed to the used data source or even completely refrained from defining their object of investigation.

Even if researchers' behavior might be partly explained due to the multiplication of topics, regions of investigation and existing definitions, it seems that some academics did not undertake efforts to uniquely define family businesses. Instead, they referred to the applied data source without citing the selection criteria used in the underlying study (e.g., McCann *et al.* 2001 [59]) or they quoted their study's specific orientation respectively intention as reasons for the eschewal of an explicit definition (e.g., King 2003 [60]). Nevertheless, the question should be raised why there is a tendency not to draw

---

[7]   The seven conceptualized types of family firms according to Westhead and Howorth are (1) cousin consortium family firms, (2) large open family firms, (3) entrenched average family firms, (4) multi-generational open family firms, (5) professional family firms, (6) average family firms and (7) multi-generational average family firms. These groups of family firms have been identified along three axes indicating the influence the family might have on the business, *i.e.*, ownership, management and financial objectives (Westhead and Howorth 2007, [57]).

on widely accepted definitions or, at least, to cite the selection criteria used in the applied data source. The described ways of handling the definitional heterogeneity do not provide readers or colleagues from other academic fields, especially those not explicitly familiarized with family business research, with sufficient information to understand the distinctiveness of family firms. Thus, publications carried out without a clear definitional demarcation of the object of investigation might suffer from a lack of confirmability and credibility which in turn does not promote the consolidation of family business research. In total, 87 out of 267 articles in this review belonging to this category have been identified.

To sum up, the clustering approach has shown that academics applied numerous different definitions of their object of investigation—not only in the early years of family business research but also in recent studies. The first three clusters encompass widely accepted definitional classifications; one initial attempt to systematically define family businesses and two subsequent approaches, focusing on specific company and/or family characteristics and gearing towards theoretical respectively empirical studies. The fourth cluster serves to gather all articles which use existing definitions to operationalize their object of investigation but do not apply one of the previously described approaches. Articles in the remaining two categories are characterized by applying a self-developed or even no explicit family business definition. While some basic definitional classifications gained in importance over several years, an increasing heterogeneity with regard to sub-classifications as well as self-developed definitions can be currently observed. The following Figure 5 illustrates the distribution of the 267 reviewed journal articles among the six definitional clusters.

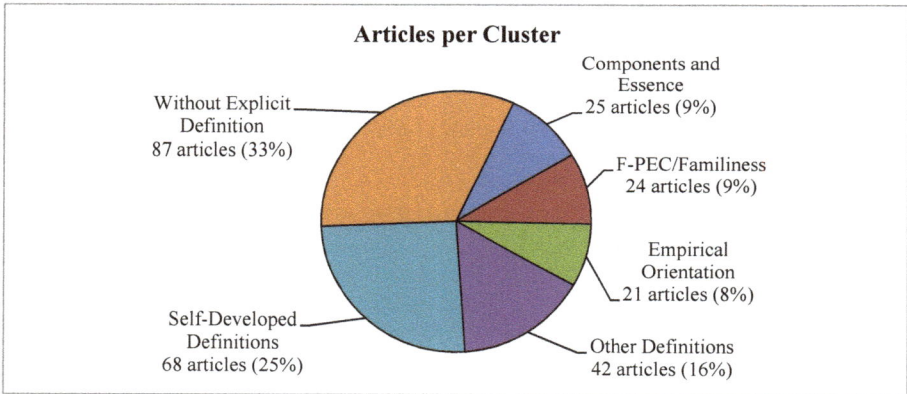

Source: own illustration.

Source: own illustration.

Figure 5. Distribution of Journal Articles among Definitional Cluster (in percentage).

6. Evaluation and Discussion of Results

After the methodological development of the clustering approach was outlined and some references with regard to definitional issues were presented, this section serves to describe and compare the distribution among the individual clusters as well as to find and explain peculiarities on selected aspects. Therefore, descriptive results over all 267 articles should be presented before a deeper analysis with a specific focus on individual clusters is conducted. It should illustrate noticeable differences in the number of articles applying certain definition concerning some analytical categories such as the region under investigation or the main topic analyzed in the articles. Subsequently, reasons for the heterogeneity in the application of family business definitions should be discussed to finally provide answers to the central research questions.

All distributions are depicted in Table A1 in and analyzed in the following segments. Thereby, only particularly conspicuous findings are outlined instead of trying to give explanations for all minor deviations compared with average values. [8]

6.1. Results over All 267 Articles

To begin with, it can be observed that the number of articles which take questions relevant for family businesses into account and delineate those firms from other groups of companies increased over the years. This growth in importance initially became apparent in family business research based in the United States (79) and in Europe (74), but can also be reflected in the relatively high number of comparative studies (25), which can be regarded as an indicator for the ongoing consolidation of the research area. Considering all 267 reviewed articles, those with an empirical focus (191) outweigh studies which concentrate on theoretical or conceptual aspects (76) of family business research. It might be taken as an indication that more recent analyses concentrate on empirical testing of previously developed concepts. While agency and/or stewardship theory were predominantly chosen as underlying theoretical structure (99), numerous studies fall back on less known theoretical approaches (56) which might be justified by the aim to integrate family business specific characteristics. Thus, the continued definitional ambiguity has been discussed from different theoretical and methodological points of view. In addition to basic approaches such as agency theory (99) or the resource-based view of family firms (14), further more recent approaches gained in importance for family business research, for instance the Developmental Model for Family Business [24], the Family Fundamental Interpersonal Relationship Model (Danes *et al.* 2002 [61]), the family orientation concept [39], the familiness perspective (e.g., Zellweger *et al.* 2010 [62]) or the family embeddedness perspective (e.g., Cruz *et al.* 2010 [63]). Regarding the main topic discussed in the reviewed journal articles, a taxonomy developed by Yu *et al.* [20] for their review on dependent variables in family business research has been applied. [9] Thereby, the majority of studies focused on performance (151), governance (142) or the role of the family (104) which reflects the central research orientations among family business academics. [10]

6.2. Results with Focus on Individual Clusters

In addition to the results with regard to all 267 reviewed articles, some indications about conspicuous findings for individual clusters should be given. Thereby, it is not intended to display statistically significant findings but rather to describe main trends within the single clusters concerning several dimensions, such as topic, region of investigation, *etc.*

In cluster 1 (25 articles in total), Chua *et al.* article builds the starting point and the number of studies based on this family business definition increased over the years and peaked between 2006 and 2010 (12). Thereby, it can be observed that studies using this definition predominantly examined family firms in the United States (13) and only occasionally in a European context (3). Moreover, the articles under review assigned to cluster 1 were mainly published in "Entrepreneurship Theory and Practice" (8), had an empirical focus (16), applied agency or stewardship approaches as underlying theory (8) and dealt with issues about performance (17), strategy (13), governance (11) and the role of family (11). However, this distribution approximately correspond to the results over all 267 reviewed

---

[8]   While all values for individual clusters could be taken from the overview about the distribution of reviewed articles displayed in Table A1 (see Appendix A), additional figures on specific relationships have not been graphically illustrated in this study, but can be provided on request.

[9]   Yu *et al.*, 2012 [20] differentiate between seven topics: performance, strategy, social and economic impact, governance, succession, family business roles and family dynamics. Two further categories (other topics and not explicitly specified) has been added for this review since some articles did not fit into Yu *et al.* taxonomy.

[10] Since some studies address multiple topics, e.g., the influence of family members on governance choices and its effects on performance, some articles have been assigned to more than one topic.

articles described earlier (see also distribution by percentage displayed in Table A1) so that the findings should not be again examined in details.

With regard to cluster 2 (24 articles in total), in which no article could be published before Klein *et al.* initial study on F-PEC in 2002, the regional focus shifts from North America (3) to Europe (6). However, in the majority of studies no explicit region was mentioned (12) which might be due to the fact that less empirical studies were conducted (12). The above-average number of theoretical contributions (12) can be traced back to the cluster layout which focuses on analyzing "soft" facts such as family characteristics and its influence on the business. Furthermore, it is remarkable that no reviewed article was published in "Journal of Business Management" or "Journal of Business Research", while more recent family specific journals such as "Journal of Family Business Strategy" (7) published a comparatively large number of articles applying family firm definitions. With respect to the underlying theory, more articles followed the resource-based view and further strategic management approaches (5) than agency theoretical methods (3) which is even more noticeable if the total distribution over all 267 reviewed articles is taken into account (14 *vs.* 99 articles). This might be explained by viewing family and company issues as structurally coupled as in the familiness concept so that these elements constitute a "unique bundle of resources" [46] (p. 11). Furthermore, the large number of studies applying other theoretical approaches (8) could stem from the integration of additional components from other scientific disciplines which are closely connected to family business research, such as sociology or psychology. This is also reflected in the analyzed topics since a higher-than-average number of articles addresses questions about the role of family (19) and family dynamics (14), but also about performance effects (17), whereas especially strategic issues (4) do not play an important role within cluster 2.

Cluster 3 (21 articles in total) consists of articles which applied a family firm definition initially yielded by Anderson and Reeb [49]. The increasing number of studies assigned to this cluster over time provides an indication that family business research has already accomplished a first consolidation because theoretical contributions usually embody the first step in the development of new research areas before the previously gathered findings can be tested in empirical investigations (Hakim 2000 [64]). Since Anderson and Reeb's study was particularly intended to find a definition suitable for empirical analyses to test the relationship between family business characteristics and performance, it is not surprising that all reviewed articles have an empirical orientation (21). Furthermore, the regional focus on the United States (16) as well as the fact that nearly all articles were published in other than family business specific journals (19) illustrate that articles following this definitional approach are well received in broader management science, especially located in the United States. However, it is astonishing that analyses were neither published in well-known family business journals nor considered other regions than the United States as area under study. In terms of topics and the underlying theoretical method, the focus on performance (15) and governance issues (18) is in accordance with the favored application of agency and/or stewardship approaches (15) and might be traced back to the intention of Anderson and Reeb's study from 2003 and subsequent analyses. This orientation again emphasizes the broader perspective of this definitional approach. It can be easier applied to an operational context than to interpersonal relations with regard to family businesses and therefore might be more attractive for other fields of business sciences.

The number of articles in cluster 4 (42 articles in total) increased over time which might be due to the cluster's layout since an already established family firm definition need to be perceived in the researcher's community before other academics could build upon this definition. At the same time, the increasing trend in the use of other than widely accepted definitional approaches (see cluster 1 to 3) could be interpreted as an indication for the non-completed consolidation of the research area. While most findings in other categories do not point to peculiarities in the distribution of articles in this cluster, the concentration of contributions published in "Family Business Review" (18) should be mentioned. It seems that this journal does not expect specific schools of thought while other journals perhaps favor certain theoretical or methodological approaches due to their general orientation. Another remarkable aspect concerns the tendency to apply definitions assigned to this cluster in comparative analyses (8). Just as the unequal distribution between theoretical contributions (5) and empirical studies (37), it might stem from the search for a suitable definition for specific investigations in terms of content. While the distribution of theoretical approaches and topics do not substantially differ from those of all 267 reviewed articles, the afore-mentioned deviations point to the existing heterogeneity in family business research.

Contrary to the first clusters, only occasional variations from the distribution pattern of all reviewed articles could be ascertained in cluster 5 (68 articles in total). Only with respects to the chronological allocation as well as regarding the region under study, differences could be detected. Some studies within this cluster applied self-developed family business definitions in early years (11 articles until 2000) which could be attributed to the non-existence of already established definitional systematizations. However, against the expectation, the number of articles grounding their studies on self-developed definitions or sub-classifications increased in the following years. Even if this development might suggest that heterogeneity still dominates family business research and a comprehensive consolidation in this field has not been reached to date, the slightly lower share of articles belonging to cluster 5 within the timeframe from 2011 compared to all reviewed articles might indicate a tendency of consolidation (14.71% *vs.* 20.97%). Regarding the considered region, an above-average proportion of articles is concerned with European family firms (29) which in turn does not seem to drive the distribution among other categories within this cluster.

In cluster 6 (87 articles in total), it is noteworthy that numerous studies without an explicit family firm definition have been published before 2000 (18) which might be due to the fact that family business research had not reached a sufficient level of consolidation at this time. However, over the course of time, the relative number of articles without explicit family firm definition—contrary to those of all 267 reviewed articles—decreased. This can be interpreted as indication for an ongoing process of consolidation since academics fell back on already well-known definitions. Furthermore, the above-average share of theoretical articles within this cluster (35) might be also due to the large number of studies published in earlier years of family business research because initial theoretical contributions are usually followed by empirical analyses with a certain time-lag. Apart from these observations, all other distributions in cluster 6 are in line with those over all 267 reviewed articles.

6.3. Summary of Findings with Respect to Definitional Heterogeneity

Overall, various family firm definitions exist which have been operationalized and applied in different contexts. This review attempts to systematize the multiplicity of definitions by developing a cluster approach based on numerous criteria. However, to fully characterize the status quo of family firm definitions, not only the chronological development should be described and discussed but also the underlying reasons for the existing heterogeneity should be considered. Therefore, the following segment serves to explore why there are still many heterogeneous definitions and for which reasons several studies had to be assigned to definitional clusters which do not contain widely accepted family firm definitions.

Already Handler [18] expressed an a priori definition of family businesses as most challenging task to researchers because previous definitions focused on different features and, therefore, were oriented into different directions. Although the difficulty to react to the complexity inherent in family businesses due to its unique characteristics has been observed in early research (e.g., [36,37,46] Sirmon and Hitt 2003 [65]), only few studies concentrated on the definitional issue.

Even if some researchers developed family businesses definitions due to disputable reasons to date and it might seem that they do not try to explicitly explain how to delineate family and non-family firms, most authors behave in that way due to comprehensible rationale. Thus, it has been detected in recent years that there is heterogeneity in family business definitions with regard to diverse reasons such as differences in the legal framework (e.g., Allouche *et al.* 2008 [66]), the culture (e.g., Getz and Petersen 2004 [67]) or the definition of family (e.g., Wennberg *et al.* 2011 [68]).

Concerning the legal framework, country-specific institutional features may affect the demarcation of family and non-family firms. For instance, the share of capital required for control, the rules to separate ownership and voting rights or legal conditions in succession processes could vary tremendously [66]. Therefore, the assumption to have the opportunity to adapt family firm definitions with minor modifications to other societal contexts might be misleading (Carney 2005 [69]). Allouche *et al.* [66] concluded that:

> "[…] a consensus definition may not represent a pertinent research goal because, by nature, FBs are contingent on the institutional legal context, which differs from country to country." [66] (p. 316)

However, to start with a broad, widely accepted definition and add some alterations or, at least, point to reasons for not applying already existing definitions might help to compare findings from family business research. As an example, Kowalewski *et al.* 2010 [70] followed this behavior by referring to several established family firm definitions and discussing necessary modifications due to specific company laws in Poland, their region under study.

With respect to cultural aspects, the organizational culture has to be regarded as influencing factor just as determinants driving the national culture. Concerning organizational facets, the decision to treat companies as family firms largely depends on the interpretation of what constitutes a family business [67]. Since these companies are always composed of two—sometimes conflicting—systems, the business and the family, cultural traits of family members play a vital role in managing a family firm (Birley 2001 [71]). If researchers take these cultural aspects into account for the demarcation of family and non-family businesses and corporate culture in family firms is regarded as unique competitive advantage (Denison *et al.* 2004 [72]), the decision which companies are included into the family firm sample may drive the results obtained for family businesses. Although researchers focusing on a single national context may not face this problem, international comparative studies have to consider the deviating corporate culture of family firms. Questions such as whether enterprises should be counted as family-driven even if no family member is still active in the company might substantially influence the findings, especially in definitions which are based on owners' or managers' self-assessment about the family firm status of their company.

Closely linked to corporate culture, aspects such as the relationship between involved family members and their distinctive national cultural background have to be considered to define family firms. Thereby, the characteristics and behavioral patterns of family businesses are shaped by attitudes business-involved family members possess which vary by country and its related national culture [71].

Taking cultural aspects into consideration to entirely capture what constitutes a family business means that certain questions, such as how family firm specific culture is transmitted to subsequent generations (organizational culture) and what factors might explain international differences in family businesses' culture (national culture), have to be addressed since these facets shape scientific outcomes [72]. Therefore, comparative analyses, especially in an international context, might require a strong discussion of the influence of cultural aspects on family business characteristics and its definition.

Another factor justifying the heterogeneous application of family firm definitions might be the differentiation of the term "family" which most researchers did not address in their studies included in this review. However, in some publications, numerous differences exist regarding the characteristics which have to be fulfilled to be considered as family member because family is deemed to be a soft factor whose interpretation varies with contextual factors such as time or culture (Bertrand and Schoar 2006 [73]). Since it depends on the national context if only nuclear and immediate family members or also those with extended kinship relations should be taken into account by thinking about family firm peculiarities, definitions might vary according to the region under study. While kinship relations are often less strong for most Northern European countries or in the United States than for Spain, Italy, Latin America or Southeast Asia, researchers should be careful in applying the same family firm definition in different regions or countries [68]. Therefore, Sharma *et al.* 1997 [74] concluded that:

"Although the field recognizes that different types of families exist, not much has been done to determine which differences really matter [...] Do not assume that what was a problem for one family business will be so in another [...]." [74] (p. 18)

Altogether, numerous comprehensible reasons for a heterogeneous application of family business definitions exist but future researchers should not be oblivious to the fact that previous efforts on systematically classifying family business definitions have already contributed to a theoretical consolidation of the entire research area.

7. Conclusions

7.1. Summary

Concerning the first research question which definitions have been frequently applied and which chronological development can be observed, this review has shown that family business research proceeds in finding a widely accepted definition since years. While the number of studies tracing back their analyses on already accepted definitional approaches (clusters 1 to 3) increased over time, the interim trend to utilize self-developed definitions, sub-categorizations or even no explicit family business definition (clusters 5 and 6) seems largely averted to date.

However, a profound consolidation on what is exactly meant by family businesses is still missing so that the key variable of interest remains vaguely determined. Thereby, the necessary condition for valid and reliable analyses, an unambiguously defined population, should not be neglected to ensure a sufficient degree of validity and reliability. This especially applies to (international) comparative studies in various disciplines, such as finance, and is of particular relevance for empirical analyses because a common understanding provides the basis for more detailed examinations, which is also important in contrast to research on small and medium-sized enterprises. Some researchers tried to unify the numerous endeavors to uniformly define family businesses after years of uncertainty and many new thoughts on family business definitions.

With respect to the second research question which are the underlying reasons for not having agreed on a widely accepted family business definition within the research field, some factors have been identified. Not only differences in the legal framework and the interpretation of the term family but also issues of organizational and national culture play a decisive role in justifying why some ambiguities in family business definitions exist. These aspects represent only a selection of important framework conditions which justify the application of individual family business definitions and they might be supplemented by several other factors contributing to the current heterogeneity of family firm definitions. Thus, some researchers consciously choose context-specific definitions to account for certain business settings as well as cultural or political environments such as the considered region or the point of time. To structure the debate about the heterogeneity among family firms, numerous review articles have been published in recent years (e.g., [9]; Basco and Pérez Rodríguez 2009 [75]; [3]; Goel *et al.* 2014 [76]; Nordqvist *et al.* 2014 [77]).

However, by searching for a definition which can be broadly accepted without being overly vague, some attempts, particularly started in the early 2000s (e.g., by [36,45]), made serious progress but did not entirely unite the research community on family-businesses. Instead, some researchers in recent years thwarted this already initiated process and tended to apply self-developed definitional approaches or sub-classifications for family firms but hardly pointed to efforts made by earlier studies.

7.2. Contribution to Theory and Practice

The lack of a clear definition or even a systematization which approach could be applied under which circumstances hampered especially cross-study comparisons but also other comparative studies with a focus on the same topic (Anderson *et al.* 2005 [78]) and interdisciplinary work. Thus, this review should contribute to a consolidation of family business research, particularly with respect to the definition of the object of investigation. Otherwise, as Dyer [56] stated,

"[. . .] some studies likely included firms in their 'family firm' sample that would not have been included in other studies' samples and this mixing of 'apples and oranges' might account for the ambiguous findings." [56] (p. 254)

If performance measures, sample size, region under study and/or timeframe additionally widely vary between studies, reliable comparisons are hardly to conduct.

By analyzing selected journal articles and thereby giving an overview about the dynamics in the chronological development and in terms of contents, the review yields that the first steps in terms of agreement and consolidation on a widely accepted family firm definition have been achieved. Furthermore, it reveals that research on a common family business definition seems to converge rather than to further diversify. While the number of articles assigned to the clusters 1 to 3 increased over time, researchers applied other definitional approaches to a lesser extent. Articles working with a self-developed or even no explicit definition were still used in recent years, but at a decreasing rate.

Hence, future research can benefit from this review article because it provides a classification of fundamental research strands in the field and reawakens the necessary discussion about a consistent family business definition. This has been demonstrated by an extensive literature review and provides future researchers an orientation which definitional approach could ideally be applied under which framework conditions. Even if no unambiguous assignment of definitional approaches to certain framework conditions is feasible and also not desirable due to the heterogeneity concerning individual family companies as well as the environmental conditions, academics could recognize which definitions have been previously used in comparable settings. Furthermore, researchers not only benefit from getting a comprehensive overview about existing definitions and its application in previous studies. They can also align their studies' underlying family firm definitions with already established definitional approaches to increase the validity and reliability of their analyses by taking this review's insights into account. Thus, results from family business research trigger the comparability with findings from research on related fields such as small and medium-sized companies or entrepreneurship. Thereby, it should not be the goal to introduce and establish an additional family business definition. It is rather intended to give other researchers, especially younger ones and those from related research disciplines, an orientation within family business research since a multitude of sometimes contradictory definitions exist. Without sufficient knowledge about the difficulties in properly defining family firms, researchers might randomly apply one of the definitions which can lead to results not being comparable to previous findings. By providing a classification scheme future research can easily match their works' target with an appropriate family business definition. This in turn increases the trustworthiness of the entire research area as well as the attention received from other (business) economic research communities and from practitioners.

If family business researchers agree upon on a broadly accepted family firm definition, company representatives will also benefit from the increased reputation of family business research due to more reliable and statistically proved analyses on family firms' differences to other companies as well as on the heterogeneity within this specific group of enterprises. Even if this step might take some more time, this review not only provides an initial starting point for this important theoretical development in family business research but also raises the awareness in practice to have a closer look at the definitional concept applied in studies on which business owners or managers plan to base their strategic decisions.

7.3. Limitations

Although the cluster approach of this review and the subsequent analysis of the reasons for heterogeneity in family business definitions contribute to the further development of theoretical foundations in family business research, some limitations have to be considered.

Firstly, there might be a sample selection bias with regard to the reviewed articles. Since only highly ranked (business) economic journals or those with a specific focus on family businesses have been included into the analysis, beneficial contributions from other sources or scientific fields were not taken into account. However, it is not feasible to integrate all studies concerned with family businesses in this review due to the large number of potentially relevant examinations on this topic. Therefore, a concentration on certain studies with a specific focus seems necessary.

Secondly, the distribution of topics within all clusters could only be interpreted in terms of percentage compared to the entire sample of 267 articles because some studies addressed multiple issues so that articles were assigned to more than one topic. Nevertheless, results are still comparable in two-dimensional analyses.

Thirdly, there might be a bias in the classification of individual articles to the six definitional clusters. For instance, it could lead to an overestimation of the clusters 1 to 4 that some authors are overrepresented in the review because they were quoted more often in the selected publications than others. However, since studies of these well-known academics represent a substantial part of family business research, this limitation can be attenuated.

Lastly, only two-dimensional relations between the considered categories and the definitional clusters have been analyzed. However, some clues on multi-dimensional linkages have been given, but not tested in this study.

7.4. Recommendations and Implications for Future Research

Regarding the depicted limitations, it seems especially relevant to control for the results of this review by using an extended database in further studies. Other researchers might conduct studies in which they integrate additional articles dealing with definitional issues or focusing on theory development, performance issues or strategic behavior. The more review articles are considered to test the analyzed relationship between the applied definitional approach in studies relevant for family business research and several categories, the earlier the objective to reach a consensus about a broadly accepted initial family business definition which researchers are willing to apply (with modifications) to operationalize family businesses will be achieved. In this context, analyses in which multidimensional relations between the considered categories and the definitional clusters would be tested might be conducted in future studies to further elaborate the underlying approach of this review.

As long as researchers are searching for additional results, it is recommended to apply one of the principle definitions displayed in the clusters 1 to 3 in a first step because these approaches identify all relevant elements (ownership structure, involvement of the family in management decisions and transgenerational issues) of a comprehensive family business definition (components of involvement, essence/intention) and they are able to take a hierarchy of single elements into consideration. In cases in which specific framework conditions, such as distinctive external characteristics regarding legal aspects or cultural traits, influence the sample selection, researchers should not closely stick to these three approaches but refer to them before modifying the family business definition or to give explanations why they apply another definition. To account for the deliberate application of heterogeneous family firm definitions due to context-specific reasons, further considerations about modifications researchers would like to integrate in their family firm definition could be taken into account in a second step. However, this review recommends all researchers to begin with one of the described definitional approaches or, at least, to explain why the application of certain other definition is more appropriate for a specific research design. This behavior would reduce the fuzziness regarding family firm definitions and contributes to a further consolidation of the entire research field

Appendix A

Table A1. Overview of Distribution of Journal Articles.

Definitional Cluster	In …	1	2	3	4	5	6	Aggregate
No. of Journal Articles	absolutes	25	24	21	42	68	87	267
	%	9.36%	8.99%	7.87%	15.73%	25.47%	32.58%	100.00%
Year	absolutes	25	24	21	42	68	87	267
	%	100.00%	100.00%	100.00%	100.00%	100.00%	100.00%	100.00%
until 2000	absolutes	1	0	0	3	11	18	33
	%	4.00%	0.00%	0.00%	7.14%	16.18%	20.69%	12.36%
2001–2005	absolutes	4	7	2	7	14	25	59
	%	16.00%	29.17%	9.52%	16.67%	20.59%	28.74%	22.10%
2006–2010	absolutes	12	12	11	23	33	28	119
	%	48.00%	50.00%	52.38%	54.76%	48.53%	32.18%	44.57%
from 2011	absolutes	8	5	8	9	10	16	56
	%	32.00%	20.83%	38.10%	21.43%	14.71%	18.39%	20.97%
Journal	absolutes	25	24	21	42	68	87	267
	%	100.00%	100.00%	100.00%	100.00%	100.00%	100.00%	100.00%
ETP	absolutes	8	4	0	1	2	10	25
	%	32.00%	16.67%	0.00%	2.38%	2.94%	11.49%	9.36%
FBR	absolutes	5	5	0	18	29	31	88
	%	20.00%	20.83%	0.00%	42.86%	42.65%	35.63%	32.96%
JSBM	absolutes	2	0	0	2	3	4	11
	%	8.00%	0.00%	0.00%	4.76%	4.41%	4.60%	4.12%
JBR	absolutes	2	0	1	1	2	6	12
	%	8.00%	0.00%	4.76%	2.38%	2.94%	6.90%	4.49%
JBV	absolutes	1	2	0	1	3	3	10
	%	4.00%	8.33%	0.00%	2.38%	4.41%	3.45%	3.75%
JFBS	absolutes	4	7	1	4	4	4	24
	%	16.00%	29.17%	4.76%	9.52%	5.88%	4.60%	8.99%
Others	absolutes	3	6	19	15	25	29	97
	%	12.00%	25.00%	90.48%	35.71%	36.76%	33.33%	36.33%

Table A1. *Cont.*

Definitional Cluster	In …	1	2	3	4	5	6	Aggregate
Region								
	absolutes	25	24	21	42	68	87	267
	%	100.00%	100.00%	100.00%	100.00%	100.00%	100.00%	100.00%
USA and Canada	absolutes	14	3	16	11	15	20	79
	%	56.00%	12.50%	76.19%	26.19%	22.06%	22.99%	29.59%
European State	absolutes	3	6	3	14	29	19	74
	%	12.00%	25.00%	14.29%	33.33%	42.65%	21.84%	27.72%
Asia	absolutes	2	0	2	4	3	3	14
	%	8.00%	0.00%	9.52%	9.52%	4.41%	3.45%	5.24%
Other Regions	absolutes	0	1	0	1	4	4	10
	%	0.00%	4.17%	0.00%	2.38%	5.88%	4.60%	3.75%
Comparative Study	absolutes	0	2	0	8	6	9	25
	%	0.00%	8.33%	0.00%	19.05%	8.82%	10.34%	9.36%
Not Specified	absolutes	6	12	0	4	11	32	65
	%	24.00%	50.00%	0.00%	9.52%	16.18%	36.78%	24.34%
Type								
	absolutes	25	24	21	42	68	87	267
	%	100.00%	100.00%	100.00%	100.00%	100.00%	100.00%	100.00%
Theoretical/Conceptual Approach (incl. Reviews)	absolutes	9	12	0	5	15	35	76
	%	36.00%	50.00%	0.00%	11.90%	22.06%	40.23%	28.46%
Empirical Approach	absolutes	16	12	21	37	53	52	191
	%	64.00%	50.00%	100.00%	88.10%	77.94%	59.77%	71.54%
Theory								
	absolutes	25	24	21	42	68	87	267
	%	100.00%	100.00%	100.00%	100.00%	100.00%	100.00%	100.00%
Agency/Stewardship Theory	absolutes	8	3	15	19	27	27	99
	%	32.00%	12.50%	71.43%	45.24%	39.71%	31.03%	37.08%
RBV/Strategic Management	absolutes	4	5	0	2	2	1	14
	%	16.00%	20.83%	0.00%	4.76%	2.94%	1.15%	5.24%
Organizational Theory	absolutes	4	3	3	3	5	5	23
	%	16.00%	12.50%	14.29%	7.14%	7.35%	5.75%	8.61%
Behavioral Economics	absolutes	2	2	0	3	2	1	10
	%	8.00%	8.33%	0.00%	7.14%	2.94%	1.15%	3.75%
Others	absolutes	4	8	1	7	17	19	56
	%	16.00%	33.33%	4.76%	16.67%	25.00%	21.84%	20.97%
Not Specified or No Single Approach	absolutes	3	3	2	8	15	34	65
	%	12.00%	12.50%	9.52%	19.05%	22.06%	39.08%	24.34%

Table A1. *Cont.*

Definitional Cluster	In . . .	1	2	3	4	5	6	Aggregate
Topic	absolutes	65	69	45	102	171	191	643
	%	260.00%	287.50%	214.29%	242.86%	251.47%	219.54%	240.82%
Performance	absolutes	17	17	15	27	41	34	151
	%	68.00%	70.83%	71.43%	64.29%	60.29%	39.08%	56.55%
Strategy	absolutes	13	4	7	17	26	20	87
	%	52.00%	16.67%	33.33%	40.48%	38.24%	22.99%	32.58%
Social and Economic Impact	absolutes	3	3	0	10	11	13	40
	%	12.00%	12.50%	0.00%	23.81%	16.18%	14.94%	14.98%
Governance	absolutes	11	9	18	24	39	41	142
	%	44.00%	37.50%	85.71%	57.14%	57.35%	47.13%	53.18%
Succession	absolutes	3	2	0	4	9	13	31
	%	12.00%	8.33%	0.00%	9.52%	13.24%	14.94%	11.61%
Role of Family	absolutes	11	19	5	12	27	30	104
	%	44.00%	79.17%	23.81%	28.57%	39.71%	34.48%	38.95%
Family Dynamics	absolutes	7	14	0	8	14	26	69
	%	28.00%	58.33%	0.00%	19.05%	20.59%	29.89%	25.84%
Others	absolutes	0	1	0	0	3	9	13
	%	0.00%	4.17%	0.00%	0.00%	4.41%	10.34%	4.87%
Not Specified	absolutes	0	0	0	0	1	5	6
	%	0.00%	0.00%	0.00%	0.00%	1.47%	5.75%	2.25%

 Values of single clusters 1-6 larger than value for aggregate sample

Appendix B

Table A2. List of Journals with Reviewed Articles.

No.	Journal		No. of Articles	% of Sample
1	Family Business Review		88	32.96%
2	Entrepreneurship Theory and Practice		25	9.36%
3	Journal of Family Business Strategy		24	8.99%
4	Journal of Business Research		12	4.49%
5	Journal of Small Business Management		11	4.12%
6	Journal of Business Venturing		10	3.75%
7	Journal of Management Studies		7	2.62%
8	Betriebswirtschaftliche Forschung und Praxis		6	2.25%
9	Entrepreneurship and Regional Development		6	2.25%
10	Journal of Family Business Management		6	2.25%
11	Academy of Management Journal		5	1.87%
12	Journal of Corporate Finance		4	1.50%
13	Journal of International Business Studies		4	1.50%
14	Journal of Accounting Research		3	1.12%
15	Journal of Banking and Finance		3	1.12%
16	Journal of Economic Perspectives		3	1.12%
17	Organization Science		3	1.12%
18	Review of Financial Studies		3	1.12%
19	Small Business Economics		3	1.12%
20	The Journal of Finance		3	1.12%
21	American Economic Review		2	0.75%
22	Asia Pacific Journal of Management		2	0.75%
23	Journal of Accounting and Economics		2	0.75%
24	Journal of Financial and Quantitative Analysis		2	0.75%
25	Journal of Financial Economics		2	0.75%
26	Journal of Management and Governance		2	0.75%
27	Managerial and Decision Economics		2	0.75%
28	Strategic Management Journal		2	0.75%
29	Zeitschrift für KMU und Entrepreneurship		2	0.75%
30	Academy of Management Review		1	0.37%
31	Accounting. Organizations and Society		1	0.37%
32	Administrative Science Quarterly		1	0.37%
33	Asia-Pacific Journal of Financial Studies		1	0.37%
34	Corporate Governance: An International Review		1	0.37%
35	European Finance Review		1	0.37%
36	European Financial Management		1	0.37%
37	European Management Review		1	0.37%
38	Financial Markets and Portfolio Management		1	0.37%
39	Finanz Betrieb		1	0.37%
40	International Journal of Entrepreneurship and Small Business		1	0.37%
41	International Journal of Production Research		1	0.37%
42	Journal of Business Ethics		1	0.37%
43		Journal of Business Finance and Accounting	1	0.37%
44		Journal of Enterprising Culture	1	0.37%
45		Journal of International Financial Management and Accounting	1	0.37%
46		Journal of the European Economic Association	1	0.37%
47		Management and Accounting Research	1	0.37%
48		Review of Finance	1	0.37%
49		Strategic Entrepreneurship Journal	1	0.37%
Sum			267	100.00%

Conflicts of Interest: The author declares no conflict of interest.

References

1. Kayser, G.; Wallau, F. Industrial family businesses in Germany-situation and future. *Fam. Bus. Rev.* **2002**, *15*, 111–115.
2. Chrisman, J.J.; Chua, J.H.; Litz, R.A. Comparing the agency costs of family and non-family firms: Conceptual issues and exploratory evidence. *Entrep. Theory Pract.* **2004**, *28*, 335–354. [CrossRef]
3. Sharma, P.; Chrisman, J.J.; Gersick, K.E. 25 years of family business review: Reflections on the past and perspectives for the future. *Fam. Bus. Rev.* **2012**, *25*, 5–15. [CrossRef]
4. Chittoor, R.; Das, R. Professionalization of management and succession performance? A Vital Linkage. *Fam. Bus. Rev.* **2007**, *20*, 65–79. [CrossRef]

5. Chrisman, J.J.; Kellermanns, F.W.; Chan, K.C.; Liano, K. Intellectual foundations of current research in family business: An identification and review of 25 influential articles. *Fam. Bus. Rev.* **2010**, *23*, 9–26. [CrossRef]
6. Siebels, J.-F.; zu Knyphausen-Aufsess, D. A review of theory in family business research: The implications for corporate governance. *Int. J. Manag. Rev.* **2012**, *14*, 280–304. [CrossRef]
7. Rutherford, M.W.; Kuratko, D.F.; Holt, D.T. Examining the link between "familiness" and performance: Can the F-PEC untangle the family business theory jungle? *Entrep. Theory Pract.* **2008**, *32*, 1089–1109. [CrossRef]
8. Sacristán-Navarro, M.; Gómez-Ansón, S.; Cabeza-García, L. Large shareholders' combinations in family firms: Prevalence and performance effects. *J. Fam. Bus. Strategy* **2011**, *2*, 101–112. [CrossRef]
9. Astrachan, J.H.; Zellweger, T. Performance of family firms: A literature review and guidance for future research. *ZfKE* **2008**, *56*, 1–22.
10. Frank, H.; Lueger, M.; Nosé, L.; Suchy, D. The concept of "Familiness". *J. Fam. Bus. Strategy* **2010**, *1*, 119–130. [CrossRef]
11. Pukall, T.J.; Calabro, A. The internationalization of family firms: A critical review and integrative model. *Fam. Bus. Rev.* **2013**, *26*, 323–332. [CrossRef]
12. Mazzi, C. Family business and financial performance: Current state of knowledge and future research challenges. *J. Fam. Bus. Strategy* **2011**, *2*, 166–181. [CrossRef]
13. Bhattacherjee, A. *Social Science Research: Principles, Methods, and Practices*, 2nd ed.; Createspace: Tampa, Florida, FL, USA, 2012.
14. Dekker, J.C.; Lybaert, N.; Steijvers, T.; Depaire, B.; Mercken, R. Family firm types based on the professionalization construct: Exploratory research. *Fam. Bus. Rev.* **2013**, *26*, 81–99. [CrossRef]
15. Sharma, P. An overview of the field of family business studies: Current status and directions for the future. *Fam. Bus. Rev.* **2004**, *17*, 1–36. [CrossRef]
16. Donnelley, R.G. The family business. *Harv. Bus. Rev.* **1964**, *42*, 93–105.
17. Zachary, R.K. The importance of the family system in family business. *J. Fam. Bus. Manag.* **2011**, *1*, 26–36. [CrossRef]
18. Handler, W.C. Methodological issues and considerations in studying family businesses. *Fam. Bus. Rev.* **1989**, *2*, 257–276.
19. Lansberg, I.; Perrow, E.L.; Rogolsky, S. Editors' notes. *Fam. Bus. Rev.* **1988**, *1*, 1–8.
20. Yu, A.; Lumpkin, G.T.; Sorenson, R.L.; Brigham, K.H. The landscape of family business outcomes: A summary and numerical taxonomy of dependent variables. *Fam. Bus. Rev.* **2012**, *25*, 33–57. [CrossRef]
21. Litz, R.A. The family business: Toward definitional clarity. *Fam. Bus. Rev.* **1995**, *8*, 71–81.
22. Wortman, M.S. Theoretical foundations for family-owned business: A conceptual and research-based paradigm. *Fam. Bus. Rev.* **1994**, *7*, 3–27.
23. Shanker, M.C.; Astrachan, J.H. Myths and realities: Family businesses' contribution to the US economy-a framework for assessing family business statistics. *Fam. Bus. Rev.* **1996**, *9*, 107–123.
24. Gersick, K.E.; Davis, J.A.; Hampton, M.M.; Lansberg, I. *Generation to Generation: Life Cycles of the Family Business*; Harvard Business School Press: Boston, Massachusetts, MA, USA, 1997.
25. Wall, R.A. An empirical investigation of the production function of the family firm. *J. Small Bus. Manag.* **1998**, *36*, 24–32.
26. Westhead, P.; Cowling, M. Family firm research: Need for a methodological rethink. *Entrep. Theory Pract.* **1998**, *22*, 31–56.
27. Daily, C.M.; Dollinger, M.J. An empirical examination of ownership structure in family and professionally managed firms. *Fam. Bus. Rev.* **1992**, *5*, 117–136.
28. Chrisman, J.J.; Chua, J.H.; Sharma, P. Trends and directions in the development of a strategic management theory of the family firm. *Entrep. Theory Pract.* **2005**, *29*, 555–576. [CrossRef]
29. O'Boyle, E.H.; Pollack, J.M.; Rutherford, M.W. Exploring the relation between family involvement and firms' financial performance: A meta-analysis of main and moderator effects. *J. Bus. Ventur.* **2012**, *27*, 1–18. [CrossRef]
30. Kraus, S.; Filser, M.; Götzen, T.; Harms, R. Familienunternehmen—Zum State-of-the-Art der betriebswirtschaftlichen Forschung. *Betr. Forsch. Prax.* **2011**, *63*, 587–605.
31. Sharma, P.; Carney, M. Value creation and performance in private family firms: Measurement and methodological issues. *Fam. Bus. Rev.* **2012**, *25*, 233–242. [CrossRef]

32. Schrader, U.; Hennig-Thurau, T. VHB-JOURQUAL2: Method, results, and implications of the german academic association for business research's journal ranking. *Bus. Res.* **2009**, *2*, 180–204. [CrossRef]

33. Chua, J.H.; Chrisman, J.J.; Sharma, P. Defining the family business by behavior. *Entrep. Theory Pract.* **1999**, *23*, 19–39.

34. Fiegener, M.K. Locus of ownership and family involvement in small private firms. *J. Manag. Stud.* **2010**, *47*, 296–321. [CrossRef]

35. Audretsch, D.B.; Hülsbeck, M.; Lehmann, E.E. The benefits of family ownership, control and management on financial performance of firms. Available online: http://dx.doi.org/10.2139/ssrn.1690963 (accessed on 27 April 2014).

36. Chrisman, J.J.; Chua, J.H.; Litz, R. A unified systems perspective of family firm performance: An extension and integration. *J. Bus. Ventur.* **2003**, *18*, 467–472. [CrossRef]

37. Habbershon, T.G.; Williams, M.; MacMillan, I.C. A unified systems perspective of family firm performance. *J. Bus. Ventur.* **2003**, *18*, 451–465. [CrossRef]

38. Marchisio, G.; Mazzola, P.; Sciascia, S.; Miles, M.; Astrachan, J.H. Corporate venturing in family business: The effects on the family and its members. *Entrep. Reg. Dev.* **2010**, *22*, 349–377. [CrossRef]

39. Lumpkin, G.T.; Martin, W.; Vaughn, M. Family orientation: Individual-Level influences on family firm outcomes. *Fam. Bus. Rev.* **2008**, *21*, 127–138. [CrossRef]

40. Sirmon, D.G.; Arregle, J.-L.; Hitt, M.A.; Webb, J.W. The role of family influence in firms' strategic responses to threat of imitation. *Entrep. Theory Pract.* **2008**, *32*, 979–998. [CrossRef]

41. Basco, R.; Pérez Rodríguez, M.J. Ideal types of family business management: Horizontal fit between family and business decisions and the relationship with family business performance. *J. Fam. Bus. Strategy* **2011**, *2*, 151–165. [CrossRef]

42. Lumpkin, G.T.; Brigham, K.H. Long-Term orientation and intertemporal choice in family firms. *Entrep. Theory Pract.* **2011**, *35*, 1149–1169. [CrossRef]

43. Uhlaner, L.M. The use of the guttman scale in development of a family orientation index for small-to-medium-sized firms. *Fam. Bus. Rev.* **2005**, *18*, 41–56. [CrossRef]

44. Björnberg, Å.; Nicholson, N. The family climate scales? development of a new measure for use in family business research. *Fam. Bus. Rev.* **2007**, *20*, 229–246. [CrossRef]

45. Astrachan, J.H.; Klein, S.B.; Smyrnios, K.X. The F-PEC scale of family influence: A proposal for solving the family business definition problem. *Fam. Bus. Rev.* **2002**, *15*, 45–58.

46. Habbershon, T.G.; Williams, M.L. A resource-based framework for assessing the strategic advantages of family firms. *Fam. Bus. Rev.* **1999**, *12*, 1–25.

47. Danes, S.M.; Loy, J.T.-C.; Stafford, K. Business planning practices of family-owned firms within a quality framework. *J. Small Bus. Manag.* **2008**, *46*, 395–421. [CrossRef]

48. Klein, S.B.; Astrachan, J.H.; Smyrnios, K.X. The F-PEC scale of family influence: Construction, validation, and further implication for theory. *Entrep. Theory Pract.* **2005**, *29*, 321–339. [CrossRef]

49. Anderson, R.C.; Reeb, D.M. Founding-Family ownership and firm performance: Evidence from the S&P 500. *J. Financ.* **2003**, *58*, 1301–1327. [CrossRef]

50. Villalonga, B.; Amit, R. How do family ownership, control and management affect firm value? *J. Financ. Econ.* **2006**, *80*, 385–417. [CrossRef]

51. Nam, Y.-H.; Herbert, J.I. Characteristics and key success factors in family business: The case of korean immigrant businesses in Metro-Atlanta. *Fam. Bus. Rev.* **1999**, *12*, 341–352.

52. McConaughy, D.L. Family CEOs *vs.* nonfamily CEOs in the family-controlled firm: An examination of the level and sensitivity of pay to performance. *Fam. Bus. Rev.* **2000**, *13*, 121–131.

53. Davis, P.S.; Harveston, P.D. Internationalization and organizational growth: The impact of internet usage and technology involvement among entrepreneurled family businesses. *Fam. Bus. Rev.* **2000**, *13*, 107–120.

54. Danes, S.M.; Stafford, K.; Loy, J.T.-C. Family business performance: The effects of gender and management. *J. Bus. Res.* **2007**, *60*, 1058–1069. [CrossRef]

55. Heck, R.K.Z.; Trent, E.S. The prevalence of family business from a household sample. *Fam. Bus. Rev.* **1999**, *12*, 209–224.

56. Dyer, W.G. Examining the "family effect" on firm performance. *Fam. Bus. Rev.* **2006**, *19*, 253–273. [CrossRef]

57. Westhead, P.; Howorth, C. "Types" of private family firms: An exploratory conceptual and empirical analysis. *Entrep. Reg. Dev.* **2007**, *19*, 405–431. [CrossRef]

58. May, P.; Koeberle-Schmid, A. Die drei dimensionen eines Familienunternehmens: Teil I. *Betr. Forsch. Prax.* **2011**, *63*, 656–672.

59. McCann, I.E.; Leon-Guerrero, A.Y.; Haley, J.D., Jr. Strategic goals and practices of innovative family businesses. *J. Small Bus. Manag.* **2001**, *39*, 50–59.

60. King, S. Organizational performance and conceptual capability: The relationship between organizational performance and successors' capability in a family-owned firm. *Fam. Bus. Rev.* **2003**, *16*, 173–182.

61. Danes, S.M.; Rueter, M.A.; Kwon, H.-K.; Doherty, W. Family FIRO model: An application to family business. *Fam. Bus. Rev.* **2002**, *15*, 31–43.

62. Zellweger, T.M.; Eddleston, K.A.; Kellermanns, F.W. Exploring the concept of familiness: Introducing family firm identity. *J. Fam. Bus. Strategy* **2010**, *1*, 54–63. [CrossRef]

63. Cruz, C.C.; Gomez-Mejia, L.R.; Becerra, M. Perceptions of benevolence and the design of agency contracts: CEO-TMT relationships in family firms. *Acad. Manag. J.* **2010**, *53*, 69–89. [CrossRef]

64. Hakim, C. *Research Design: Successful Designs for Social and Economic Research*, 2nd ed.; Routledge: London, UK; New York, NY, USA, 2000.

65. Sirmon, D.G.; Hitt, M.A. Managing resources: linking unique resources, management, and wealth creation in family firms. *Entrep. Theory Pract.* **2003**, *27*, 339–358. [CrossRef]

66. Allouche, J.; Amann, B.; Jaussaud, J.; Kurashina, T. The impact of family control on the performance and financial characteristics of family versus nonfamily businesses in Japan: A matched-pair investigation. *Fam. Bus. Rev.* **2008**, *21*, 315–330. [CrossRef]

67. Getz, D.; Petersen, T. Identifying industry-specific barriers to inheritance in small family businesses. *Fam. Bus. Rev.* **2004**, *17*, 259–276. [CrossRef]

68. Wennberg, K.; Wiklund, J.; Hellerstedt, K.; Nordqvist, M. Implications of intra-family and external ownership transfer of family firms: Short-term and long-term performance differences. *Strateg. Entrep. J.* **2011**, *5*, 352–372. [CrossRef]

69. Carney, M. Corporate governance and competitive advantage in family-controlled firms. *Entrep. Theory Pract.* **2005**, *29*, 249–265. [CrossRef]

70. Kowalewski, O.; Talavera, O.; Stetsyuk, I. Influence of family involvement in management and ownership on firm performance: Evidence from Poland. *Fam. Bus. Rev.* **2010**, *23*, 45–59. [CrossRef]

71. Birley, S. Owner-Manager attitudes to family and business issues: A 16 country study. *Entrep. Theory Pract.* **2001**, *26*, 63–76.

72. Denison, D.; Lief, C.; Ward, J.L. Culture in family-owned enterprises: Recognizing and leveraging unique strengths. *Fam. Bus. Rev.* **2004**, *17*, 61–70. [CrossRef]

73. Bertrand, M.; Schoar, A. The role of family in family firms. *J. Econ. Perspect.* **2006**, *20*, 73–96. [CrossRef]

74. Sharma, P.; Chrisman, J.J.; Chua, J.H. Strategic management of the family business: Past research and future challenges. *Fam. Bus. Rev.* **1997**, *10*, 1–35.

75. Basco, R.; Pérez Rodríguez, M.J. Studying the family holistically: Evidence for integrated family and business systems. *Fam. Bus. Rev.* **2009**, *22*, 82–95. [CrossRef]

76. Goel, S.; Jussila, I.; Ikäheimonen, T. Governance in family firms: A review and research agenda. In *The SAGE Handbook of Family Business*, 1st ed.; Melin, L., Nordqvist, M., Sharma, P., Eds.; SAGE Publications Ltd.: London, UK, 2014; Chapter 12; pp. 226–248.

77. Nordqvist, M.; Sharma, P.; Chirico, F. Family firm heterogeneity and governance: A configuration approach. *J. Small Bus. Manag.* **2014**, *52*, 192–209. [CrossRef]

78. Anderson, A.R.; Jack, S.L.; Dodd, S.D. The role of family members in entrepreneurial networks: Beyond the boundaries of the family firm. *Fam. Bus. Rev.* **2005**, *18*, 135–154. [CrossRef]

MDPI AG
St. Alban-Anlage 66
4052 Basel, Switzerland
Tel. +41 61 683 77 34
Fax +41 61 302 89 18
http://www.mdpi.com

International Journal of Financial Studies Editorial Office
E-mail: ijfs.@mdpi.com
http://www.mdpi.com/journal/ijfs

www.ingramcontent.com/pod-product-compliance
Lightning Source LLC
Chambersburg PA
CBHW041216220326
41597CB00033BA/5980